The Living Classroom

SUNY series in Transpersonal and Humanistic Psychology
Richard D. Mann, editor

The Living Classroom

Teaching and Collective Consciousness

Christopher M. Bache

State University of New York Press

Cover image photo by Steve Satushek.

Published by State University of New York Press, Albany

© 2008 State University of New York Press

All rights reserved

Printed in the United States of America

For information, contact State University of New York Press
www.sunypress.edu

Production by Ryan Morris
Marketing by Michael Campochiaro

This book was printed on acid-free, 50% recycled paper.

Library of Congress of Cataloging-in-Publication Data

Bache, Christopher Martin.
    The living classroom : teaching and collective consciousness / Christopher M. Bache.
        p.   cm. — (SUNY series in transpersonal and humanistic psychology)
    Includes bibliographical references and index.
    ISBN 978-0-7914-7645-1 (hardcover : alk. paper)
    ISBN 978-0-7914-7646-8 (pbk. : alk. paper)
1. Consciousness. 2. Transpersonal psychology. 3. Teaching. 4. Classroom environment. I. Title.

BF311.B253 2008
153—dc22

                                                                    2007052827

10 9 8 7 6 5 4 3 2 1

For reasons we don't yet understand, the tendency to synchronize is one of the most pervasive drives in the universe, extending from atoms to animals, from people to planets.

—Steven Strogatz, *Sync*

This book dedicated to

the great circle of learning

CONTENTS

FOREWORD

William James would love this book. Because he was a vigorous empiricist, someone who trusted his own experience and the varied experience of others, James would love the courageous, patient, modest, and convincing empiricism on display in this book. For the last thirty years of his career, as founder and dedicated leader of the American Society for Psychical Research, James was in search of what he referred to as "one white crow," one person whose experience might slay the enemies of empiricism—dogmatic religion, skepticism, materialism, and what has come to be called scientism, the dogmatic use of science to prevent the full range and variety of experience from breaking into thought and culture. James would have loved the way that the author of this book lets his surprising and significant experiences, and the amazing experiences of his students, chip away at the prevalent flatland, monodimensional academic worldview.

Similar to James's philosophical project, Chris Bache's argument is primarily focused against the position that presently dominates the academy, the position that regards the human mind as singular, isolated, and incapable of either a transcendent or depth experience precisely because there is no transcendent or depth reality to experience. Materialistically inclined scientists and philosophers of science typically assume that their methodologies are true to experience, truly empirical; this is the whole point of the scientific method, to observe and theorize on the basis of observation. Bache's entire book opposes this too easy claim. Where scientism sees flatland, Bache presents and argues for multiple levels, a variety of dimensions, a rich panoply of influences and effects. Bache's is not a very tidy worldview, but it is rich and exciting.

As the methods of scientists tend to focus on potentially replicable experience and repeatedly verifiable observation, they tend to leave out experiences that are not measurable. Consequently, important dimensions of experience are often missed by the scientific purview. Not so with the empiricism in this book: here the experiences of a professor and his students, over more than two decades, are respectfully attended to, critically analyzed, and in the end honestly and modestly affirmed. Published on the centenary of James' *Pluralistic Universe* (1908), this book finds meaningful relations between minds where most professors would be oblivious to such connections or deny them because their worldview simply would not allow such robust interaction at an unconscious and unintended level. James, of course, would say "listen to the experts," the ones who are having such experiences and then articulate a worldview faithful to such experience.

Bache's careful recounting of his wakefulness to the varied dimensions of psychic experience in his "living classroom," and his students' vivid descriptions of their experiences, though anecdotal, combine to bring into question the conventional view of mind—that minds are fundamentally isolated from one another. They also bring into question the conventional view of the universe as essentially dead, a view first formulated in the eighteenth century by Isaac Newton. Breaking through this comfortable worldview—though comfortable only because we are used to it, not because it is healthy or enlivening—to one unbounded, astonishing, and wildly pluralistic, Bache's universe is profoundly open, enchanting, and startling. Bache and his students comprise exhibit A of James's "white crows."

C. G. Jung would love this book. In addition to being a thoroughly Jamesian book, *The Living Classroom* is also deeply Jungian. Probably more than anyone else, C. G. Jung has brought to the twentieth century West revolutionary insights concerning the deep psyche's wisdom, persistence, and ability to communicate. Jung calls the most basic of these foundational influences "archetypes." These archetypes influence human awareness, carrying significant messages from the depths of the unconscious to normal consciousness. This worldview is important background for the experiences reported in this book because Bache, following Jung, has an eye to see what most professors cannot see, or refuse to see, namely, the active role of the unconscious in the collective conscious experience shared by teachers and students. In his interpretation of such surprising experiences, Bache is of course totally at odds with the Cartesian-Newtonian dualistic view of the mind. His entire project is supported by the worldview articulated brilliantly by Jung and subsequent archetypal thinkers such as Stanislav Grof, James Hilllman, and Richard Tarnas.

As we have learned from Jung, synchronicity is one of the primary instruments by which the depth of the unconscious communicates significant coincidences to the conscious life of individuals and groups. What most people take to be coincidences are in reality meaningful acausal events. According to Jung and others, synchronicities are subtle ways by which an intelligent universe brings about a startling juxtaposition of events, the kind that awakens a person to a new truth or an important meaning that would otherwise have been missed. Synchronicities can happen at any time and to anyone, but the kind of synchronicities Chris Bache is describing in this book occur inside groups that meet and share ideas regularly, such a college class.

Rupert Sheldrake would love this book. A lecture that Bache delivered in class included essentially the same event a student had experienced two days prior: the student had not mentioned the event to anyone, and Bache used the example spontaneously, unaware of the student's experience. How is the world constituted so that this kind of sharing could happen regularly? It would seem to be constituted in such a way as to include Rupert Sheldrake's concept of morphic fields, a subtle realm that weaves together discrete centers of consciousness. The experiences that Bache presents in this volume suggest that, there is a field of consciousness within which we function, from which we draw, by which we send messages—and, according to the examples given, a consciousness through which messages are received without a person having consciously sent them! Bache leads us to the idea that, in this field of consciousness, the part of consciousness that is the professor receives the part of consciousness that is the student. Once led to consider this unorthodox idea, the thoughtful reader wants more evidence and argument on behalf of this idea. Many examples and arguments are given both here and in the published research of Rupert Sheldrake.

It makes all the difference whether the reader accepts that the experiences reported here actually happened as described or whether they reject them out of hand as impossible. The first are genuine empiricists, inquirers who are faithful to experience, to what is truly happening in the room insofar as possible before interpretation, analysis and argument. The second response issues from a worldview that disallows these phenomena, no matter how accurately they might have been reported. In writing this book about teaching, Chris Bache had college professors most clearly in view, but the phenomena he is describing and interpreting are profoundly relevant for teaching at any level, and for anyone who participates in groups with any regularity. In principle, any teacher can gain the ability to see and hear beneath the usual level of discourse but this is unlikely if that teacher holds a view of reality that lops off the far sides and the peaks of experience.

The phenomena described in this book depend on the teacher's openness to subtle modes of consciousness and a subtle field of consciousness that develops over the course of a semester, even growing stronger from semester to semester. The first condition for the emergence of these phenomena seems to be a buildup of shared experience, some kind of bonding between student and professor. It might be important that the remarkable experiences Bache reports generally did not happen the first day of class, but rather surfaced as a result of shared experiences that developed over weeks and months, the time necessary for the class to build a subtle body. It is also noteworthy that in one case an elderly recently widowed woman who was taken to class by her friend for only one night experienced an opening that proved to be deeply healing for her. It would seem that the morphic field of the class cocreated by Professor Bache and his students served as a live environment for that woman's healing. She brought her living situation to the living relationship between professor and student.

Parker Palmer would love this book. Parker Palmer is prized for his ability to encourage and empower teachers to develop the courage to teach out of their own experience. Chris Bache has taken this ideal to its furthest limits. When Bache was a young professor after finishing his Ph.D. in philosophy of religion at Brown, he held an agnostic view concerning the divine and thought that profound religious or mystical experience was for others. He says that at that stage of his life he considered himself to be a "psychic brick." He needn't have worried; by the time he wrote this volume, his third, he is more like a psychic switchboard. As this book demonstrates so vividly and convincingly, Bache is alive to the consciousness (memories, thoughts, feelings) of his students and, perhaps more remarkably, they to his and to each other's.

The essential component of the phenomena described in this book is the distinctive ability of the professor. Perhaps at one time (in his early agnostic days) Bache's consciousness really was as dense as a brick, but now that he has been meditating for several decades, his consciousness is porous, extended, and acute. He has eyes to see and ears to hear what most professors neither see nor hear. Professors tend not to hear the unspoken largely because their worldview prevents them from listening to the unconscious of the student, or to their own unconscious as it registers a student's thoughts or recent experience. In this case, the adage is reversed: believing is seeing (or empowers seeing), and not believing, which of course is the dominant academic paradigm, inevitably results in neither seeing the invisible nor hearing the inaudible.

When professors comment, as they often do, that individual classes have personalities—whether alive or deadly, contentious or pacific, harmonious or factionalized—they are referring to observable traits that become dominant, usually slowly but occasionally from the first day. What this book is describing, however, is not so much a personality trait as an emergent psychic capacity, an access to thoughts, words, and images that are shared at a mysteriously deep level, a level that leaves everyone involved both amazed and sometimes confused. If that really happened, how did it, how could it? Similarly, in this book we experience a professor who doesn't just have a good sense of a class or a facility for language and affect, but rather an openness to the unconscious of his students, a capacity to hear and reflect back a student's thoughts and memories even though the student had not previously communicated them to the professor. In principle, every professor and teacher can bring this sensitivity to the classroom, but such teaching will take courage.

The Dalai Lama would love this book. Quite simply, this book is a stunning advertisement for the efficacy of meditation, the kind that the Dalai Lama practices and teaches. As thousands of his admirers attest, the mental space around the Dalai Lama tends to be unusually alive. Professor Bache states that the kinds of experiences of connectivity between his students and himself that surfaced in his classroom can be had by any professor, teacher, or person who works with groups. In principle, this is probably so, but it must also be said that such experiences favor meditators and those who consciously engage the deep psyche. For three decades Bache has spent some time every day clearing his mind of the mundane and opening his consciousness to its deeper levels. It would appear that the inherent connectivity of consciousness has a better chance to surface within his mind than with those who don't do these exercises. He would seem to be a receptor. The unconscious of his students can reach him due to his ability to hold a living space between himself and his students for such nonordinary modes of connectivity and communication. He is the key ingredient in making his classroom "living."

Some individuals, called psychics or clairvoyants, have this same ability, or more, but because their ability is so rare and controversial they tend not to find a home in the academy. Because their ability is opposed by the many who espouse a materialist worldview, they usually set up shop outside the academy. In addition to innate clairvoyants, some, such as Bache, must work diligently for the ability to hear the inaudible. As a result of his spiritual practice throughout the thirty years that he has been a professor, Bache is able to see and hear extraordinarily well, so well that his experience challenges the dominant worldview and will probably generate in some readers an "I don't think so" reaction.

Not everyone will love this book. Certainly some professors will decide in advance, whether by the endorsements or by the titles of Bache's previous two books or by this foreword (if they get that far), that they would not like this book—and will not read it. During the twenty years that I was a professor of philosophy (including a dozen years as chair of the philosophy department at Baruch College, CUNY), I knew very few professors who would be willing to read this book. To a professor who rigidly holds the dominant academic worldview, the several hundred pages of reports of unconscious connectivity between Professor Bache and his students, together with his insightful reflections on these reports and his arguments on behalf of the worldview that makes these reports comprehensible, would simply not be strong enough to overturn a worldview that is so widely shared and into which so much human capital has been invested.

This worldview has held the dominant position in Western thought as long as it has because it has been so effective, so productive of valuable results. As James and other pragmatists would say, "it works"; and it really does work for most purposes. And yet, following James, Jung, Sheldrake, and many other contemporary thinkers, Bache argues that any worldview that denies the unconscious and the kind of inherent connectivity celebrated by this book does not work for the edges or the heights or the depths of human experience. It does not work for the synchronicities of life or for the "something More through which saving experiences come" of which James wrote so brilliantly.

Many readers will love this book. There are at least two groups of readers who will benefit from this book—those who are already comfortable affirming such phenomena as Bache presents and those who are unaware of or only dimly or tentatively aware of such events. If, as seems likely, professors and students in other colleges and universities have observed such experiences as Bache has described, why are they so seldom acknowledged? Certainly some professors and students have observed such phenomena themselves, but with little or no fund of similar experiences being reported by others, they would not know how to interpret them nor would they be in a position to affirm their validity.

In this respect, the kind of experiences presented in this book, and the worldview that supports them, are rather like the visions of an afterlife that surface during a near-death experience, for example, in a near-drowning or during surgery. Though countless individuals have had these experiences, they were not publicly acknowledged until Raymond Moody, Elizabeth Kubler-Ross, and Kenneth Ring brought them to the attention of the reading public and provided a convincing explanation of them. In a similar manner, Chris Bache wisely recognizes the need for a critical mass of professors to acknowledge, when true, that they too are picking up on the thoughts of their students. As more professors report these experiences, they will come to be regarded as intelligible and valuable. Once they are so regarded, professors and students alike will join in more regularly observing these synchronous moments and will give them the significance they deserve.

Once the observation and sharing of synchronous moments become widely shared, the worldview that prevented their being seen and understood will be replaced by a worldview that accounts positively for such phenomena. Whatever else that worldview will affirm and deny, it will recognize the subtle communication that takes place between students and teachers. And if experienced by a professor and his or her class, why not with teachers and their elementary and high school classes, conductors and their orchestras, coaches and their teams, pastors and their congregations? Such experiences do take place, but, like near-death experiences, until they are written about in a series of convincing books, they will not be recognized as the significant events they are. This book stands as a powerful case on behalf of such experiences.

—ROBERT MCDERMOTT

ACKNOWLEDGMENTS

There are many persons who helped bring this book into being. First, I want to thank my colleagues in the Department of Philosophy and Religious Studies at Youngstown State University for their friendship and encouragement, especially Thomas Shipka and Bruce Waller who as chairpersons supported this project at different stages of its development. I also want to thank the university community for the sabbatical leave during which the core of this book was written. Numerous friends and colleagues outside the university read portions of the manuscript and gave me valuable feedback, including Juanita Brown, Jody Bryan, Anne Dosher, Duane Elgin, Sheryl Erickson, June Katzen, Bob Lyman, Randi Pappa, Dean Radin, Kaia Svien, and Tom Zinser. Thank you for your contagious enthusiasm and for the many improvements you helped me make to the text. Many thanks also to Jane Bunker, my editor at State University of New York Press, and her staff for their wise advice and counsel.

I especially want to thank Claire Russell who believed in this project from its early stages and supported the writing with a generous summer grant. Her belief that these ideas needed to be brought forward meant a great deal to me. In a similar manner, many thanks to Carol Horn, trustee of the Delmar Sacred Garden and Healing project, for both her financial support and her vision of the role of gardens in reawakening our sense of interconnectivity.

Those closest to the act of creation bear the greatest burden, for few people are more self-absorbed than an author working on a book. It is in this vein that I want to thank my wife and coconspirator, Christina Hardy, for believing in me, for her patience with my long absences, and for her many helpful suggestions on the manuscript. Without her this project would not have been nearly as much fun.

Last and most important, I want to thank my students at YSU for taking the adventure of learning with me. Thank you for your courage, for the fun we had along the way, and for the memories that will stay with me forever. I especially want to thank those students who shared with me the stories that appear at the end of this volume. May readers be as nourished by them as I have been.

Introduction

This book is an invitation to explore the deep interiority of teaching and the dynamics of collective consciousness. It studies the subtle mind-to-mind and heart-to-heart connections that spring up between teachers and students in the classroom, unbidden but too frequent and too pointed to be accidental. It investigates what I call the field dynamics of mind, examining influences that radiate invisibly around us as we teach. It explores the emergence of a true collective intelligence that skillfully integrates the many minds present into larger patterns of discovery and transformation. In short, it invites teachers to meet their students in a classroom that is more alive and more interconnected than we had previously thought possible and in the process to take their teaching to a more conscious level.

I've been a university professor for nearly thirty years, and the longer I have taught the more convinced I am that there is a form of collective consciousness operating in my classroom. For years I have watched a collective intelligence surface there, connecting individuals in semihidden projects and patterns. In the beginning I did not understand what I was seeing; my belief system simply could not accommodate such a thing. Gradually, however, I was forced to confront the impossible, to think the unthinkable. Groups have minds. They show signs of a true consciousness and intelligence. I watched as fields of influence grew around the courses I was teaching, the learning taking place in one semester influencing the learning taking place in subsequent semesters. But this is impossible, I objected. These are different students with separate minds and this is a new semester. We should be starting from scratch every term. But we weren't. There seemed to be a punctuated rhythm of learning that pulsed beneath the cycle of semesters, a connectivity that linked one class to another in subtle but discernible ways.

1

Of course, teachers experience the truth of the private mind every day. Our students don't know what we know, and sometimes it's devilishly hard to get them to see what we see. Everyone knows this. And yet, at a deeper level, there seems to be an underlying connectivity to our minds that can emerge unexpectedly and dramatically in our classrooms.

Sometimes when I'm lecturing, thoughts show up in my presentations that appear to be lifted straight from someone else in the room. An example I randomly choose to illustrate a particular concept turns out to precisely mirror a student's recent experience. When they hear their life coming back at them in my lecture, it snaps them to attention, as though our minds were secretly collaborating to produce precisely this result. But surely this must be just coincidence, we cry. To suggest otherwise is academic heresy. The absolute separation of our minds from one another is an axiom of modern thought, one that I too internalized in my academic training. And yet, here it was, not once but many times. How many "coincidences" does it take to overturn an axiom? Whatever the number, I have passed it. The connectivity of mind has demonstrated itself so frequently in my classroom over the years that something more than chance must be operating here.

I love teaching. I love introducing students to new ideas, challenging their assumptions and helping them discover new ways of seeing the world. And for as long as I have been a teacher, I've also been a spiritual practitioner, someone who does spiritual practice on a regular basis. I began meditating when I was in college and have continued to do various types of transformative practice ever since. For me, spiritual practice at its core is not about religion, creeds, or dogma but simply the cultivation of self-awareness and the systematic exploration of the deep psyche, relaxing the knots that bind us and gradually opening to the deeper clarity that lies within. When these two passions came together—teaching and spiritual practice—events were set in motion that thirty years later produced this book.

As a matter of professional ethics, I always kept my personal spiritual life out of my professional academic life, and yet over time I found that one began to influence the other. Things started to happen in my classes that seemed triggered by events unfolding in my practice. Breakthroughs at home were causing shockwaves among my students on campus. Over the years as I entered progressively deeper states of consciousness, the number of students being affected grew and the impact intensified. It was as though *depth* was triggering *breadth*, as though depth and breadth were two different dimensions of a seamless fabric of consciousness. As a professor of religious studies, I knew that the world's spiritual traditions celebrated a Oneness that lies beneath life's diversity, but I thought of this Oneness as a purely spiritual phenomenon. I naively thought that if I were fortunate enough to actually experience this reality, it would take the form of absorption into some state of unity consciousness or non-dual awareness. I did not expect it to have reverberations in the tangible world I earned my daily bread in. I certainly did not expect it to involve my students. But it did.

With consciousness-expanding practices becoming a growing feature of our cultural landscape, I suspect that other teachers are experiencing similar resonances springing up between themselves and their students. And I'd be willing to bet that many of them have been as shocked by these events as I was. The cultural paradigm we inherited from our training does not help us understand these matters; in fact it often blinds us to what is taking place right in front of our noses.

Over time these synchronistic resonances became such a prominent part of my teaching experience that I had no choice but to address what was driving them. I carefully observed what was taking place in my classes and experimented with how to work with the powerful forces that were involved. With the support of a research leave from my university, I formulated the first draft of my understanding of these dynamics in a chapter in my book *Dark Night, Early Dawn*, published in 2000. There, however, it was embedded in a larger philosophical inquiry that limited its circulation among educators. Further refinements of the ideas followed. I began to find more scientific documentation for the concepts I was proposing. A recent sabbatical has allowed me to bring forward this more complete presentation of the proposal aimed specifically at teachers. My hope is that this book will reach beyond the consciousness community and find an audience among teachers at all levels of the curriculum.

Collective consciousness is an idea that appears to be gaining traction in our culture. In 1994, the Princeton Engineering Anomalies Research lab at Princeton University began studying whether groups could mentally influence nearby random number generators. A year later, Roger Nelson and Dean Radin began to extend those studies to look for large-scale patterns of global coherence when mass attention was focused on major news stories through the international media. (See chapter 3.) In 1998, the Institute of Noetic Sciences and the

Fetzer Institute, two nonprofit organizations engaged in consciousness research, cosponsored two national dialogues exploring group consciousness. In 2003, Fetzer published a report on collective wisdom entitled *Centered on the Edge* and a year later established a Web site dedicated to that topic. In 2003, Rupert Sheldrake published an important book on the "extended mind," and a year after that the magazine *What Is Enlightenment?* devoted an entire issue to the topic of collective intelligence. In 2006, a German conference on collective intelligence attracted 800 participants and Dean Radin published *Entangled Minds*, perhaps the best survey to date of the scientific research on the subtle connectivity of consciousness. An Internet search for collective consciousness in January 2008 returned 1,400,000 hits.

This growing interest in collective consciousness suggests that this is an idea whose time has come. A new paradigm appears to be emerging that is taking us beyond our previous models of consciousness. Because this new paradigm will be unfolding for years to come, we cannot see all its implications yet, but the inadequacy of the old paradigm is becoming increasingly obvious to many thinkers. I believe that we are standing on the threshold of a new understanding of the collective dynamics of consciousness and a new way of working with the awesome forces that are generated when people work together in groups.

The Paradigm of the Private Mind

As you can see from the above list, most of the inquiry into collective consciousness is being carried out at present by nonprofit institutes and independent researchers. With some exceptions, the academic community still remains largely committed to the paradigm of the private mind. I was reminded of this when I visited my son at Harvard as I was completing this book. He's an undergraduate studying psychology and taking full advantage of the incredibly talented professors who surround him there. And yet none of his professors are speaking to him about collective consciousness or the field dynamics of mind. I suspected that this would be the case because it's the same where I teach and at universities across the country. By and large, the academic and scientific communities are strongly committed to the view that our minds are ontologically separate from one another. Whatever consciousness is—and we're still not sure exactly what it is or how it is "produced"—there is a general consensus that it's basically a private affair. *One mind per brain.* This consensus was forged through a long sequence of historical developments too complex to summarize here. Indeed, one might argue that the entire trajectory of Western thought from the ancient Greeks to modern science aims in this direction. While not attempting to do justice to these developments, I would like to identify a few contributing factors.

Surely the most important reason the paradigm of the private mind has met with wide acceptance is the fact that it accords with the majority of our everyday experience. Each day we experience the privacy of our thoughts and the challenge of communicating across the gap created by our mental isolation. The occasional experience of bleed-through between minds, if credible at all, only seems to confirm the general principle that our minds are separate from one another.

Of course, experience is not always a reliable barometer of truth, but in this case our experience of mental isolation has been reinforced by one of the deepest convictions of modern thought, namely, the belief that the physical world is the only world that exists. In this view, generally known as materialism, matter is what is truly real, everything else rests upon it. Accordingly, in the "decade of the brain" a relentless barrage of fMRIs and other sophisticated imaging technologies has reinforced the perception that our consciousness is nothing more than the subjective by-product of our neuroanatomy, that our minds are being produced by our brains. According to this view, brain is the fundamental reality because matter is the fundamental reality. If our minds are being generated by our brains, it follows then that they should take their shape and characteristics from our brains. Simply put, *if our brains are physically separate entities, our minds should also be separate entities.*

The metaphysical view that matter is the only reality is often presented on our campuses today as the "scientific view" of reality, and the rise of materialism is closely associated with the rise of science in the seventeenth to nineteenth century. Even though as a metaphysical hypothesis about the nature of reality, materialism goes considerably beyond the actual findings of science, it is primarily our confidence in science that underpins our cultural confidence in materialism. It is their respect for the achievements of science that leads many academics to reject out of hand the suggestion that there could be such a thing as a collective consciousness. Where is the physical substrate, they ask, that could be generating such a collective entity?

The premise that mind is essentially a private enterprise was also encouraged by a series of philosophical developments during this period that shaped the emergence of the modern self, a self that was understood to be radically separate from everything that surrounded it, including culture, nature, and other human beings. During the Renaissance a complex tapestry of intellectual streams converged to champion the individual, empowering the emergence of individual genius to an historically unprecedented degree. If we were to cite only one name in the long list of thinkers who contributed to this trend, it might be Descartes, whose thought was seminal in this regard. In his book *The Passion of the Western Mind*, Richard Tarnas summarizes Descartes' impact as follows:

> Here, then, was the prototypical declaration of the modern self, established as a fully separate, self-defining entity—doubting everything except itself, setting itself in opposition not only to traditional authorities but to the world, as subject against object, as a thinking, observing, measuring, manipulating being, fully distinct from an objective God and an external nature.[1]

If we go further back in history, we find that the roots of thinking of ourselves as separate and distinct entities reach back to the religious foundations of Western culture. For two thousand years, Christianity has emphasized *individual* salvation (or damnation) and Islam concurs. Very simply put, if God can divide the human race at the last judgment and send some souls to heaven and others to hell, this is possible only because souls are being seen as separate entities, like marbles scattered across a table. Both these religions, which together account for more than half of the world's population, have affirmed the view that the individual soul working out its individual destiny is the working unit of God's kingdom.

When this long philosophical and religious tradition of emphasizing the autonomy of the individual entered the modern era and combined with the new conviction that matter was the only reality, the stage was set for seeing our minds as fundamentally self-enclosed, separate entities—like so many stand-alone PCs, not networked, not integrated except by physical words and gestures.

This conclusion was further encouraged by the general tenor of the physics of the times. The assumption of the private mind came into its own when Newtonian science was at its peak and we were in the hypnotic grip of its atomistic vision of reality. By "atomistic"

I mean that this vision saw the universe as being composed of fundamentally separate, irreducible parts. Ultimately, the world Newton envisioned was not the world of quantum entanglement and nonlocality but a world of separate atoms moving about in mathematically precise patterns. The psychology that emerged in the context of this physics had a similar atomistic quality, emphasizing our separateness. In the end, *the unquestioned assumption that educators inherited from the modern era was the assumption of the private mind.*

It will take a long time for philosophers, psychologists, and historians to tease apart this complex history and decide which parts of it we should preserve and which we should discard. Here, however, I want to emphasize that the concept of collective consciousness does *not* undermine the value our culture places on human individuality— either a secular individuality or one rooted in theological discourse. *Individuality does not require ontological isolation.* I deeply affirm the value and importance of human individuality and see it as an emergent property of our universe, one that marks an evolutionary threshold of great significance. Such an individuality is not compromised by recognizing an underlying connectivity of consciousness that integrates individuals into larger landscapes of awareness. On the contrary, as we will see, the collective dimensions of mind actually nourish and support our complex individuality.

Newtonian physics has yielded to quantum mechanics and the rights of the individual are today discussed in the context of a growing appreciation of our collective obligations to each other and to other species, but the conviction that matter is the only reality continues to exert enormous influence on the intellectual life of our universities. The conviction that we can explain everything in the universe in terms of physical reality alone has shaped a narrative on our campuses that is usually presented as the "scientific view" of life. Students are regularly told by their professors that science has "proven" that there is no deeper purpose behind existence other than blind chance and that the survival of the fittest is the basic law governing all evolution and therefore all existence. Ethics are merely culturally embedded habits and our genes determine our destiny. In the context of this relentless reductionism, students are taught that when their physical brain dies, they die, period. Students are free to "believe" whatever they want about postmortem existence, but they are also told that if they want to think critically, there is only one rational conclusion they can come to. To affirm any form of survival of death is either to indulge in wishful thinking or to carry over pre-modern religious beliefs into the scientific era where they no longer belong.

It pains me that most of my students don't know that the cutting edge of science has already deconstructed this reductionistic materialism and that many of the givens of that worldview are considered false by a growing chorus of scientific voices. As the philosopher of science Karl Popper observed in his book *The Self and Its Brain*, materialism "transcended itself" in the twentieth century. At a time when physicists are suggesting that only 4 percent of the universe's energy is actually visible and superstring theorists are proposing that there are not three but eleven dimensions to the universe, many of the traditional arguments for materialism sound naïve at best. Today we seem to be in the process of disentangling the scientific method from the metaphysical hypothesis that was dominant during the birth of science, but changes of this magnitude take time.

If there is one theme that stands out in this rapidly changing intellectual landscape, I think it is the theme of connectivity. Everywhere we turn it seems that we are finding that systems we had previously thought were separate from each other are actually interconnected. For decades now we have been absorbing the strangely holistic world described by quantum mechanics. Bell's theorem, now empirically confirmed, reveals a universe that is instantaneously aware of itself across vast distances. Quantum entanglement was originally thought to be restricted to the subatomic realm, but now scientists are finding that its effects "scale up" into our macroscopic world, meaning that the world we walk around in shows signs of quantum connectivity. Other disciplines are concurring. Chaos theory has shown us that the macro-realm we live in is awash with holographic patterns and fractal iteration. Feminist writers have persuasively argued that the concept of an atomistic self is an inherently masculine creation that contrasts sharply with what some have called the "connective self" that flows more naturally from women's experience. Meanwhile, the science of ecology has shown us that in the natural world, life-systems interpenetrate so profoundly that it is heroically difficult to isolate one species from another in this matrix. While not collapsing the distinctions between these disciplines, the seminal insight that is emerging seems clear—*life's parts cannot be meaningfully isolated from the systems in which they are embedded*. The postulate of existential separation is at odds with practically everything we are learning about how nature actually works.

And yet, when we turn to teaching, it is as though we still live within a Newtonian universe of separate selves and isolated minds. The quantum revolution has not yet soaked through to our mainstream psychological models. The revolution of connectivity has not yet transformed how teachers engage their students. The momentum of the materialist paradigm and the dominance of egoic experience keep us looking only at the more tangible aspects of teaching while missing the more subtle interactions that are taking place everywhere around us.

The paradigm of the private mind has taught us many things, but many truths fail to rise in such a landscape. In fact, most of the truths I want to recommend in this volume cannot rise in this landscape. Having worked in universities all my professional life, I understand how the proposals made here may sound to persons trained in the older way of thinking. And yet we must move beyond the atomistic model of consciousness for two fundamental reasons: (1) because that model is seriously incomplete and (2) because it is constraining our capacity as teachers.

We are facing many critical challenges in the world today—global warming, collapsing ecosystems, the convulsive ending of petroleum culture, resource wars, and growing international conflict. In this context, it seems indulgent to write a book on such a seemingly esoteric topic as the dynamics of the collective psyche. Surely there are more pressing problems that demand our attention. And yet, if we follow these problems to their source, we find that many of them are rooted in a failure to grasp a fundamental truth about our lives. *An isolated self is an unnatural self; a divided self creates a divided world.* As we enter the century in which the future of our planet will be decided on many fronts, it is critical that we recognize the truth of our interdependence and interpenetration, a truth so penetrating that it reaches to the very core of our being. If this book makes even a small contribution to this shift in our collective self-understanding, it will not be a wasted exercise.

Educational Setting

Because the ideas I am going to present fall outside mainstream thinking, I've decided that the best way to introduce them is to tell the story of how they surfaced in my work as a college professor. I've tried to provide a fair amount of scientific evidence in support of these ideas, but what follows is primarily a narrative of personal discovery.

To tell this story, therefore, I should give the reader a little background on where and what I teach.

I teach at Youngstown State University, an open-enrollment public university in northeastern Ohio with about 13,000 students. Typical of many second-tier state universities, YSU's primary objective is undergraduate education with a scattering of MA programs and one doctoral program. Most of our students commute and most are the first in their family to attend college. I work in the department of Philosophy and Religious Studies. Academically, I'm a generalist, having spent a significant proportion of my time teaching survey courses in world religions and Eastern thought. I also teach courses in psychology of religion, transpersonal studies, Buddhism, and comparative spirituality. The connecting thread that runs through all these courses is consciousness. The recurring question that fascinates me is: What is the nature of consciousness? What are its potentials and patterns? What are its boundaries?

Youngstown State University is situated in a challenging economic and social environment. The core of the local economy in Youngstown was steel until 1977 when that industry collapsed, a year before I arrived. On September 19 of that year, known locally as "Black Monday," the largest steel plant in the city closed its doors and more than 4,000 workers lost their jobs. Other steel plants and related industries followed, sending Youngstown into a downward economic spiral with job losses eventually numbering in the tens of thousands. A way of life had ended; the city was hemorrhaging. Over the next twenty-five years, its population fell from 140,000 to 80,000, a grueling experience for any city to endure.

Even before all this took place, Youngstown had acquired a reputation for being one of the most politically corrupt cities in the United States. An article in the *New York Post* in 1963 called Youngstown "Crimetown U.S.A." Reaching back to the prohibition era, the mob held the city in its clutches for three generations, infiltrating its public institutions to an unprecedented degree. Eventually, in 1999, a four-year FBI probe of organized crime in Mahoning County indicted forty-six people; forty-two took plea bargains. "I couldn't believe there was a place as corrupt as Mahoning County," said Assistant U.S. Attorney Julia Stiller as she left the courtroom.[2] The worst is now over; the rebuilding has begun.

In such an environment, YSU stands as a symbol of hope for a more promising future for the citizens of northeast Ohio. Our students come to college to create a better life for themselves, and they bring a hardnosed pragmatism to the task. Here, teaching is not a gentle game of scholars and would-be scholars, but a rough and tumble world of give-and-take. I teach where the Rust Belt meets the Bible Belt with sometimes warping effects, where remedial education programs patch holes in inner-city transcripts, and where nontraditionally aged men and women come back to school in large numbers, comprising over 35 percent of our student population—a picture not unlike many state universities across the country. This is frontline education in America.

I mention these things to make the following point. If what I'm going to describe can happen here in these challenging circumstances, it can happen anywhere. It is not the result of a privileged academic environment or a selective student population. The potential I'm describing is inherent in the human condition.

If you teach to have a genuine impact in such a setting, you have to be willing to push some edges. It's what I call full-contact teaching. It's gritty and it's fun. I offer no apology for wanting to make my students' experience with me one they will remember. I want them to work hard and to think deeply about life. I want them to re-think their assumptions and question sacred truths. The students may not realize it, but when they enter my classroom they have entered a *dojo*—a school for training in the martial arts—where everything is on the line. My classroom is something like this. Here students will be shown every respect and courtesy, but they will also be tested, their defenses probed, their limits stretched. I'll do just about anything to get through to that student in the back of the room with the "wake me when it's over" look in his eyes.

Because some of the experiences I'll be describing in the chapters that follow may appear unusual, it might be worth mentioning that my personal background and academic training were very traditional. I grew up in the deep South, in Vicksburg, Mississippi, icon of the Civil War and home of the largest branch of the Corp of Engineers in the country, where my father worked as an administrator. I was raised in a middle-class neighborhood on the outskirts of town. Nature was my second home, and though I eventually set aside the gentlemanly arts of hunting and fishing that my father taught me, I have always kept a love of the outdoors. From there I went on to do my undergraduate work in theology at the University of Notre Dame, followed by a master's at Cambridge University and a doctorate in philosophy of religion at Brown University. Despite all this higher education around religion, or perhaps because of it, by the time I completed my graduate training I was a deeply committed agnostic. Though I had a fledgling interest in the deeper capacities of human consciousness, my mainstream roots and traditional education made me the last person you would expect to find writing the book you are holding in your hands.

Looking back, if I ask myself what brought about the change in thinking reported here, I have my students to thank for a lot of it. Over the years they broke me down and rebuilt me, tore me apart and put me back together. My entire view of what happens in a classroom has deepened because of them, and I am forever grateful for the gift of their companionship on this journey. The ideas presented in this book are not my discovery but *our* discovery.

In the story that follows, I'll tell you some things that have gone right in my classroom, but I'll skip over days when things didn't go as well, when I was tired or distracted, when the students were heavy and inspiration was hard to find. Every teacher knows those days. What I want to share with you goes beyond good days and bad days. It's about the underlying reality that we are grounded in on both good and bad days. It's about something that is always *trying to happen* underneath our feet when we teach, always pushing upward in the room. It's about the forces of nature that weave our minds together as we work, entangling the edges of our being into collective patterns that are clearly visible if step back and know what to look for. This connectivity is our natural condition. Teaching brings it to the surface, but it does not create it. It is always present, waiting for an opportunity to manifest itself.

Structure of the Book

The main body of the book is divided into three sections. Part I—The Emergence of Fields of Consciousness—has three chapters. The first chapter discusses the phenomenon of *resonance* in the classroom. The second describes the emergence of *group fields* surrounding entire courses, true "group minds" that encompass all the students in the room. Chapter 3 explores the science of fields. Here I step away from personal narrative to consider what science is telling us about the mind's capacity for connectivity.

Part II—Working with Fields of Consciousness—is a practical, hands-on discussion intended for teachers who want to begin working with fields of consciousness in their classrooms. In chapter 4 I outline a series of strategies that I've developed through the years for working with these fields, dividing them into four clusters—preparing the field, nourishing the field, visualization exercises, and closing the field. Chapter 5 introduces a fifth strategy—café conversations. The World Café is the creation of Juanita Brown and the World Café Community. It is a powerful conversational architecture that is specifically designed to tap fields of collective intelligence.

Part III—Teaching in a Living Universe—steps back in the direction of theory to reflect more deeply on the spiritual dynamics of teaching. Having described the emergence of fields of consciousness and given some practical suggestions for working with them, in chapter 6 I turn to consider some of the deeper existential implications of these fields. I place the concept of the living classroom inside the vision emerging in science of a living universe and speak to the underlying wholeness that grounds our lives in a larger cosmic order.

This discussion is then followed by a collection of student stories that forms something of an addendum to the book. Here I share with the reader a series of poignant stories that my students have shared with me about various experiences they've had. Often these experiences were the deepest experiences of their lives. They describe, for example, the day they died and lived to tell the tale, or the day that something beyond their reckoning reached out and touched them, changing their life forever. They write about hard choices they've made and mistakes they've lived with. Given the nature of these stories, let me clarify their role in this volume.

The fields of consciousness that I am addressing in this book have nothing to do with my specific discipline. They will appear whenever and wherever the requisite conditions are present, and these conditions cut across all academic lines. The stories contained in this last section of the book, however, *do* reflect my particular discipline. They address issues that come up regularly in courses in religious studies, such as encounters with death, conversion experiences, and personal existential discoveries. In this section of the book, therefore, I am putting on a different hat and inviting readers on a different journey. Here my wish is simply to share a series of intimate exchanges between a religious studies professor and his students. Here the students will do the primary speaking, and I will simply provide context and light commentary.

Most of these stories, therefore, are not directly related to the theme of collective consciousness. For this reason, I encourage the reader to treat these chapters as a separate conversation. More specifically, I want to emphasize that I am *not* offering these anecdotal accounts as evidence for the theory of collective consciousness presented in the main body of the book. For that theory I will provide careful argument and supporting observations from science. In these stories, I am simply bringing some of my students' experiences to public attention, experiences they were often reluctant to speak about, given the current philosophical temper of our universities. I have included these stories here primarily because they are so beautiful that I did not want to be the only person who has the privilege of reading them. They are divided into six short chapters. You may dip into them as you read the primary six chapters of the book, or you may save them until the end.

Though these stories differ in their project from the discussion of collective consciousness, they overlap with it in two ways. First, they vividly illustrate the personal depths that students are sometimes moved to explore by the mysterious alchemy that takes place in the classroom. I did not deliberately seek to evoke these remarkable essays from my students, but something called them forward. In this respect, they give witness to the depth of the transformative processes I'm describing in this book. Second, many of these essays clearly suggest the inadequacy of the materialist paradigm, as lived experience often does. They show us that the lives of well-educated, ordinary citizens regularly brush up against a larger reality that lies beyond the physical world. Thus, these stories place another pebble on the scale of public opinion, making a small contribution to the eventual collapse of this outdated way of thinking.

The Living Classroom represents the distillation of many years of reflecting on the transpersonal dynamics of teaching. It has been personally clarifying for me to develop the ideas presented here, and I sincerely hope they will be helpful to other teachers. I also hope they will contribute to the development of a truly integral approach to education. Not only must educators teach the whole person, but *how we teach* should reflect the inherent wholeness that permeates our universe.

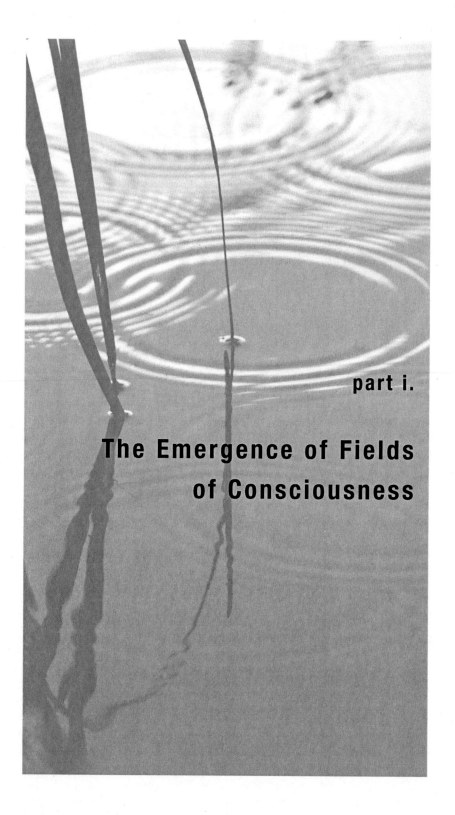

part i.

The Emergence of Fields
of Consciousness

CHAPTER 1

Resonance in the Classroom

There is more to intelligence than a solitary capacity exercised within the life of one entity. As it attunes to life, intelligence evokes a fuller, deeper intelligence in and around it. Resonant intelligence is intelligence that grows stronger or fuller as it resonates with other sources of intelligence.

—Tom Alee, "Resonant Intelligence"

It started this way. I was giving a lecture in one of my courses when a student asked a question. This was many years ago when I was a young professor fresh out of graduate school. I can't remember which course it was or the student, but what happened next is engraved in my memory. It was an ordinary question, one that I had fielded numerous times in previous semesters. On this particular day, however, instead of giving the answer that immediately popped into my mind, I stopped for a moment to mull over the possibilities. There was a pause in the flow of my thinking, a break in continuity as I asked myself, "Which answer has the best chance of getting through to this particular student?"

Suddenly I had a visual image of a small door in the back of my mind. The door opened and a slip of paper came through it with a suggestion written on it, an answer I had never used before. A different slant on a familiar topic. I tried it and it worked. In fact, it worked exceptionally well. Not only was the student satisfied, new ideas were sparked in the room. Learning had happened.

People experience these creative moments in different ways, but this is how I often experience them—a pause, a letting go, an emptiness, and a little door opening in the back of my mind. That was almost thirty years ago and intuition was less studied then than it is today, and even today many of my colleagues would raise their eyebrows at this story. We are, after all, rational people, highly trained professionals with advanced degrees, and rational people (with advanced degrees) don't have little doors in the back of their mind. I was a product of respected universities, well trained in research and dialectic, and not once in many years of graduate education had anyone spoken to me about intuition, about how it worked or how to integrate it into my teaching. But here it was.

In the beginning, I barely noticed these moments. Being a conscientious academic, I came to class with reams of carefully prepared notes and outlines to put on the board. I worked my students hard, covering the material thoroughly. (I still do.) In those early years, as soon as a student asked me a question, my memory banks would kick in and automatically generate the "correct answer." I didn't yet appreciate that there are a dozen versions of the "correct answer," each with a different nuance, a different emphasis, and from among all these possibilities there is one answer that is perfectly shaped to unlock this particular mind. Gradually I came to see that these moments were choice points, opportunities for intuition to transform an otherwise predictable lecture into a lively improvisational exchange tuned to a specific audience.

So I learned to work with these moments. I found that if I slowed down when asked a question and took the time to interrupt my stream of thoughts, the door would appear and little pieces of imaginary paper would be passed to me from some deeper place with suggestions written on them—an idea, a picture, an example. I found that if I took the risk and used these gifts, some of which seemed strangely off target at the time, something magical would happen. Something new and unexpected would come forward. My answers seemed to hit the mark or ignite a vigorous conversation. Like that solid "whack" when you make perfect contact with a well-thrown pitch, the ideas that emerged often triggered a "perfect moment" in the classroom. The energy in the room would rise, students would brighten up, and we would move together in a creative excursion instead of a predictable loop.

Now you may think that this was just an instance of a boring lecturer getting away from his scripted notes and maybe it was, but I don't think so. I've always loved teaching and I've always had the gift of gab. I know how to work a room, how to pace an audience and take them through the material in a way that builds to peaks and crescendos. This was something different. This was about cooperating with some mysterious process that brought out what was inside me in a way that was exceptionally fine-tuned to my audience. So for the next five years I experimented with these moments and learned how to weave them into my lectures. I learned how to integrate my prepared material with the novelty they unleashed. Then something new began to happen.

About the time I was jumping my first major academic hurtle—going up for tenure and moving from assistant to associate professor—students started coming up to me after class, when the room had emptied and they were sure no one would hear them, and saying things like, "You know, it's strange you used the example you did in class today, because that's exactly what happened to me this week." Sometimes it was, "That's exactly what happened to my Mom recently" or some other close family member.

The first time this happened, I thought it was interesting, but shrugged it off. Then it happened a second and third time. In the years that followed, it became a not uncommon occurrence in my classes. Not that it would happen every time I lectured, thank God, but it happened often enough that I couldn't dismiss it. Students were finding pieces of their personal lives showing up in my lectures in ways that startled them, sometimes jolting them. If my colleagues would have raised their eyebrows at the story of the little door in my mind, you can imagine what they would have done with this. So being a rational person (with advanced degrees), I kept it to myself. But it kept happening, just often enough to force me to pay attention to it.

An Example

One evening I was teaching a night course on Eastern religions. There were about thirty students in the class. In the middle of my lecture, I found myself taking a little unexpected detour in which I described an account of Zen master who had an accurate precognitive intuition of his impending death. I had never done this before in this lecture. It was just a little aside, something dropped in to add a little anecdotal interest to the discussion we were having about the powers of the mind from an Eastern perspective.

After class, a silver-haired elderly woman came up to talk with me. I had never seen her in class before. She explained that she was not in the course but had come tonight with her friend, another elderly woman who was enrolled. The two of them explained that her friend had dragged her to class that night because she was worried about her. Her husband had died three months before, and her friend thought she was languishing at home and needed to get out of the house.

In the conversation that followed, she told me this story. Her husband had been a used car salesman in good health; his death was completely unexpected. Shortly before he died, he had cleared out most of the cars from his lot without explanation and gotten all his financial paperwork in order. A few days later, he and his wife were watching television in the evening when he put down his newspaper and, in a way that was quite out of character for him, turned to his wife and said, "Darling, I just want you to know that if I died tomorrow, you've made my entire life worthwhile." A week later, he died in his sleep.

What she wanted to know was whether I thought her husband might have been unconsciously aware that he was going to die, like the person I had described in my lecture. I said that it certainly sounded like a possibility and this thought was comforting to her. This led to a longer conversation in which she described the challenges and opportunities his passing had created for her. After touching her grief, she got in touch with how overprotective he had been and how she was now being given the opportunity to develop herself in ways that his well-intentioned care had always prevented. To make a long story short, she decided that night to come back to college. She did so and thrived here for several years.

Was this just a coincidence as most of my colleagues would insist or was something more going on? My colleagues would likely say that if you lecture to thirty people week after week, sooner or later you're bound to hit a few bull's-eyes even with your eyes closed. And they have a point. If you think about all the life experiences tucked inside all our students, surely we're going to bump into someone's experience some of the time. Do the math and it looks less significant than it feels. That's what rational people say. For a long time that's what I said to myself. But the question kept bothering me. Was what was happening really just a series of coincidences? A woman who wasn't even a member of the course had her bell rung. Something touched her and she changed the direction of her life. How do you do *that* math?

As I experienced more incidents like this in my courses, eventually I came to disagree with the academic consensus, a dangerous thing for any junior faculty member who has to answer to peer review committees for promotions, grants, and sabbaticals. This had to be more than chance. The hits were too frequent and too well crafted. But if something more was involved, what was it and how did it work? I felt like I was being dragged dangerously close to the edge of a cliff.

A Second Example

This example comes one from a public lecture I gave in Minneapolis a few years ago. In this lecture I happened to mention as an aside that a number of students who were mothers have told me that they felt their babies had named themselves, that their incoming children had somehow communicated to them during the pregnancy their wish to be given a particular name. This usually took place in a dream or during a quiet moment. In making this point, I said with some humor and a raised voice, "I don't want to be called *Shirley*; I want to be named ..." (leaving the sentence unfinished). The line drew the expected chuckle from the room and we went on.

The choice of the name Shirley was entirely spontaneous and random for me. I don't remember ever talking about children naming themselves in my lectures, and I certainly had never used the name Shirley before. I don't personally know any Shirleys, and there are no Shirleys in my family. However, my "random" comment struck a nerve with someone in the audience, an elderly lady in her seventies. She later took the trouble to write me a letter about it.

After telling me a bit about her family history, she mentioned the Shirley-line and said it had struck a chord with her. Her name *was* Shirley, but she had always felt that Shirley wasn't her "real" name. In her heart she was Dorothy. All her life she had secretly identified with the name Dorothy, though she did not share this with others. Then she went on to write:

About 25 years ago, when I was a juvenile probation officer in Minneapolis, I passed one of our referees in the hall. At that time, he was also Clerk of Court for our county. Harold said, "Hi, Dorothy." Then he quickly apologized and said, "I made that mistake because you and Dorothy D. started work the same week." That fact was true—but ever since that day, many, many people have said to me, "Hi, Dorothy." They are people I know well or people I've never met (for example, an attorney who called to discuss a case), etc. There have been times when I was introduced to someone as Shirley—and the person to whom I was introduced has turned around and introduced me to another, saying, "Meet Dorothy."

Shirley felt that in her case her mother did not get the message. Though she had been named Shirley, she felt that she still gave off a Dorothy "vibe" that other people sometimes picked up on unconsciously.

Another coincidence? Perhaps. Certainly another unusual story. Being a well-read person, Shirley interpreted the episode in terms of C. G. Jung's concept of synchronicity. Synchronicity is the idea that two events can be meaningfully connected even though they are not causally connected by any physical medium that we have identified. She felt a connection between my choice of the name Shirley in my throwaway line and the deep ambivalence she had carried all her life about having been named Shirley, and it had led her to get more engaged in my presentation.[1]

The Magic

When these things first started happening in my classes, I was shocked because I was completely unaware of making any "paranormal" contact with my students, if you want to call it that, and certainly had not intended any. In fact, I had always thought of myself as something of a psychic brick, incapable of such things. Nevertheless, the trickle of such reports grew until these synchronistic coincidences became a not uncommon occurrence in my classes. The students also began to tell me that it was uncanny how often my lectures answered as if on cue questions they were feeling but were not asking out loud.

Not only were students finding pieces of their lives in my lectures, but as the previous examples illustrate, these events often touched sensitive areas in their lives. It was as though a radar was operating below the threshold of our awareness that zeroed in on some part of their life that was hurting or constricted. Sometimes it touched a question they had been holding for a long time or triggered an insight they had been searching for, something they needed to find before they could take the next step in their lives. Sometimes it lanced a private pain that had been festering inside them for years. It was as if their souls were slipping messages to me, giving me hints on how I might reach them—telling me where they were hiding, where they were hurting, and, most important, what ideas they needed to take the next step in their development. This process, whatever it was, was obviously intelligent and it was obviously collective.

At home I started to call this mysterious interweaving of minds "the magic." When the magic happened, the walls of our separate minds seemed to come down temporarily, secrets were exchanged, and healing flowed. When the magic happened, my students and I tapped into levels of creativity beyond our separate capacities. On a good day the room was so filled with new ideas that after class I too copied down the blackboard. In these elevated conversations, I would some-times catch glimpses of a deeper trajectory of ideas coming forward and working themselves out in our dialogue.

As you can imagine, these occurrences often affected my students deeply. Imagine that you are an undergraduate taking a class simply looking for three more credits toward your degree when suddenly the professor is using your recent history to illustrate a point he is making. Buried in the back of the room, safely anonymous in the crowd, suddenly your life is exposed, your heart pierced by words that seem aimed directly at you. Given such a personal invitation, how could you not sit up and pay attention? How could you not get more deeply involved in the course?

As my students continued to come to me with these reports and I saw how deeply they were being affected by this mysterious alchemy that was taking place between us, I was more than a little shaken myself. What were these powerful processes that were linking me to them in such an intimate manner? Neither of us had solicited the connection, yet here it was. Did I need to protect them from what was happening? Obviously this was not what they had signed up for. How does one ensure informed consent when the dynamics are so involun-tary and beyond the pale of academic discussion?

The only control I had over the situation was whether to close and lock this door in my mind and cut off contact with this deeper source of information, wherever it was coming from. Though I considered taking this drastic step, in the end I decided against it. If I cut myself off from my intuition in order to avoid these "complications," I would also be cutting myself off from a creativity that was benefiting my teaching in very tangible ways. Furthermore, I instinctively realized that it would be foolish and perhaps even damaging to cut myself off from this well of creativity just as my career was getting started. I did not know where this was leading, but I decided to stay with it and keep the door open. I chose to continue the experiment but to monitor my students carefully, watching for signs of impact and possible distress. As I subsequently learned, these synchronicities were the over-ture to a still deeper connection with my students that was beginning to emerge and would continue to deepen for many years to come.

Spiritual Practice

Now I need to put another piece of the puzzle on the table, a piece that brings us to the very heart of the issue this chapter is raising. For as long as I've been an academic, I've also been a spiritual seeker. Sometimes I think of these as my two jobs—one I get paid for, the other is volunteer work. In my paid daytime job, I'm a university professor in a department of philosophy and religious studies. My work is education; my tools are reason, critical reflection, oratory, lots of reading, and a sense of humor. In my unpaid nighttime job, I'm a spiritual practitioner. Here the tools are silence, prayer, meditation, and from time to time immersion in deep, introspective, cathartic states of consciousness. Though I began meditating when I was in graduate school, it was only after I came to YSU when I was twenty-nine that I settled into the discipline of a sustained spiritual practice, about the same time I started my marriage and settled into the rhythms of home and children.

So as I took out my first mortgage and changed the first of many diapers, I created a carefully divided world between being a professor and a spiritual practitioner. I spent my weekdays teaching and many of my weekends in various exercises designed to explore what Abraham Maslow called the "farther limits of human nature." I do not think the details of my specific spiritual practice are important to the story I'm telling here, and I've written about them elsewhere.[2] There are many forms of spiritual practice, many techniques and systems of transformation that sensitize the mind and body and push back the boundaries of conscious awareness. Far from recommending one system over others, I think that *all of these systems have the potential to evoke the kind of phenomena I am reporting here.*

I started my life as a Roman Catholic, but over time have drunk from many spiritual streams. Like many practitioners today, I have combined teachings and practices from several different spiritual lineages, hopefully without compromising any of them. The strongest influences in my contemplative life have been Christianity, Buddhism, and shamanism. I would also include science in this list as a form of *jnana* yoga. In taking this eclectic approach to spirituality I'm a child of my generation, part of the wave of social entrepreneurs Paul Ray and Sherri Anderson describe in their book *The Cultural Creatives*, individuals who draw from a variety of spiritual traditions as they try to live a more centered, more harmonious life in today's global environment.

Spirituality is distinct from institutionalized religion, of course, but because the two sometimes get conflated, let me clarify what I mean here by spiritual practice. As I understand it, spiritual practice is about cultivating an experiential opening to the larger patterns of life and the deeper roots of one's existence. It is not primarily about faith, creeds, or ritual, though these may play a role in one's practice. Pragmatically, spiritual practice is about systematically engaging the constrictions within one's heart, mind, and body that keep awareness trapped within the narrow, repetitive cycles that constitute the private self and allowing one's being to relax into its deeper currents and its innate purity, eventually opening to the crystalline clarity that is the ever-present context and source of all experience. As this opening unfolds, one discovers many insights, encounters many truths, but the fundamental movement is simply to experience life as it is—in its fullness and immediacy, free of the constrictions of self-reference.

When one experiences life as it is—in its "suchness" as the Zen Buddhists say or as a "grace" as the Christians put it—one is inevitably struck by its wholeness, by the fact that at this profound and utterly simple level, life is not divided into parts. The things that usually fascinate us, the countless objects dangling in store windows or catalogued in our encyclopedias, the people walking down the street each with their different story, all these cease to exist as isolated, separate phenomena. Underneath and within this rich diversity, life lives and breathes as One. Its inherent wholeness is not fragmented by its emergent diversity.

The essence of spirituality then, at least as I understand it and try to practice it, is to open this living Oneness or Totality that encompasses and subsumes all distinctions. Wholeness, therefore, is the essence of the art. I hope other practitioners will feel their own experience echoed in this description.

Now let's return to our story. Honoring the time-tested wisdom of keeping one's personal beliefs out of one's professional life, I kept my two jobs separate. I did not talk about my spiritual practice in my classes and revealed my personal convictions only rarely and in carefully bracketed situations. My work at the university is not to instruct students in what I personally believe and certainly not to try to interest them in my particular spiritual path, but to expose them to some of the best minds in the intellectual and spiritual traditions I am responsible for in our curriculum. While my spiritual practice has no doubt influenced what questions I think are deserving of my students' time and attention and what books are worthy of study, the choices I make always must pass academic muster. Every course one puts into the curriculum is carefully screened by several committees of one's peers, every syllabus is reviewed by one's department chair.

As a matter of professional ethics, therefore, I did not speak about my spiritual practice to my students, and yet with the passage of time

I discovered that these two worlds I had kept apart so carefully were beginning to interact. As my spiritual practice deepened through the years, the synchronistic events I've been describing became more frequent and more intense. Despite my best effort to keep these two sides of my life separate, they seemed to be reaching out and touching one another. Not only were the synchronicities increasing, but students were beginning to have unusually deep experiences around the concepts I was presenting in class. It was as though their lives were being activated by more than just the ideas I was lecturing on. It was as if they were somehow being touched by the actual experience of these realities that now lived in me to some degree because of my practice.

Experiences of Resonance

Truth spoken directly from the heart and skillfully illumined by the mind has an enormous power that cannot be eliminated, even in the academic setting. This applies to spiritual truths as well as to other kinds of truth. Because I teach survey courses in world religions, I have spent many years conveying to thousands of students the insights of what some scholars have called the "perennial tradition." The perennial tradition is the name given to a collection of common insights that run throughout all the world's religions. The discovery of this common core was seeded by Aldous Huxley's pioneering work *The Perennial Philosophy*, published in 1944. Like perennial flowers, these ideas keep showing up wherever human beings have pushed beyond the boundaries of ordinary, sensate consciousness and explored the deeper dimensions of consciousness. Thus, the perennial philosophy reflects the experiences of the world's contemplatives more than it does the teachings that circulate among the masses of the faithful, which appear relatively diluted by comparison. This common spiritual ground would take considerable space to describe in detail, but it can be safely said to include the following concepts, which I've framed here in a contemporary vocabulary.

The perennial vision is that our physical universe is a living, multi-tiered, self-emergent universe originating in a rich plenum of pure potentiality, the source of the big bang. Because our universe is rooted in and continuously replenished by this infinitely rich plenum, a creative intelligence permeates and saturates all existence, allowing it to function at a deep level as a single, integrated, living Totality. Accordingly, underneath our transitory egoic identity there exists a deeper identity that is our True Self, and this Self is sourced in this deeper reality. Thus, the perennial tradition recognizes the human capacity to penetrate beneath the surface of the personal mind and to awaken to these deeper dimensions of consciousness.

From the perennial perspective, the trajectory of evolution is for humanity to experientially realize its deeper transcendent nature and to fully embody it in space-time, progressively transforming the planet in the process. This journey of discovering and embodying divine consciousness is long, leading us to live on Earth not once but many times. From the universe's perspective, our species is an infant, emerging just 100,000 years ago inside a cosmic garden that has been unfolding for 13.7 billion years and will continue to unfold for many billions of years to come. Given the vast scale of the evolutionary project of the universe, we are only beginning to glimpse the depths of the reality that has birthed us and is birthing us still.[3]

When students hear the perennial truths of the world's spiritual traditions simply spoken, when they are reminded of things long ago forgotten but always present at the edge of their awareness, there is sometimes a spark of recognition that can explode into a flame. This flame is contagious and sometimes stimulates sympathetic resonances with other students in the room. Students may collectively feel their energy shift to higher centers of awareness, though they may not understand what is happening. Symptoms of chakra-opening and kundalini-type arousal may begin to manifest. Energy runs, hearts open, and insights arise.[4]

These can be very powerful experiences for students. One sophomore described such an experience in an essay she wrote. It happened to her in an introduction to Eastern religions course when I was describing the Buddhist understanding of the relationship of the individual mind to the awakened mind. To convey this point, I sometimes do a visualization exercise with the students in which I develop an analogy with a tree, contrasting leaf-consciousness (the private self) with tree-consciousness (the Totality). In this analogy, we imagine that the leaves are individually conscious, but not yet conscious of the life of the tree they are part of until the moment of breakthrough occurs. It's a powerful exercise that I save until I think the class is ready to absorb its full import. On this particular day, this young woman experienced the following:

> The thing that hit me the hardest of all that we talked about in class was tree-consciousness and leaf-consciousness. It was what brought everything together for me. What made me understand everyone's

interdependence and stopped me from living in fear. I was so moved that it took everything that I had not to cry in class, not from sadness but from being hit by a life-altering realization. It made an emotion rise in me that I had never felt before and I wasn't really sure how to react to it.

Another student, a woman in her mid-thirties, summarized her experience in a different class in the following way:

Sitting in class, I felt like I was inside one of those glass ball snow scenes that folks use as paperweights. Shake the ball and mass confusion begins with flakes of fake snow swirling all around.... I couldn't *hear* the lecture. My mind struggled to focus and stay with your words, but I was missing it....

Later ... at home ... alone. It would all return to me, the lecture ... Mostly feelings. Tears. Recognition. Understanding after I let it simmer for a while. Realization that if I didn't grab at it, it would be there waiting, this knowledge. These tiny bright spots of revelatory insight. I'd journal. I'd cry. Sometimes light and gentle, warm feel-good crying. Sometimes sobs, wracking and exhausting. *I thought I was losing my mind a few times.*

Instead of hearing your lectures with my Brain-Mind-Intellect, I actually heard you from somewhere else.... Heart-Soul maybe? Ears of a type that I hadn't been exercising. They had atrophied. You gave them a workout. Or the class field was so intense that it penetrated my controlling dominant brain-mind and vibrated my heart-soul like cardiac shock paddles to bring it to life.

The result? I'm becoming who I was *long* ago. The field by-passed my intellect and went directly to my heart to pry it open....I now know what I had deeply buried in me for years, and the gift of the pick and shovel for the ongoing process comes from being in the energy of the folks in our classroom. It didn't come from me alone.

A third student, a seasoned middle-aged woman—is it significant that I'm quoting more women than men here?—described her experience more succinctly: "I have difficulty sitting in this class sometimes. I get so spiritually high that I start to tremble internally. I think that I might lift out of my body and float up."

Again I want to emphasize that it was not my intention to trigger these deep existential reactions. In fact, fearing that they were out of place in a university setting, I often tried to damp them down. This was impossible, however, without damaging the teaching process itself. Whenever we would come together and simply cover the assignment, these things would spontaneously occur, without premeditation or contrivance. It was as though fire was lighting fire. When my students and I would gather and simply focus on the task of sharing under-standing, these *resonances of living experience* would occur unpredictably—not always but often—drawing the students into heightened states of awareness.

Like all insights, these "Aha" experiences can be elusive. One student, a male this time, wrote an essay in which he tried with much frustration to convey the awakening he had experienced in one class. Those who have walked the edges of inspiration will empathize with his dilemma.

> Do you know how close I was today?! I touched it! I felt it breathe! I grasped it with my mind! I knew it was there! It started when you lectured on nature vs. supernature. The Western world was vividly displayed to me....
>
> What was it? It was only there for short spans of time. Damn my Western mind! No sooner would I feel it, I'd lose it. I cannot tell you what it was. Or even what I knew. But I know I knew something! It made sense. *It was as though everything I'd been fighting for and fighting against lay down, side by side.* I knew the answers to my questions, but the answers so overwhelmed me, I forgot the questions. Then I'd lose it. I came *SO* close to breaking down some barriers.

Teaching at Two Levels

Over the course of time, I began to realize that I was beginning to function on campus at two different levels, with each level attracting a different group of students. For most students, I was a conventional professor. This group took my courses looking for academic instruc-tion and they usually walked away reasonably satisfied. Our relationship was primarily about information exchange, the usual undergraduate give-and-take. As the years passed and the magic deep-ened, however, a second group of students emerged with whom I had a different relationship. With these students the exchange of academic information seemed to become a vehicle for a deeper transformational process that triggered significant psychological confrontations, heal-ings, and sometimes spiritual openings. This was happening not because of any conscious design on my part but simply from our coming together and doing the work of education.

This second group of self-actualizing students, to borrow Maslow's phrase, was much smaller in number. They were sprinkled throughout my introductory classes and then signed up for my more specialized upper division courses where their numbers increased, tilting the balance in their favor. Balancing the pedagogical needs and interests of these two groups can be challenging, for both groups are entitled to the college experience they expect. While I always took care to satisfy the intellectual needs of the first group, the second group seemed to be in touch with the course content and with me at a deeper level. It was these students who were to initiate me into a new way of teaching that carried with it new responsibilities. It was they who eventually taught me about the dynamics of collective consciousness.

Teaching at this level in an academic setting, especially at a state university, quickly becomes a very delicate matter. You have to watch carefully to make sure that you have not crossed the line between explaining and persuading. Those who don't know me may suspect that these students responded as they did because I crossed this line or blurred the distinction between education and indoctrination. I understand this concern. In response I can only say that I know and affirm the boundaries of responsible instruction at a state university serving a pluralistic student body. I have diligently honored the separation of church and state in my classes, and my department chair will back me up on this. It is not misdirected missionary zeal that produced these results, but something far more subtle and difficult to comprehend.

More challenging than keeping church and state separate is dealing with student projections. When students are this deeply touched by something that comes out of your mouth, they tend to project all manner of things onto you and it often becomes necessary to protect them from their own enthusiasm. If you don't keep your feet solidly planted on the ground, you can easily get distracted by self-inflation, which is a waste of time, of course, and a waste of a precious opportunity. These things happen not because of our charming personalities but because of something much deeper and larger operating under our feet. Here teachers must be guided by the same principle that guides physicians—"Do no harm"—and indulging our ego is always harmful to our students. Their welfare must be our first, second, and third concern. Fortunately, all these things developed slowly, and my students taught me what I needed to understand about the process as we went along.

Deepening Resonance

So strongly conditioned was I by the Newtonian-Cartesian paradigm that it took years before I was able to admit what now looks to me to be the obvious and natural interpretation of these events—that my spiritual practice outside of class was somehow sparking what was happening inside my classroom, not by my talking about it but silently, covertly, energetically. *The expansive states of conscious that were emerging in my private life seemed to be triggering incidents of sympathetic resonance in my public life.* The transpersonal states of consciousness I was entering at home seemed to be activating the transindividual fabric of life around me, energizing the meridians of the collective psyche and triggering a collective intelligence that was latent in my classroom.

My life and the lives of my students seemed to be moving in sync with each other. I remember one particular incident that dramatized this pattern. One night I had a dream that involved one of my students, a complex dream that did not make any sense to me. On my way to work, I decided that if this particular student showed up at my office hours that day, I would share the dream with her; otherwise I would let it go. (That's how cavalier I had gotten about these things.) Well, the student did show up at my office, and she wanted to tell me about a dream *she* had had that same night in which I had been a player. When she told me her dream, I realized that our two dreams formed two halves of a larger whole. By themselves, the two half-dreams made little sense, but when we put them together, the resulting whole-dream did make sense, and it contained a significant message for her. The whole-dream was not about her and me and there was nothing romantic going on between us. I had simply been enlisted to help her unconscious communicate a point to her conscious awareness. When she left my office that day she had much to think about, and I moved on to what came next. Something was always coming up next.

These synchronicities became particularly pronounced during a period of several years when I was undergoing a series of powerful inner experiences in my spiritual practice that were breaking me down at very deep levels. All spiritual traditions describe a phase of inner work that involves dissolving the boundary between self and other. They describe a membrane that marks the boundary between the individual and the surrounding universe, the interface of the personal and the transpersonal psyche. On the near side of this membrane, the world appears to be composed of separate beings, each with their own private existence. On the far side of the membrane, the world appears as an integrated whole, a continuum of energy that shows itself to be a massive, unfathomably complex, extravagantly beautiful, single organism. Hence, this boundary membrane is the domain of "death and rebirth," death to the world of the private self and rebirth into a larger transcendental order of wholeness that underlies and saturates life's diversity. When a practitioner is transitioning through this territory, standing at the interface of these two paradoxically compatible realities, powerful synchronicities with other persons sometimes manifest.[5]

As my inner work came to focus on this boundary, as it does sooner or later for every practitioner, some of my students seemed to be simultaneously undergoing particularly difficult challenges in their own lives. Most of my students did not enter these waters, of course, and passed through my courses untouched by these dynamics. But some did enter them. Those who did sometimes felt themselves coming to a breaking point in their lives or a moment of supreme risk-taking. It was as though they and I were together being drawn through a collective *death-rebirth vortex*, a vortex that was breaking all of us down in different ways, uprooting deeply buried pains, and crushing restrictive barriers in our lives.

Conscientious students who took my courses during this period were sometimes drawn into deep personal transformation as their systems strained to break the bonds that were holding them back from some richer, more authentic life. Some chose to end bad marriages or to heal wounded ones. Others left careers they had outgrown but were still holding onto. Some began to confront their addictions and others to re-approach persons from whom they had been estranged for a long time. One woman in her mid-forties hints at the profound disruption of her inner and outer world that occurred during this period when she began to spontaneously recover painful memories of child abuse, in a course on Buddhism, of all places:

> During and after having been in your classes, my internal world became increasingly chaotic as demons from painful psychological gestalts began to emerge, and eventually coloring my external world too, challenging everything I thought I was and dissolving familiar reference points. . . . As I struggled to break through powerful gestalts of pain, you spoke to and nourished my soul, making it possible for me to move more deeply into my spiritual journey.

While these kind of reactions may be expected in certain types of courses, such as a counseling course, for example, this was not the case for the courses I was teaching. Rather, these events seemed to be the *indirect effect* of our simply coming together to study. It was not the content of the course that seemed to be driving these effects but something deeper. It had to do with the juxtaposition and interaction of our life energy at a deeper level.

Eventually I came to realize that the fact that my inner and my outer life, my "private" spiritual practice and my public professional life, could not be kept entirely separate from each other was *demonstrating an important truth about the nature of consciousness and the deep structure of reality*. It was actually demonstrating the validity of one of the core axioms of the perennial perspective—the inherent wholeness of existence, the integrated, interpenetrating nature of the universe. Beneath the surface of appearances there are energetic exchanges that connect our lives to those around us, subtle threads that weave our lives into larger wholes. From one perspective, consciousness is clearly differentiated into separate lives, and yet from this deeper perspective it functions holistically, pulsing with a deeper intentionality that ignores the boundaries between self and other.

Seeing Through Two Eyes

It is as though we can see the universe through two different eyes. Through one eye we see the usual world of separate beings. Through this eye of the physical senses we see separate selves—individual human beings learning, growing, challenging themselves, becoming more than they were. Through the other eye, we see the exquisitely intricate patterns that weave these separate lives into larger wholes. When seen through this second eye, consciousness—and life itself—is not something that can be divided into separate bits and pieces but is a seamless whole. It is like the air that is in your lungs one minute and mine the next and in the trees the minute after that. From this perspective, there are no private minds. The very concept of a private mind is seen as an illusion, or, to put it more carefully, as only one half of a greater truth. The challenge is to learn to see through *both* eyes simultaneously, to affirm *both* the truth of individuality *and* the truth of wholeness.

The truth of wholeness and interconnectivity was not a truth that was invited or welcomed in the philosophical landscape I had internalized in graduate school. Like most of my colleagues, I had internalized a worldview that had been born when Newtonian science was at its peak influence. It was a vision of life that was deeply "atomistic," by which I mean that it sees a world composed of separate parts, where the big parts are made of smaller parts that are made of smaller parts still until eventually you come down to some irreducible nugget. For Newton, this nugget was the atom. In this intellectual landscape, the key to understanding the world lies in finding the smallest bits and pieces of life and the laws that govern their properties and movements. From there we can piece together the movements and characteristics of all the larger units life has assembled.

Even after we split the atom and discovered the strangely interconnected and entangled world inside, this tendency to view the world as composed of discrete parts continued in many disciplines. In psychology it combined with other intellectual currents to coalesce into the conviction that the human mind is fundamentally a discrete entity, a private affair. From my perspective, however, this is life as seen through only the first eye. Persons who hold this view of consciousness have simply not yet opened their second eye. They see clearly through the eye of the senses, but the eye that sees wholeness is still closed.

In this atomistic worldview, which is still the default view of most academics even seventy years after the revolution of quantum mechanics, teaching is conceptualized as the transfer of information between ontologically separate minds, minds that do not touch. Teachers pass along to their students the knowledge they have accumulated, or, if they are more gifted, they awaken their students' hunger for learning and then help them satisfy that hunger through a combination of readings, lectures, and discussions. This exchange is always conceptualized as taking place between minds that are fundamentally separate entities. Information must be taken out of one mind, packaged in words or pictures, and projected into other minds where it is taken in, decoded, and assimilated. If all goes well and the transplant takes, our students walk away with something growing inside them that wasn't there before.

It is an unquestioned tenet of most pedagogical thinking today that this exchange takes place between separate beings who are not connected in any way other than through physical channels. The commonsense perception that there are separate minds housed within separate bodies is reinforced daily by the simple fact that our students don't know what we know, that they have to work hard to learn what we have already mastered. However, while this model obviously captures much that goes on in the classroom, it also misses much. It misses what one sees through the second eye. It captures what I would call the "front yard" of teaching but it misses entirely the more subtle dynamics of the "back yard" of teaching. In my classroom, something more was happening, something that went beyond this model.

In contrast to the atomistic model, the understanding of life emerging in many disciplines today—ecology, quantum-relativistic physics, chaos theory, systems theory, feminist theory, and transpersonal psychology, to name only a few—stresses interconnectivity and interpenetration. The living systems model points to a world of fractal iteration and coparticipation, of networks operating within networks within networks, of wholeness sustaining partness. Theory is echoed in human experience. People who meditate or who cultivate other forms of spiritual practice often report that as they shift to deeper levels of consciousness, a new awareness opens. In this awareness they discover that their lives are threads in a single intentional fabric of complex design. These threads are so tightly woven together that they cannot be meaningfully separated from each other.

These observations suggest that *when one person begins to throw off the layers of conditioning and awakens to deeper, more inclusive states of consciousness, surrounding persons will necessarily be affected.* We can picture this if we imagine this deeper Mind, which I capitalize here to distinguish it from the personal mind, as a large tablecloth spread out on a table. If the tablecloth is pulled up at any one point, the entire fabric is drawn up to some degree. Similarly, when any one of us "rises" into clarity, we are all uplifted to some degree and those near us are lifted more than others.[6]

Though this suggestion is still heretical in most academic circles, it raises fewer eyebrows in spiritual communities, which have long been aware that persons undergoing deep spiritual transformation affect those around them. When deep levels of the psyche are activated, the effects radiate outward to touch surrounding persons, like circles rippling across a lake. Satprem, for example, discusses this phenomenon in his biography of Sri Aurobindo entitled *Sri Aurobindo or The Adventure of Consciousness.* There he writes:

> Sri Aurobindo and the Mother would realize that transformation is not just an individual problem but one involving the earth and that no individual transformation is possible (or at least complete) without some degree of collective transformation.... It should be noted that each time Sri Aurobindo and the Mother had some experience indicating a new progress in the transformation, the disciples, without their even knowing anything about it, experienced in their consciousness a period of increased difficulties or even revolts and illnesses, as if everything were grating. Now we begin to understand how things work.[7]

Mike Sayama also mentions this phenomenon in his book *Samadhi*. In his discussion of the dynamics of "vital energy" or *ch'i*, Sayama quotes the Japanese healer Kaneko Shoseki who made the following observation:

> Apart from the normal communication between men through language and action there is another quite different sort of mutual influence. It is that of the rhythm of the Original Strength which permeates all human beings and Nature. Through it every individual thing ... is connected with every other. If then one who is further removed from the working of the Primordial Force is close to one who lives more in accord with it, the rhythm of the Primordial Force will certainly be transmitted from the one to the other. The latter without knowing it exerts a good influence on the other.[8]

In this chapter I am emphasizing the role of the teacher's consciousness as an initiating catalyst, but it goes without saying that initiation requires the participation of two parties, not just one. The professor alone cannot make this happen. Most of my students, remember, did not enter these waters. For this deeper transformation to take place, the students must step forward from their side and seize the opportunity. There must be an openness and receptivity on their part, a felt need to engage or to express themselves more authentically. They may not have been aware of this need before the course began, but somewhere along the way they must make the decision to engage the material more deeply.

Transpersonal Psychology and Teaching

The discipline of transpersonal psychology weaves together psychological theory, scientific research, philosophical analysis, and classical and contemporary spiritual inquiry to outline a worldview that holds the following. Beneath the levels of consciousness in which our minds are separate and distinct lie hidden depths where they begin to interpenetrate until they eventually are enfolded within an unbroken, seamless field of consciousness that I am here calling Mind.

If we view teaching as an activity taking place within this Mind, or perhaps better put, within this Mind-Field, our model of classroom dynamics expands dramatically. Just as our individual minds are intelligent, this larger Mind possesses a *collective* intelligence. The incidents of energetic resonance and informational bleed-through begin to look less anomalous and more natural, even expected. From this perspective, there is no ontological gap between our minds, no juncture or tear in the fabric of being, only a psychological gap that creates the appearance of separation. A starting point that affirms the existence of a seamless field of consciousness underlying our quasi-separate minds gives us a new context within which to view what takes place when minds "meet" in earnest exchange in the classroom.

If mind is a field phenomenon as this study proposes, if it registers not only as our particlelike, sensory awareness but also as a wavelike awareness that extends beyond our bodies, then teaching is more than just sending out information across an ontological chasm for our students to catch. In addition to this, teaching involves the *direct energetic engagement of the mental fields of our students*. It is mind directly engaging other minds within the unified field of Mind. Through this direct engagement, bridges of resonance sometimes spring into existence underneath, supporting the exchange of information taking place at the conscious level. Usually these deeper resonances are so subtle that they pass undetected, like most of the operations of the collective psyche. Under certain conditions, however, they can surface and make their presence consciously felt in the classroom.

From the perspective of many spiritual systems, both ancient and contemporary, there is no such thing as an entirely private mind and for that reason there is no such thing as an entirely private spiritual practice. Every practice emerges from and reaches back into the extended fabric of Mind. Its effects spread out around us in circles, like ripples spreading across a pond. In chapter 3, I will review some of the scientific research that supports this model of consciousness. For the moment, let me continue to speak using metaphor more freely.

When a person begins to sink into oneness with life through sustained spiritual practice, it is as though it creates a depression in the spiritual-gravitational field around that individual. Other persons are sometimes drawn into this field of influence often without seeming to choose it. Why this happens is easier to understand from a transpersonal, integral perspective than from an atomistic, materialistic perspective.

In the transpersonal vision, life is deeply and inherently integrated at the start. Though we rightly value our boundaries and celebrate our differences, the deeper currents of life nourish the connective tissue of our integrated existence. Our personal intelligence participates in a larger collective intelligence. Therefore, when one person enters into communion with this deeper intelligence, it is as though it generates an energy that radiates through the underlying fabric of life in which we are all suspended. *Clarified states of consciousness are contagious.* This is an utterly natural phenomenon, an unstoppable effect. Our spiritual ecology simply does not allow private awakening.

This radiating effect is particularly noticeable when one is standing in the center of one's work in the world. Performing artists, musicians, athletes, and ministers have all reported experiencing the collective waves that sometimes pulse through them when they work. The same is true for teachers. There is a subtle collective pulse that sometimes registers inside our work, a meaningful and complex interweaving of lives and insights. As a teacher, I have learned to trust this mysterious process, to not be afraid of it, and to respect its power. It demands impeccable conduct and complete surrender to the good of our students.

Though I left my spiritual practice at home every morning when I went to work at the university, I could not leave myself at home, and my spiritual practice seemed to be changing my energetic constitution at deep levels. It appears that my "private" attempt to actualize a more authentic existence and deeper communion with life was causing my person to act as a kind of lightning rod triggering sparks of a similar awakening among those students who were receptive to this influence. And this was happening automatically, without my conscious intention or direction.

As the second group of self-actualizing students began to be drawn toward their own deeper potential, they began to wake up to new possibilities in their lives. Most of them experienced this as a pleasant, even ecstatic experience, an "Aha!" moment or series of moments. For some of them, however, the waking up process presented them with difficult personal challenges. Without either of us intending it, taking a course with me triggered their own transformational process. Before they could become the "more" that they had the potential to become, they had to confront whatever it was that was keeping them stuck in the "less" position.

When their systems were activated by what I believe is a life-affirming, life-enhancing energy, these students began a spontaneous process of detoxification—a shedding of old patterns, old ways of thinking and feeling. Why this happens is rather straightforward. In order to make room for new growth, they had to confront the habits, convictions, and choices that had been holding their lives in some stuck position. I do not believe that this would have happened if they had not been ready for it to occur and even inviting it at a deeper level. They entered this transformational process not because they were forced to but because they were ripe for it.

This transformational initiation did not happen to all my students, of course. Most of my students, those in the first group, simply experienced an intellectually stimulating course. "Thanks for a great course, Doc. See ya!" It was the students in the second group who felt something more happening and signed up for more courses with me. The most powerful synchronistic effects showed up primarily in my upper division courses, where the majority of students were repeat business. These students *chose* to expose themselves to this activation. They wanted more, not less, of what was happening to them.

While the activation my students experienced was sometimes quite powerful, there were no casualties and many positive breakthroughs. On the rare occasion when a student's self-transformation became particularly turbulent, I referred him or her to a gifted therapist in the area with whom they were able to process what was emerging in a safe therapeutic environment. The woman who wrote that she thought she was "losing her mind" is glad she lost it. She used our time together to make important changes in her life and has become a good family friend.

I understand how strange this story may sound to readers who, like me, were educated to think of the mind as compartmentalized and physically constrained to the brain. And yet I believe that this conventional way of thinking is simply false, and it does educators a great disservice because it desensitizes us to the subtler collective textures of the teaching experience. By failing to legitimate our lived experience, it obstructs our ability to make sense of what is actually taking place in our classroom and thus stifles the full transformative potential of the student–teacher relationship. It is not that people's minds don't function separately in a "stand–alone" mode because they obviously do, but it appears that this is not the whole truth. There is also a more subtle dynamic operating in the classroom, a *collective* dynamic that reflects the wavelike features of mind that transcend and integrate the particlelike mind, a *collective* intelligence that surrounds our personal intelligence.

Teaching and Spiritual Practice

With a growing number of educators taking up different forms of spiritual practice today, the interactions I have been describing in this chapter are likely to become more common in the years ahead if they are not that way already. The spiritual disciplines people are practicing are many and varied—yoga, meditation, shamanic initiation, vision quest, sacred medicine work, prayer and fasting, trance dancing, and experiential psychotherapy. This list may be putting too exotic a spin on it, for surely a life of service to the collective good has the potential to produce similar results. Even so, there is no denying that powerful techniques for expanding consciousness and engaging the deep psyche have become part of our cultural landscape. Before the last century, many of these practices were the carefully guarded secrets of small contemplative circles or the lifeblood of cultures far distant from our shores. But how quickly our spiritual terrain has changed. For better or for worse, self-transformation is a highly marketed, widely distributed commodity today. Previously secret lore is being passed along to a hungry public through an international network of workshops, institutes, and retreat centers.

Educators who engage in transformative practice can expect these connections with their students to surface in a variety of forms. I have been describing how I happened to experience them, but there are countless ways for these subtle dynamics to surface around us. As unique beings from the moment of our birth, we each have distinct constitutions that lead us to meet the world in different ways, causing different configurations of experience to crystallize around us. Furthermore, the spiritual practices we do vary widely and impact consciousness in different ways, encouraging this deeper fabric of connectivity to surface in a variety of patterns. The subtle training of Buddhist mindfulness meditation, for example, may lead some teachers to begin to notice the delicate dance of synchronicity pulsing quietly within the ever-changing flow of circumstance. Alternatively, the powerfully evocative states of shamanic immersion may trigger more explosive sparks. The underlying fabric of life can express itself in many modalities.[9]

If there is a message that my students and I wish to share with the reader that comes from our experience, it is this. *If you are an educator who has chosen a form of spiritual practice that has the capacity to activate deep levels of the unconscious, you can expect to stimulate sympathetic resonances in at least some of your students.* Separate minds are an illusion of the senses, how life appears if you look at it through only one eye. If you begin to immerse yourself in the inherent wholeness of life and to stimulate the purification processes that inevitably occur when self seeks True Self, you will not make this journey alone. As an educator, you must anticipate that at least some of your students will move in rhythm with your descent. You must expect it and you must prepare for it. Like ripples on water, these resonances are inevitable, and the better teacher you are, the more powerful you can expect them to be.

These observations apply to more than teachers, of course, and I hope they will be picked up and used by persons in other occupations. They apply to anyone who works with or lives in groups, which includes just about all of us. The resonances described in this chapter can spring up wherever persons gather in well-focused collective projects—in think tanks, board rooms, on playing fields, and around the dining room table.

I do not think we need to be afraid of the energetic resonances that spread out around us as a result of our spiritual practice. We need to be careful, of course, and to act responsibly and compassionately at all times, but I think we can trust that we are where we are supposed to be. Furthermore, I do not believe that what happened in my classes was the result only of energetic resonances springing up between my students and my person. This is only half of the story. There was something else that was contributing to these events. This is what we will explore in the next chapter.

CHAPTER 2

Group Fields, Group Minds

We have all known that simple physical systems exhibit spontaneous order. . . . What is new is that the range of spontaneous order
is enormously greater than we have supposed. Profound order is
being discovered in large, complex, and apparently random
systems.

—Stuart Kaufman, *At Home in the Universe*

When the synchronistic resonances described in the previous chapter
began manifesting in my classes, I first thought of them as paranormal
exchanges taking place between separate minds. The isolation of our
minds from one another seemed to me to be the "natural condition"
and these instances of bleed-through were the exception that needed
to be explained. In speaking about them to others, I often used the
language of "sparks" and "bridges," images that suggested spanning
or jumping over gaps. Like invisible radio waves connecting radio
operators miles apart, what fascinated me was the idea that separate
beings could occasionally bridge the chasm that separated them. The
chasm felt primary; the bridges were the exception to be explained.

As deeper patterns of interconnectedness emerged, however, I
began to recognize that these events were better thought of as the
manifestation of something more fundamental than this. A profound,
organic, preexisting interconnectedness seemed to be surfacing. I
began to make a fundamental pivot in my thinking—that the chasm
of separation may not be the natural condition after all, that underneath the truth of separation another truth might be trying to emerge.

In describing the characteristics of light, Niels Bohr said, "The
opposite of a profound truth may well be another profound truth."
This seems to be true of consciousness as well. The truth of our
psychological separation is an obvious and important truth that

anchors something quite precious, our individuality. In my courses, however, this truth was being confronted with another truth, the truth of an underlying wholeness. Eventually it simply became more elegant to conceptualize these phenomena as symptoms of the emergence of a unified field that incorporated the class as a whole, a *group mind* if you will.

There were several features of what was happening that pushed me in this direction. Students were becoming more porous not only to me but to each other. They sometimes showed up in each other's dreams in significant ways. Synchronicities between them were increasing, and life-expanding coincidences were becoming almost routine in my classes. As one male student who returned to college after a twenty-year absence reported to me:

> Each quarter seemed to bring new and unexpected changes and synchronicities. I entered into a web of personal relationships and meetings with people that profoundly influenced my life. I was "finding" individuals whose circumstances were eerily similar to my own; people who knew friends of mine from obscure places in the world; people who seemed to be reading the same books at the same times and having experiences that were transforming them in the same shattering yet exhilarating ways.

A female student sent me the following description of the connectivity she experienced with other students during the same time period.

> All of us who have been in your classes feel a deep connection to one another. We don't know what it is. We only know that it is there. All that I know is that I have felt something binding us all together. I remember things going on around me in class with the other students. We were sensitive to each other's thoughts and feelings. There were times when I would pick up bits and pieces of certain people's thoughts. We could see the connections being made and we acted accordingly. I always wondered if you knew what was going on because you never said a thing in class! Strange things were happening. The students closest to you expected them to happen. Were we crazy? "What the hell is going on?" we questioned. Imagine all of this taking place on a college campus. A college class that wasn't only a class it was a community, semester after semester.

The most important observation that pushed me toward a collective reading of these events was the sheer magnitude of the forces that seemed to be involved. Too many people's lives were being too deeply affected for me to conceptualize what was happening solely in terms of resonances with my individual energy. If my person was in some way a catalyst for these experiences to surface among my students, what was actually surfacing was something much larger than I could be generating. As I made the shift to thinking of this larger "something" in terms of a collective field or collective mind, a variety of conceptual and experiential pieces began to fall into place.

The emergence of a group mind is not restricted to the classroom, of course, and is more common than one might think. In her doctoral dissertation, Renee Levi studied thirty-two episodes of "collective resonance" that occurred in contexts as different as a singing group, a construction crew, a strategic planning retreat, and a senator's election campaign.[1] Other writers concur. Michael Novak described the emergence of a group mind in sports in his book *The Joy of Sports* (published in 1976):

> When a collection of individuals first jells as a team, truly begins to react as a five-headed or eleven-headed unit rather than as an aggregate of five or eleven individuals, you can almost hear the click: a new kind of reality comes into existence at a new level of human development.... For those who have participated in a team that has known the click of communality, the experience is unforgettable, like that of having attained, for a while at least, a higher level of existence.[2]

Los Angeles Lakers coach Phil Jackson has observed the same thing. In an interview he said:

> When a player surrenders his self-interest for the greater good, his fullest gifts as an athlete are manifested.... It changes things for everybody. All of a sudden, the rest of the team can react instinctively to what that player is doing. And it just kind of mushrooms out from there—the whole begins to add up to more than the sum of its parts. We see this a lot in critical situations. When players are totally focused on the *team* goal, their efforts can create chain reactions. It's as if they become totally connected to one another, in sync with one another, like five fingers on one hand.[3]

Catherine Baker, a professional musician, described the emergence of a similar psychic connection in a chamber music orchestra: "It does seem that when a chamber group orchestra gets this psychic 'link' in a performance, the audience genuinely knows that it has been part of something special (as do the players!)."[4] William Rowe, an engineer interested in studying what he calls "episodes of focused group energy," summarized their appearance in the following manner:

> Every so often we hear of a group of people who unite under extreme pressure to achieve seemingly miraculous results. In these moments human beings transcend their personal limitations and realize a collective synergy with results that far surpass expectations based on past performance. Anyone hearing a fine symphonic or jazz group hopes for one of those "special" concerts, that uplift both the audience and the performers.... These occurrences, although unusual, are much more frequent in American business than is commonly suspected.[5]

Concerning such moments of collective synergy, Emerson wrote:

> And so, in groups where debate is earnest, and especially on high questions, the company becomes aware that the thought rises to an equal level in all bosoms, that all have a spiritual property in what was said, as well as the sayer. They all become wiser than they were. It arches over them like a temple, this unity of thought.[6]

If athletes, musicians, philosophers, and business people experience transient episodes of integrated, collective mental functioning, is it that unusual that they should also surface in a classroom?

Sometimes when I am simply doing my job as a professor, covering the day's assignment, it's as if the floor suddenly falls away. The atmosphere in the room becomes supercharged, and everyone seems to congeal into a unified state. My mind becomes unusually spacious and clear, and my students' eyes tell me that they have moved into a particularly receptive state. Our hearts seem to merge, and from this open field of compassion comes a slow stream of thoughts that I, as spokesperson for the group, unfold and work with.

In these transient moments of heightened awareness, I sometimes have the acute sensation that there is only one mind present in the room. It's as if the walls that usually separate us have become gossamer curtains. Individual persons melt into a softly glowing field of energy, and this unified energy thinks and feels and hungers to speak. Because this field incorporates the life experience of everyone present, of course we sometimes find the details of our separate histories surfacing spontaneously in it. Because it embodies our private hopes and fears, of course we are sometimes deeply touched by what comes out of it.[7]

Rupert Sheldrake and Morphic Fields

The concept of a centralized, integrating intelligence, an *anima mundi* or "world soul" underlying our individual lives, is an ancient idea, but the attempt to provide empirical evidence for its existence is a relatively recent undertaking. Beginning with C. G. Jung's early attempt to demonstrate the existence of a collective unconscious through the cross-cultural study of ancient myths and comparing these to the spontaneous dreams of his clients, the movement to give empirical precision to this concept has gathered momentum rapidly in the last century. Quantum theory either invites or at the very least tolerates such an "implicate" intelligence, depending on whose interpretation of the calculus one reads. J. E. Lovelock's Gaia hypothesis directs us to a planetary intelligence in order to make sense of otherwise enigmatic shifts that have taken place in the Earth's ecosystem over billions of years. John Barrow and Frank Tipler's anthropic cosmological principle invites us to look afresh at the extraordinary series of highly improbable coincidences that have led to our existence and reintroduces the notion of a goal-oriented intentionality operating inside evolution.

One of the important attempts to give empirical precision to the concept of an integrating, collective intelligence has been Rupert Sheldrake's theory of formative causation and morphic fields. Sheldrake more than any other writer helped me take the step of thinking of the events taking place in my classes as a manifestation of a collective intelligence. Sheldrake uses the term "morphic field" as a general category that includes several different types of fields, including morphogenetic fields, behavioral fields, social and cultural fields, and mental fields. Here I am primarily concerned with the field Sheldrake calls the "group mind."

In an important series of books—*A New Science of Life* (1981), *The Presence of the Past* (1986), and *The Rebirth of Nature* (1991)— Sheldrake has argued that the individual members of every species are networked in a group mind that constitutes the dynamic blueprint of that species. He has presented a powerful body of evidence to propose that each species has a morphic field associated with it that contains the blueprint of the species' physical form. Going against the assumptions of mainstream biology, Sheldrake argues that these fields, not just DNA alone, influence the species' morphological development. This innovation allows him to solve a number of paradoxes that biologists had previously been unable to resolve.

Sheldrake goes on to propose that these fields are essential to understanding not only the morphology of a species but its behavioral tendencies as well because they hold the collective learning of the species as a whole. He sees the collective mind of a species as incorporating the new experiences of its individual members, constantly synthesizing at a central level the diverse experiences of its many members. In short, the species-mind learns as its individual members learn. This learning is carried and transferred through a process of *morphic resonance*, which Sheldrake has described as the influence of like on like, the influence of patterns of activity on subsequent similar patterns of activity, an influence that passes through or across space and time from past to present.

According to Sheldrake, all experience and all learning registers at two levels—at the individual level and at a centralized, collective level. When members of a given species are learning a new behavior, the learning curve is low because the new learning of the few is outweighed by the prior cumulative learning of the many. As more individuals learn the new behavior, however, a critical mass is eventually reached. The system comes to a tipping point where the learning curve of the group shifts. It's as if the collective mind suddenly "gets it." From that point on, it gets progressively easier for members of the species to learn this behavior. Future learners still have to exert themselves to acquire the skill, but it's as if at some deep level of consciousness the path has been marked, the skids greased. Learning gets easier. Sheldrake insists that his theory is empirically testable because we can test the rate at which new skills are acquired by a species. The early reports of attempts to carry out such tests are encouraging.[8]

Sheldrake thus proposes that the individual and its species are constantly involved in a complex, two-way feedback process, with the individual contributing to the learning of the whole and the whole structuring the learning of the individual. His theory suggests that the mental processes we see operating within an individual human being are paralleled by similar processes operating in the species as a whole, making allowances for the enormous differences involved. Just as we remember in a coherent fashion our individual experiences, the species mind remembers the experiences of its many members. Just as the integration and management of our individual experiences reflects intelligence and choice, the species mind possesses a higher order of the same capacities.

In essence, Sheldrake believes that groups have minds and that these minds can be described as fields. Fields have been an increasingly prominent concept in scientific discourse beginning with Michael Faraday's introduction of electromagnetic fields in the nineteenth century and extending to contemporary discussions of the zero point field. In essence, a field can be thought of as a *self-organizing region of influence*, a matrix or medium that connects two or more points in space, usually via a force whose properties may or may not be initially understood. The concept of field is often invoked as a way of speaking about what scientists call "action at a distance," the apparent influence between separate objects with no detectable substance connecting them.[9]

Between the individual and the field of the species mind, Sheldrake suggests that numerous intermediate fields exist corresponding to various subgroups that the individual is part of—family, community, nation, race, and culture, to name a few. The species field is in turn nested in a series of larger fields that encompass the planet, the solar system, the galaxy, and so on. As in general systems theory, Sheldrake's vision is of fields nested within fields nested within fields, with lines of communication running from the largest to the smallest and back again.

McDougall's Rats

Because the concept of a group mind jars so many of our sensibilities, let me briefly summarize an important series of experiments Sheldrake points to for support of this hypothesis. There are many pieces of research that Sheldrake uses to make his argument, but this experiment is particularly telling.

Mechanistic biology sharply distinguishes between innate behavior, which is genetically programmed, and learned behavior, which is acquired. It is a widely accepted axiom of biology that these are two separate systems and that learned behavior cannot be passed on genetically. In the 1920s, William McDougall at Harvard University decided to test this axiom in what became a highly controversial experiment.

McDougall designed a water maze in which he tested white rats from the Wistar strain. In his maze were two gangways leading out of the water to two doors that were alternatively lighted at random intervals. The lighted door led to a shock; the unlighted door led out of the maze. The learning task was to exit the water by avoiding the lit door. The rate of learning was calculated by counting the number of tries it took each rat to exit the water through the correct door.

McDougall would train a generation of rats, tabulate their scores, then breed them and test the next generation in the maze. He wanted to see whether the learned behavior of one generation was being passed along genetically to their children, allowing them to learn the maze more quickly than their parents.

All in all, McDougall tested thirty-two generations of rats in an experiment that ran for fifteen years. His results showed that, contrary to expectations, successive generations of rats did in fact learn the maze more quickly than their parents. His conclusion was that learned behavior could be passed along genetically.[10]

Because these experimental results challenged a deeply entrenched scientific belief, they provoked a hailstorm of criticism, some of it deserved and some of it not. The most serious failing of McDougall's experiment was his failure to provide a control group—rats that were bred under the same conditions as the rats that were taught the maze but who were not trained. Members of the control group could be periodically tested to determine whether any other variable in how the rats were being treated might be influencing the results.

In Scotland, a research team at Edinburgh University led by F. A. E. Crew attempted to replicate McDougall's results while correcting for this omission. Crew's team reproduced McDougall's water maze exactly and worked with the same strain of rats for eighteen generations, though not ones genetically descended from McDougall's rats. Unfortunately, Crew's results were inconclusive, possibly because he allowed intense inbreeding among his rats. One startling observation did emerge from Crew's research, however. His team found that the average score of Crew's rats from the very beginning was similar to McDougall's rats after thirty generations of training. It was as though Crew's rats began their learning where McDougall's rats had left off.[11]

A second and definitive attempt to replicate McDougall's findings was subsequently carried out by W. E. Agar and his colleagues at Melbourne University in Australia. Agar's team used better methods than Crew and included a control population in their study. They kept their research going for twenty years, testing fifty generations of rats and publishing their final results in 1954. They too found that successive generations learned the maze more quickly than their parents, thus vindicating McDougall's findings. However, in a dramatic turn of events, they found the same tendency in the control population, at a slightly reduced rate. Rats that were untrained were also learning the water maze faster and faster through successive generations. Agar therefore rejected McDougall's conclusion that learned behavior was being passed along genetically and drew an even more radical conclusion. Learning was being transferred, he said, through a nongenetic, nonphysical medium. That is, learning was being transferred from mind to mind, or psychically.[12]

Morphic Fields in the Classroom

I had read Sheldrake's books and embraced his concept of morphic fields operating at the species level, but it was some time before I saw the relevance of his theory to what was taking place in my classes. At its core, Sheldrake's theory addresses the mind of an entire species. When he focuses on human beings, he extends his theory to include various subgroups within the species, but these subgroups are deeply entrenched in history. Family, community, nation, race, and culture are patterns of association that form over decades, centuries, and millennia. My classes seemed to be too short-lived to be included in this list. My students and I met for only a few months, and it did not seem that anything that developed in so short a period of time could participate in the processes Sheldrake was outlining.

This shifted for me in 1994 when I had an experience that dramatically expanded my frame of reference for understanding these events. At that point I realized that Sheldrake's concept of morphic fields could be used to illumine many of the puzzling experiences my students and I had been having. The dynamics of the species mind that he had been tracing seemed also to apply to the short-term groups I was working with—to a more modest degree. The key insight that I took from Sheldrake was the idea that not just individual persons have minds, *groups also have minds*. This revolutionary premise encouraged me to take his conclusions one further step—even *transient* groups can manifest a kind of group consciousness. Sheldrake gave me permission to interpret the phenomena that had been surrounding me as symptoms of a collective mind emerging in my classroom.

Looking back, I am amazed that it took me so long to recognize what has now become obvious—that there is a living intelligence operating in groups, a subtle field that weaves those present into a larger operational whole, a true mind that receives and integrates our many life experiences, an intermediate structure between the individual and the still larger patterns of life. My personal resistance to this concept no doubt reflected the deep resistance of my profession and my culture to thinking about mind in this way.

Let me insert a qualification. When I say that a group has a "group mind," I don't mean to suggest that it has a center of prehension or agency that controls its many members in ways comparable to how "I" control the limbs of my body. Nor am I suggesting that it is self-aware in the same way or to the same degree that we are self-aware. As a field of influence, a group mind does not usurp or eliminate the freedoms, rights, or responsibilities of its members. It does not "take over" or suppress the individual minds that compose it, as in the Star Trek series when the Borg take over the minds of the species they assimilate into its mono-mind, reducing them to subhuman, zombie-like automatons—half human, half machine. (From my perspective, the Borg look like the fear-filled projection of the Western ego that cannot imagine anything larger than itself that it is part of, except in reductionistic terms that diminish its own freedoms.) The challenge is to stretch our thinking to imagine forms of integral intelligence that do not diminish but *augment* the human abilities we rightly value so highly.

In a traditional philosophy department, you quickly step beyond the pale of acceptable conversation if you suggest that anything other than an individual being with a highly developed nervous system has a mind. Such an idea is often interpreted as regression to a premodern, prescientific mode of thinking rather a move toward a postmodern, postquantum sensibility. The mainstream position is that humans have minds because we have complex brains. We're not sure how far down the evolutionary ladder you have to go before mind drops out and you're left with "just biology," but it is a near axiom of the modern worldview that our minds derive from and are generated by our brains.

Historically, this conclusion represents the culmination of a long cultural progression in which we gradually disenchanted the universe by removing consciousness from all inorganic life forms and restricted it to only those organic life forms that had highly complex nervous systems. Invoking what we believed were sound reasons at the time, we stripped mind from the universe and located it entirely in ourselves, setting us apart from everything around us. Because human beings were mindful in a seemingly unique way—reasoning, calculating, and, above all, self-aware—we concluded that nothing else in the universe was mindful, certainly not in the way that we were. Nothing else was truly intelligent, imaginative, and purposeful. The universe was coming to be seen as an unconscious machine moving with mathematical precision and driven by blind chance and natural selection. As a result, we came to view ourselves, and perhaps some of our near evolutionary cousins, as the only beings in the universe that are conscious and could "have minds." We saw ourselves living in a dead universe, meaning a universe lacking in mind, which curiously enough has produced a species extraordinarily full of mind. How this happened has never been explained. (It pains me to take so many liberties summarizing such an important series of developments. Historians forgive me.[13])

When I extended Sheldrake's observations about group minds to include the more transient groups I was working with as a teacher, many pieces of the puzzle that I had been wrestling with began to fall into place, leading me to formulate the following provisional hypotheses.

Learning Fields

I believe that regularly taught courses have distinct mental fields associated with them. These fields reflect the activity we are engaged in, which in my case is learning, so I think of the fields that surround my work as an educator as *learning fields*. If I were a physician working in a hospital, I would be talking about healing fields, reflecting the repeated acts of healing that take place every day in hospitals. If I were a coach, I would be speaking about team fields. But, since I work at a university, the fields generated by my work are learning fields.

Following Sheldrake, I suggest that a learning field reflects and embodies the cumulative learning of all the students through the years who have ever taken a specific course with a specific professor. I tend to view these fields as connected to individual professors because of the highly personalized nature of teaching. The same course taught by different professors in a department will typically end up being different educational experiences. This is especially true in the humanities where the nature of the discipline allows us wide latitude for individual tailoring of how we approach our subject. Each professor brings his or her distinctive strengths and perspectives to the task of teaching. They may select different readings, give different assignments, and ask their students to extract different lessons from the material.

For these reasons, I tend to give more weight to the professor as the anchor of these learning fields than the course itself, though clearly there is overlap here. While my primary objective is to analyze the base unit of fields associated with the courses of individual instructors, I think that these fields combine with other learning fields at more comprehensive levels. Individual faculty fields compound into department fields that compound into college and university fields. In a hospital, the fields of individual doctors compound into department fields and so on.

In this view, the learning fields associated with a professor's courses reflect and embody the cumulative exercise of learning that has taken place inside their courses over many years. Thus, they are *informational fields*, meaning that they are content specific. They register and carry the mental exertion that previous students have invested in understanding specific ideas—their breakthroughs and their resulting insights. They reflect both the depth of learning that has occurred and the quantity. Where the learning has been greater, the fields will be stronger, and they continue to grow stronger through the years as more and more students take the course.

Two Layers of the Field

I recommend that we distinguish two layers of these learning fields— what I call the *course field* and the *class field* or, alternatively, the *course mind* and the *class mind*. This is an important distinction for the theoretical discussion of fields. What I have been describing thus far is the course field—the energetic field that holds the cumulative learning experience of *all the students who have ever taken this course with this professor*. The class field or class mind is the layer of this field being generated by the *current group of students* who are taking the course this semester. I think of the class field as the outer membrane of the course field, the living edge of that larger field. We might draw an analogy with a tree. The class field can be compared to the tree's outer cambium ring while the course field is the tree in its totality. The more rings a tree has, the larger and stronger it is, but its present growth is always taking place at its outer edge.

The distinction between the course field and the class field allows us to describe some of the dynamics of these fields more precisely. While the course field is the standing field surrounding a course, the class field is the new layer being generated and added this semester. I believe that being an intentional field, the class field begins to congeal during registration when the students are choosing their courses, weeks before the class actually begins to meet. If we wanted to be more precise, we could say that the class field begins to form when students first set their mental intention to take a particular course.

The class field gets stronger as the students go through the various steps required to take the course—registering for the course, arranging their work schedules, buying their books, and paying their tuition. Each step strengthens their commitment to taking the course and invests the field with more energy. Because many of my students pay their own college bill, writing a check for their tuition represents a significant commitment on their part and therefore strengthens the field considerably. By the time the students show up on the first day, the class field has been growing for some time. On that day I meet the physical body of a field I have been in dialogue with for weeks. (More on this in chapter 4.)

I think of the course field as being more powerful energetically than the class field, or it becomes so over time. Generalizations about the course field's strength relative to the class field are hazardous and hard to justify. How do we compare the cumulative energetic residue of thousands of students from the past with the energy of thirty living students who are present in the room now? One might argue that present energy trumps past energy, that the living energy of those present today is actually more potent than the energetic traces left by students who are no longer present.

I understand this position and there is much to recommend it. Nevertheless, my intuition is that the cumulative power of the course mind *eventually* trumps the power of the class mind at some point in the course's history. If not in the beginning, in time the energy that collects around activities repeated over many years with many people develops a momentum that begins to influence the behavior of subsequent groups in powerful and sometimes dramatic ways. When old learning begins to influence new learning, this is a sign of its greater power.

When the semester starts and we get down to work, the older and more potent course field begins to suffuse and integrate with the recently formed class field, unleashing its powerful currents into this new group of students and from there into the minds of individual students. When the course is under way, the energy that these students will encounter will be not just their professor's energy and not just the collective energy of the students present in the room but also the energetic residue of the learning of all the students who have taken this course before them.

I believe that these fields are always present whenever collective intention is focused in group projects of sustained duration and repeated form. Usually they operate below the threshold of awareness, and most of my colleagues, even very conscientious instructors, are not aware of their existence. They appear to vary enormously in strength, reflecting a variety of factors, including the commitment and focus of the students, their level of enthusiasm for the subject matter, and the vitality of their engagement in the classroom. Under certain conditions, these fields can become strong enough to trigger a variety of phenomena that are "paranormal" only from the perspective of an outworn atomistic psychological paradigm. Within an integral, transpersonal paradigm, these phenomena are entirely normal. *They are simply the natural effects of the gradual surfacing of the deeper levels of collective mind in group contexts.*

Changes in the Learning Curve

Applied to the university setting, Sheldrake's theory of morphic fields suggests that the learning that previous students have achieved should sooner or later make it easier for subsequent generations of students to acquire the same concepts. At this point, we don't know how many students a professor has to teach or how many times he or she has to teach a course before the learning field surrounding it reaches a state of critical mass that could trigger such a shift in the students' learning curve. Careful longitudinal studies are required to test this hypothesis and those studies have yet to be performed. However, I can report that this expectation is consistent with my experience in the classroom, and other educators have told me that they have observed the same phenomenon in their classes. I find that every so many years, I have to adjust my lesson plan because the students are more easily grasping concepts that previously had required lengthy explanation and argument.

Teaching a course is something like climbing a mountain (says one who has never gone mountain climbing). You study the mountain and plan your ascent. First you will establish a base camp at A, then a second and third camp at B and C. You plan the route, calculate the supplies and number of Sherpas you will need for each phase of the climb, and you set the schedule. If all goes well, you'll be ready to launch your final push for the summit on a particular date. Teaching is something like this. You have an objective that must be reached in stages. You calculate what the students will need to accomplish each stage, what information, resources, and skill sets they will require. You anticipate what problems they will likely encounter and build the solutions into your lesson plan. And because time is always limited, you create a schedule. You have to have a schedule if you're going to give the students the full experience of the course's vision in fifteen short weeks. Without a schedule, you may waste precious time in the early weeks and have to rely on luck to pull things out at the end, or you'll have to turn back early with the summit not reached.

After you've taught a course for several years, you've pretty much worked these details out. You've put the course through its shake-down cruise, learned what does and doesn't work, and have hopefully shaped a successful course. You bring your climbing schedule to class on the first day in the form of a syllabus, but sometimes your students throw you a curve. You show up with a carefully prepared agenda that has been a consistent winner in previous years, but your students signal you in the first week that they do not need some of the prelim-inaries you've planned. They are ahead of you in the syllabus. This can be a very disconcerting experience for an instructor. After years of using a proven route to a specific intellectual objective, it's as if the students have suddenly found a shortcut and are bored if you insist on taking them the long way around. It requires making some quick adjustments if you're going to stay in true dialogue with them.

Obviously, many factors could be contributing to this develop-ment. It could be that the students are reflecting general shifts in cultural insight. Previously challenging ideas may have become more culturally accepted over time and so need less preparation and argu-ment. It could be that students are a self-selecting population. A professor gets a reputation on campus for being interested in certain ideas and this draws to your courses students who are also interested in these ideas and are therefore predisposed toward them. It could also be improved pedagogical delivery—you've simply gotten better at getting the point across in less time.

While all of these influences may be contributing to the situation, after watching this cycle repeat itself many times through the years, I'm convinced that more is going on. In my experience, these shifts take place too suddenly and too frequently for them to be fully accounted for by these explanations. The students can turn the tables on you in one semester, remain stable for several years, then suddenly shift again. It's almost as if they've gotten smarter all of a sudden, as if certain ideas are just easier for them to take in and come to terms with—which is what Sheldrake's theory predicts should happen. If I stick with the tried and true program because it's easier or more certain, it's usually a disaster. Pedagogically, it's a new day and they want me at their edge. This is where the energy is strongest, when we meet at our true edges.

Another observation from my experience that correlates well with Sheldrake's theory is the way that the influence of these learning fields developed gradually in my course. Sporadic instances of resonance began showing up in my courses after I had been teaching for about five years, but it took another five years or so before the fields gathered sufficient strength to become a significant collective force in the room. This pattern of progressive strengthening matches Sheldrake's predictions. These fields begin small and become stronger with each group of students who take the course.

If the hypothesis of learning fields is correct and reflects a true dynamic of nature, we should see improvement in the learning curves of not just students but other kinds of groups as well—employees, athletic teams, work details, and so on. Such cognitive shifts are often overlooked, I think, because we haven't had a paradigm that taught us to be on the lookout for them or that could make sense of them when they did occur. Observant group leaders, however, have sometimes noticed and made note of them. I came across one such report from a musician named Colin Hall. Hall taught a series of drumming workshops in South Africa and observed an unexplained improvement in the quality of drumming that took place across these workshops. He wrote:

> We started adding a drumming session to our Program about 8 months ago. During each session we invite the participants to "go solo." The first session was embarrassingly bad. So, too, was the second and the third—although slightly less so. We considered leaving the solos out. After twelve Programs the solos have become progressively better and they are now quite extraordinary—the absolute highlight of the drumming session—indeed, one of the highlights of the whole Program. The Programs are from two weeks to two months apart; each has a different group of diverse South Africans, only the facilitators and the drum master offer continuity and the facilitators are not trained drummers. We have experimented with the ambience a little. But nothing easily explains the incredible improvement in the solo drumming.

Interestingly enough, an African participant in the last program was not at all surprised by this development. "The skins of the drums are learning the tunes," he explained. "The drummers change but they leave their learning in the skins of the drums and in the flames of the fire around which we drum."[14]

Creating Strong Fields

Exactly what conditions are required for these learning fields to manifest in the classroom is a matter of ongoing inquiry for me, and I don't yet have a definitive list of conditions. For a while I was tempted to think that it may in part be a function of the subject matter of the course, that courses that address the existential mysteries of life activate deeper levels of our being than are stirred by discussion of semiconductors, logarithms, and differential equations. Eventually, however, I decided that this just reflected my personal bias and was not a general principle. If a professor lived and breathed these technical subjects and injected their passion for them into their teaching, if their students caught and returned this passion, how could learning fields not form and make themselves felt here as well?

As I understand the process, three key ingredients must be present for these fields to emerge as potent forces in the room:

1. Collective intention focused in an emotionally engaging group project
2. A project of sustained duration
3. Repetition of the project in approximately the same form many times

Collective intention, sustained duration, and repetition. If any one of these elements is missing, the field will likely be so weak as to be undetectable. The key insight is that what we do together repeatedly, enthusiastically, and with focused collective intention generates an energy that accumulates around these activities. Teaching is only one of many activities that meet these conditions, and I'm sure readers will find other settings in which these same dynamics arise.

Because it is less emphasized elsewhere, I want to underscore the contribution that *repetition* makes to the emergence of detectable fields. Teaching the same course semester after semester, year after year, deepens the energetic groove and potentiates the learning field— repeatedly asking the same questions, challenging the same assumptions, pushing the same boundaries, orchestrating the same rhythmic exchange of ideas, mind engaging mind in the same dance. What we do repeatedly generates stronger fields than what we do occasionally.

What beyond this basic rubric is required for strong learning fields to emerge? It's simple, I think. Strong teaching makes for strong fields. There are no tricks involved, no gimmicks. What contributes to powerful teaching contributes to powerful fields. Pedagogy that stimulates strong student participation and meaningful engagement, that places a premium on critical thinking and individual reflection, will encourage the development of stronger fields than pedagogy that emphasizes regurgitative learning and passive absorption of the material. When students care about the subject they are studying, the fields will be more charged than when they don't. As intentional fields, they always reflect the intellectual and emotional vitality of the activities that generate them. When the learning is robust, the fields will be stronger; when it is cramped or damped down, they will be weaker.

I love teaching, but I don't think I have any special secrets to share about doing it well other than what I will discuss in chapters 4 and 5 where I will describe certain methods that I've developed for working with these learning fields. As an educator, I do my best and on some days I succeed and on others I fail. With some groups of students I hate to see the semester end, while with others it comes as a great mercy, allowing us both to move on to the next semester where we'll try again. So be it. You win some, you lose some, but you always keep trying to do it better.

To be honest, I haven't read many books on pedagogy, but one that has moved me deeply is Parker Palmer's *The Courage to Teach*. My approach to teaching is deeply aligned with the values and ideals he articulates so beautifully. I affirm his conviction that good teaching is not a matter of technique but emerges from the fundamental identity and integrity of the teacher. With Parker, I believe that great teaching emerges from great depth and reaches out to that depth in others. If I were to point readers to the kind of teaching that makes for strong learning fields, I would point them toward this eloquent book. Here are a few favorite passages:

> Good teaching requires self-knowledge; it is a secret hidden in plain sight.

> Deep speaks to deep, and when we have not sounded our own depths, we cannot sound the depths of our students' lives.

> The courage to teach is the courage to keep one's heart open in those very moments when the heart is asked to hold more than it is able so that teacher and students and subject can be woven into the fabric of community that learning, and living, require.

I always thought that passion made a teacher great because it brought contagious energy into the classroom, but now I realize its deepest function. Passion for the subject propels that subject, not the teacher, into the center of the learning circle—and when a great thing is in their midst, students have direct access to the energy of learning and of life.[15]

The Emergence of Fields

Usually the learning fields I've been describing remain below the threshold of our conscious awareness, their effects so subtle as to escape detection. When the right combination of circumstances converge, however, they can become a powerful force in the classroom. In my experience, part of the right mix is when these learning fields are sparked by the energetic resonances between teacher and students described in chapter 1. When these two processes come together—strong learning fields generated by engaged students and an instructor with deep experiential knowledge of his or her subject matter—striking things sometimes happen.

One might draw an analogy to a car engine. The learning field of a class is like the gas vapor in the cylinder being pressurized by the stroke of the piston; the professor is the spark plug that delivers the spark that ignites the gas. If either component is missing or if the timing is off, the engine doesn't fire; when both conditions come together in perfect rhythm, the combination can be explosive.

Though discussed as separate phenomena, these two processes are subtly intertwined in real life. If the instructor has personal familiarity with transpersonal states of consciousness, their very presence seems to encourage these fields to emerge in a room. It is as though, by virtue of their immersion in transpersonal fields of being, the instructor becomes a seed catalyst that encourages these collective mental fields to come forward in group settings. Nascent fields are always present whenever and wherever people gather, but for them to emerge as a powerful force in the room, some sort of catalyst seems to be required. A teacher with a substantive and deep spiritual practice is one such catalyst. The overlap of these two processes is further reinforced by the fact that both processes are driven by resonance. You will remember that Sheldrake describes morphic fields as being created through morphic resonance. I have similarly used the concept of resonance to describe the cognitive permeability that blends the minds of students and teacher in poignant exercises of self-actualization.

When these learning fields make themselves felt in a room, they can unleash a power that can overwhelm the student or the instructor and therefore they require careful management. When they emerge, it is sometimes as if the walls of one's mind suddenly fall away. New vistas of understanding can arise spontaneously and without effort. The depth of the human condition can suddenly be laid bare, and the intensity of the collective feelings that sweep through you can throw you off balance if you are not prepared for it.

If students are overwhelmed by this intensity, they can retreat into the solitude of their private reactions, but professors have no such retreat available and must maintain their stance in the front of the room. Professors must keep their operational focus and smoothly integrate into the work at hand the gifts that these fields can confer. Restraint is often called for. Ideas can come pouring in more quickly than can be shared with the students. Ego can tempt you to use these heightened states of awareness to deepen your personal understanding rather than advance your students' understanding. You may be tempted to follow the flow of illumination when it veers away from the subject matter of the course or when it moves too quickly for the students to keep up with. If one is dedicated to using this energy to serve one's students, however, both these distortions will naturally be shunned.

Attention is energy, and in the field of the class mind enormous amounts of energy become available to the instructor. If the instructor is comfortable with these states and capable of focusing this energy for the collective good, an escalating cycle of energetic exchange is sometimes set in motion—a perfect storm of learning. Animated by the collective field of the class mind, the instructor's own mind opens and begins to function at a slightly higher level of awareness. As the insights that rise from this higher level find their hidden targets in the room, the responses of the students release more energy into the class field, which then empowers the instructor to open to still higher levels and the cycle repeats itself. When working with motivated and well-focused students, the energy can swell to enormous proportions. The surest indicator that the magic has happened is when students don't want to leave the room after the bell rings.

When all goes well, there is a crystalline quality to what emerges that everyone in the room can feel. Like a great symphony that lifts the soul, what arises comes from depths that cannot be measured and is guided by an invisible hand that finds its mark. What could not be accomplished separately becomes available to those who work together, and the wholeness that surfaces in the deepest of these moments is characterized by a luminescent transparency. This transparency is contagious and its gifts precious. Each person draws from it gems unique to his or her situation. For me personally, the most precious gift of all is the transparency itself, as it is a token of the true nature of mind—consciousness in its pure and natural condition.

Great Learning

When the quality of engagement is high, the instructor and students have an opportunity to accomplish something both will remember for years. This powerful collective energy makes possible an exceptional kind of learning. When a high level of student engagement can be focused in a sustained way on intellectually challenging and worthwhile projects, *great learning* can sometimes occur.

Great learning is learning that will stay with the students long after they've forgotten all the lesser details of their college career, the way a team's exceptional performance in one bowl game will stay with them all their lives. It is learning that reaches into their hearts as well as their minds, that lifts their vision to a new horizon and gives them insights they will draw on for years to come. Great learning has occurred when students find the courage to confront the inadequacies of their old ways of thinking and heroically turn to explore new options without necessarily knowing where these will lead. Great learning is present when students write essays that surprise even themselves, that reach deeper than they had thought they were capable of or that say things they had been holding back for years. Great learning has taken place when students keep their papers and journals after a course has ended and use them as reference points in their lives, when they have heard their soul speaking to them as they struggle with their essays late at night, and when a shattering "Aha!" lifts them out of their well-forged confusion. Great learning has happened when students fall in love with the open-ended journey of perpetual learning.

Engagement generates energy and university courses focus large quantities of energy in coordinated group projects lasting many months. When several courses are coupled into larger learning sequences, these extended projects may last years, with students taking multiple courses with the same instructor. This sustained and repeated focusing of many minds on a single educational trajectory creates strong currents within the larger field of mind.

In some ways, we can imagine the comprehensive field surrounding a university community as a large lake. Imagine that you are standing in a still lake, patting the water with your hand. The waves created by a single slap of your hand quickly die out, but if the motion is repeated many times, it creates a pattern of standing waves in the water. In a similar way, the learning fields created by individual professors and their courses might be seen as stable whirlpools of energy spinning within the university mind, drawing people together for specific projects and then releasing them back into the larger population when the course is over.

Because universities are open systems with a constant turnover in their student body, seniors graduating and freshmen matriculating each year, we might deepen our analogy by imagining that our lake is being fed by a river that enters at one end of the lake and flows off downstream at the other end. Thus, our lake is being continuously stirred by a constant, gentle current moving through it.

This combination of stable mental fields and a slow but steady turnover of individuals is a fascinating setting in which to test Sheldrake's theory. I'm suggesting that the patterns that form in the university mind are more enduring than the constantly changing flow of students who temporarily become part of these systems. These learning fields could not have come into existence without the effort of many individuals, and yet once they exist, they have a life of their own that is larger than any of the individuals who contributed to them, including the instructor. They are true structures within the collective psyche, and they mobilize and shape our individual contact with the deeper dimensions of learning that are unfolding in the group field.

Let me inject an important qualification here. The learning fields I've been describing can augment creativity and deepen insight, but I do *not* think that they are the ultimate source of these valuable gifts. My personal conviction is that the true source of these gifts lies in a profound intelligence that permeates the universe itself. When skillfully choreographed and gracefully navigated, the course mind functions as a kind of amplifier, extending our reach into this intelligence beyond what would otherwise be possible.

When an individual is lifted into "higher" or "deeper" or "wider" states of knowing through the action of a well-focused group field, it is as though the sensitivity of their consciousness has been increased by several orders of magnitude. Like a radio receiver whose sensitivity has suddenly increased, one's mind can now draw in subtle signals from Mind-at-Large that it could not previously receive. From this perspective, the group mind is not the actual source of these signals but the vehicle through which they are accessed.

Objections

We are so deeply habituated in our culture to thinking of mind as a private entity that the invitation to recognize a collective, wavelike, field aspect of mind is likely to trigger a chorus of objections. We can immediately think of reasons why this suggestion must be wrong. First, it runs contrary to most of our daily experience. We experience our personal, isolated minds every day, but these collective fields lie outside most people's conscious experience. Surely our private mind is the norm and any bleed-through the exception that only demonstrates the strength of this norm. Second, if we open our inner life to the influence of currents within a collective mind, we may feel threatened with being overrun by mass sentiment. If our private thoughts are this porous to a collective psyche, does this not compromise the integrity of the individual? Aren't these suggestions of a "mass consciousness" going to have the effect of undermining individual effort and initiative?

I understand these objections and appreciate the possible shock that may rise when we begin to be conscious of the presence of collective fields of consciousness influencing our "private lives." But a collective field is not a "mass" of anything. It is an exquisite network of living intelligence in which we are already suspended. What is required is not that we compromise our sense of individuality but that we relocate this extraordinary individuality within a more complex psychological landscape.

From an integral perspective, our individuality is not threatened by the deeper communion described in this chapter but actually enhanced by it. Recognizing that our singular individuality is embedded in a wider and deeper web of consciousness does not make us into less than we already were or turn us into automatons. On the contrary, it challenges us to expand our self-understanding as we try to envision the generative intelligence with which we are *already* cocreating our existence.

In this respect, human individuality can be likened to what chaos theoreticians call *autopoietic structures*, an awkward term for a beautiful concept. Autopoiesis means "self-creating." In chaos theory, autopoietic structures are forms of open systems that are self-renewing, highly autonomous, and possess separate, individual identities, yet are also inextricably embedded in and merged with their environments. In *Turbulent Mirror*, John Briggs and David Peat write: "Autopoietic structures have definite boundaries, such as a semipermeable membrane, but the boundaries are open and connect the system with almost unimaginable complexity to the world around it."

Furthermore, contrary to what we might expect on commonsensical grounds, autopoietic structures achieve greater autonomy not by severing their ties to their environment but by actually increasing them. They continue: "It appears that the greater an organism's autonomy, the more feedback loops [are] required both within the system and in its relationship to the environment. This is the autopoietic paradox."[16]

Our individuality combines uniqueness and openness to others in a similar paradoxical fashion. Communion with others, far from suffocating our uniqueness, is actually necessary to sustain it. If this is the case, then deepening our communion with the fields of collective mind that I have been describing in this chapter has the potential to *augment and enhance* our individual consciousness, not compromise it.

Within the context of the conventional paradigm that still holds sway on our university campuses, what I have been suggesting in this and the preceding chapter is unthinkable. It invites charges of ego-inflation and megalomania, of endorsing magic and abandoning critical thinking. And yet it is none of these things. It is simply an attempt to begin unfolding the implications of an integral model of consciousness as it applies to education.

In this new model, mind is not the private chamber we had originally thought, but an open field where different streams of energy and information converge. Some of these streams are personal and come from our immediate and distant past. Some come from still deeper in the universe. We cannot at this early stage tell where this shift in thinking will eventually lead us. What we know with certainty, however, is that *the older paradigm of a stand-alone consciousness is hopelessly unable to deal with the full facts of human experience.* It simply trims away what it cannot explain and pretends it isn't there.

Synchronized Group Awareness and Teaching

The conventional model of the classroom is a monarchial, trickle-down model. Professors, by virtue of their longer study, have gathered a certain store of information that confers a certain privileged status on them as members of the academic aristocracy. To these educational barons, students come and knowledge is distributed, sometimes graciously and sometimes not, but always in a downward flow from a centralized source. The students don't know what the professor knows, so they have to come and get it. As Parker Palmer puts it, "In the objectivist myth, truth flows from top down, from experts who are qualified to know truth . . . to amateurs who are qualified only to receive truth."[17]

Obviously, there is a certain truth to this distributional model, but an integral model of consciousness that incorporates the transindividual field dynamics of mind opens the door to a more subtle and more intimate meeting of minds. While not ignoring the differences in experience between older and younger learners, an integral model recognizes the existence of collective fields of awareness and intelligence that are superordinate to the individuals present. Resonating with feminist proposals for revisioning pedagogy, the integral vision proposes the existence of a dynamic, living intelligence present in the room beneath the surface of dualistic appearances.

Knowledge is the reason for our coming together in the classroom, and the very act of forming groups activates dimensions of our collective being that empower the knowledge we are seeking to come forward in sometimes unexpected ways. The living power of the course mind not only injects vitality and a certain unpredictability into how information emerges in the room, it also creates an augmented field of collective intelligence within which new discoveries sometimes occur. When this happens, knowledge is not flowing down from a solitary source—the professor's mind—but rather is arising through the agency of the living presence of the course and class mind.

As already mentioned, I don't think that the group mind is the ultimate source of this creativity but a powerful vehicle that allows us to tap more deeply into the intelligence and creativity of the universe itself. When a collective field of consciousness is sufficiently strong, our personal store of knowledge can become an instrument played by a larger intelligence. Poised between things already grasped and things not yet understood, a living intelligence housed not in any one mind but evoked by the power of the group mind begins to unfold its message, taking us the next step on our individual and collective journey. In my experience, this particular magic tends to happen toward the end of one's more advanced courses, after the foundation has been carefully prepared through months and years of working together with students.

Future Potential

Having only begun to explore the field dynamics of mind, my observations on their workings are exploratory and tentative. Even so, I believe that the combined concepts of energetic resonance and morphic fields have the potential to transform not only education but a wide range of group activities taking place in our board rooms, laboratories, think tanks, and offices—wherever people meet in common cause and collective endeavor. As we become more familiar with the sinews of collective intelligence tapped by those who learn to enter into states of *synchronized group awareness*, the possibilities will expand exponentially.

For example, studies have demonstrated that creativity is augmented when the left and right hemispheres of our brain begin to function in an integrated, "whole-brain" manner. Many businesses and institutes, such as the Monroe Institute in Faber, Virginia, have for years marketed CDs that use sound waves to induce states of "hemispheric synchronization" while shifting the brain's electrical activity into the theta frequency range associated with higher creativity. Similarly, a wealth of biofeedback and entrainment technologies is using every strategy imaginable to elicit whole-brain functioning focused at specific frequencies for specific purposes. When the brain's two hemispheres are *phase-locked* and working as one, a number of known benefits result, including heightened awareness, improved recall, greater self-programming flexibility, and heightened creativity—in short, "superlearning."

From here it is a simple if substantial step to seeing our individual brains as neuron clusters within the species-brain of humanity. Our individual mind-fields are cells within humanity's collective field of Mind. When a number of minds come together and integrate their individual capacities through sustained projects of focused intention, it is as though they become phase-locked in ways analogous to how individual neurons become phase-locked in hemispherically synchronized brain states.

When people open themselves to each other and focus intensely on a common goal, their individual energies become synchronized in a way that can mediate contact with levels of intelligence and creativity that are beyond the reach of these same individuals acting alone. We must engage each other in an integrated manner for this more potent mode of knowing to emerge. The specific level of consciousness that is accessed is not as important here as the discovery of *the enhanced capacity of the integrated group mind itself*. The potential for refining this principle and applying it to new fields of endeavor seems open-ended. Whatever our individual abilities, our collective abilities are greater.

CHAPTER 3

The Science of Fields

The existence of a few basic psi effects is now sufficiently well-established to persuade anyone who studies the evidence with a critical eye, and without prejudice, that something interesting is going on.

—Dean Radin, *Entangled Minds*

Many readers will be aware of the changes in physics in the last century that have offered unexpected support for a metaphysics of interconnectivity and interdependence. Beginning with *The Tao of Physics* and *The Dancing Wu Li Masters* in the 1970s and continuing up to the present, a cascade of popular books have introduced the lay public to the strangely holistic world being revealed by quantum mechanics. The titles themselves often mark the shift taking place— *Quantum Mind* (Arnold Mindell), *Quantum Healing* (Deepak Chopra), and *The Quantum Self* (Dana Zohar).

New concepts have entered our public discourse from several disciplines—nonlocality, nonlinear systems, fractal geometry, self-organization, emergence. With them has come a deepening appreciation of what it means to be living inside a universe that many scientists are beginning to suspect is *alive* at its very core. The new cosmology is showing us a universe of not only staggering proportions but also unanticipated creativity and perhaps even foresight. As Brian Swimme—founder of the Center for the Story of the Universe at the California Institute of Integral Studies—has richly illustrated in his books and DVDs, after several hundred years of thinking of the universe as a giant machine composed of dead matter, today practically everywhere we turn we are finding signs of an intelligence and ingenuity hidden within its folds that shatter these mechanistic metaphors.[1]

It is too early to say where this profound shift in thinking is taking us, but certainly an emerging theme is *wholeness* and *connectivity*. In discipline after discipline, we are finding that systems we previously thought were independent are actually connected. Up and down the hierarchies of life, we are discovering that systems exchange information, species intertwine with other species, and things that don't touch participate in a subtle commerce. The more deeply science probes, the more the vision of a world of separate objects is being replaced by a vision of a world saturated with an extraordinary mosaic of influence. Psi appears to be simply one more example of this larger pattern of interconnectivity in nature. Right in the center of our minds, where we live and breathe, we are finding evidence of a subtle commerce with other minds.

Psi and the Scientific Establishment

The term "psi" was first used as a neutral term for psychic phenomena in 1942 by Robert Thouless. It is the first letter of the Greek word *psyche*, meaning soul or mind. Dean Radin, senior scientist at the Institute of Noetic Sciences, points out that there are words for psi in every language, reflecting the universality of psychic experience across cultures. Psi covers a wide range of experiences including telepathy, clairvoyance, precognition, and psychokinesis. In this chapter, I will be focusing primarily on telepathy, or mind-to-mind contact, because it is the form of psi most relevant to the concepts presented here.

The mainstream scientific community is deeply hostile to psi of course. Richard Dawkins, Professor of the Public Understanding of Science at Oxford University, probably speaks for the majority of scientists when he said in an interview for England's popular press in 2000, "The paranormal is bunk. Those who try to sell it to us are fakes and charlatans."[2] His colleague Peter Atkins in chemistry at Oxford put it even more strongly:

> Yes, I admit that I am prejudiced, if you like I am a bigot and I have my mind closed to this kind of research. . . . It's just a waste of time. Serious scientists have got real things to think about—we don't have time to waste on claims which we now both in our hearts and heads must be nonsense at root. . . . I think there is no known effect that cannot be explained by conventional science.[3]

A recent incident in England drives the point home. In 2001, the Royal Mail invited six British laureates to write a short paragraph about their fields to accompany a special issue of stamps commemorating the centenary of the first Nobel Prize. Brian Josephson, winner of the 1973 Nobel Prize for Physics, wrote a concise summary of quantum theory and then in his conclusion said:

> Quantum theory is now being combined with theories of information and computation. These developments may lead to an explanation of processes still not understood within conventional science, such as telepathy—an area in which Britain is at the forefront of research.

The uproar in the scientific community was immediate and predictable. "It's utter rubbish," said David Deutsch, a quantum physicist at Oxford. "Telepathy simply does not exist. The Royal Mail has let itself be hoodwinked into supporting ideas that are complete nonsense."[4]

Many scientists hold these opinions, however, *not* because they have dispassionately examined the research on psi for themselves but because they have already committed themselves to a contrary metaphysical position that they have complete confidence in. The philosopher Daniel Dennett summarizes this position in his influential book *Consciousness Explained*:

> The prevailing wisdom, variously expressed and argued for, is *materialism*: there is only one sort of stuff, namely *matter*—the physical stuff of chemistry, physics and physiology—and the mind is somehow nothing but a physical phenomenon. In short, the mind is the brain.[5]

If reality is ultimately physical and mind is the brain as Dennett says, then our minds must be private entities, compiling and compounding the information that comes into them through our hardwired five senses, not from a subtle sixth sense. If this is the way things are, then the search for psi truly is a waste of time, and everything I'm suggesting in this book is utter nonsense. But is this really the way things are?

Obviously, nothing I am going to say in this chapter will overturn such deeply entrenched resistance. That work I leave to philosophers of mind, parapsychologists, and cultural historians. My agenda in this chapter is more modest. I would simply like to survey some of the exciting work being done by scientists who are challenging the assumptions our culture has made about the boundaries of consciousness and to point readers who are interested in considering the evidence for themselves to sources where they can do so.

While it would go too far to say that science has proven all the ideas I'm proposing in this book, I think it is safe to say that there is a growing body of scientific evidence that supports them, evidence that suggests there is more going on behind our conscious awareness than we had previously thought. Despite the continued commitment of most mainstream scientists to the old conventions, the leading edge of science is more "consciousness friendly" than only a few decades ago. The annual Tucson conference on consciousness sponsored by the University of Arizona and the series of national dialogues on meditation between His Holiness the Dali Lama and the scientific community sponsored by the Mind and Life Institute are just two examples of this new orientation.[6]

Before we jump into this research, however, I want to acknowledge that many readers may not require the certification that science can provide to warm to the ideas presented in this book. Some of you may have been touched by experiences of collective intelligence operating in your own lives, or perhaps you have been influenced by the influx of Eastern philosophy that has swept our shores since the 1960s, or advances in mind–body medicine, or the emergence of transpersonal psychology, or cross-cultural studies. The list is long. Indeed, with publications such as *Tricycle, Yoga Journal*, and *What Is Enlightenment?* enjoying wide circulation, with radio programs such as *New Dimensions* on the air since 1973, and with meditation retreat centers springing up across the country, it feels almost anachronistic to defend with science what is becoming increasingly obvious to more and more people experientially—that underneath the bubble of the ego run rivers of consciousness that connect all life in an ocean of awareness. Nevertheless, science is such an important arbiter of truth in our culture, especially in our universities, that we should look carefully at what scientific research is actually telling us about the nature of consciousness.

Psi and Collective Intelligence

If psi is real, it suggests that human beings can connect with one another at very subtle levels of consciousness, and even more broadly that we are *always* connected to one another beneath our conscious awareness, participating in subtle fields of collective knowing. Before we look at the evidence for this claim, let's begin by appreciating that human beings have an extraordinary penchant for connectivity. If we look at just our physical behavior, we appear to be exceptionally porous to one another. Nature seems to have programmed us to participate in a fluid give and take that blends our edges and generates collective patterns of behavior. We quickly pick up each other's accents and mannerisms, absorb each other's ideas, convictions, and speech patterns. We even move in unconscious rhythm with each other.

The anthropologist Edward T. Hall found that children playing in a playground moved to a common beat. Filmed from a nearby hidden location, each child in the playground seemed to be doing his or her own separate thing—running, jumping, laughing, and swinging—but careful analysis revealed that the group was pulsing to a unified rhythm. "Without knowing it," Hall wrote, "they were all moving to a beat they generated themselves ... an unconscious undercurrent of synchronized movement tied the group together."[7]

Similarly, William Condon, a psychiatrist at Boston University's Medical School, analyzed films of adults chatting and noticed that the conversationalists unconsciously began to coordinate their finger movements, eye blinks, and nods. When pairs of talkers were hooked up to separate electroencephalographs, some of their brain waves were even spiking in unison. Condon's conclusion was that it didn't make sense to view humans as isolated entities. Instead, he said, we are bonded together by our involvement in "shared organizational forms."[8] Our strong tendency to merge with others even influences how we experience taste. When researchers put two to five year olds at a table for several days with other children who loved the foods that they loathed, the kids with the dislikes quickly reversed their eating habits and became enthusiastic eaters of dishes they'd previously disdained. They kept their new preferences weeks after contact with the other children had ceased.[9]

In reviewing this and other research in his book *Global Brain*, Howard Bloom concluded: "In other words, without knowing it individuals form a team. Even in our most casual moments, we *pulse in synchrony*." Bloom goes on to argue that this capacity for synchrony is deeply rooted in our evolutionary history. His position is that the global brain that Peter Russell, Joel de Rosnay, and other writers have pointed to is not the result of the Internet, global telecommunications, or any other invention of modern times. Rather, these innovations are rooted in an evolutionary ancestry that reaches back billions of years. Bloom's highly regarded book is an extended argument for the thesis that human beings are embedded *by evolution* in a networked global brain that has been developing and refining itself for more than three billion years. As he puts it: "We are modules of a planetary mind, a multiprocessor intelligence which fuses every form of living thing."[10]

Daniel Goleman would agree with this assessment of the human penchant for connectivity. Author of the best-selling book *Emotional Intelligence*, he has recently published a sequel entitled *Social Intelligence*. There he summarizes research emerging in the new field of social neuroscience and profiles in fascinating detail the neurophysiology of the synchrony Bloom refers to. He outlines the function of mirror neurons and the newly discovered spindle cells that allow us to sense *almost instantaneously* the feelings, moods, and movements of other persons. The most fundamental revelation of this new discipline, he concludes, is that human beings "are wired to connect." "Neuroscience has discovered that our brain's very design makes it *social*, inexorably drawn into an intimate brain-to-brain linkup whenever we engage with another person."[11]

Our starting point, then, for looking at the scientific evidence for psi and collective intelligence is this—*humans beings have a pronounced tendency at the physical level to mingle at their edges, to exchange information in subtle ways, and to form larger wholes*. The question we are asking is—Does this tendency extend beyond our bodies to our minds? Does this aptitude for merging extend to the psyche? What does science say?

Anecdotal evidence for psi has been around for a long time, of course. The telepathic connection between mothers and babies, for example, is well known. Mothers frequently know when their babies need them, often waking up just before their infants in the middle of the night. Sometimes this awareness is mediated unconsciously, as when mothers have a letdown response when their babies from whom they are separated are hungry. The deeper the emotional bond between subjects, the easier it seems to be for nonsensory information to make it through the filters that usually edit our incoming signals. The literature is filled with stories of people who suddenly "knew" that someone they loved had been injured or was in danger and it turned out to be correct. Hundreds of anecdotes have been collected from people who woke up at night with an accurate perception that someone they knew had just died and the timing was precise.[12]

The witnesses for these stories are often so credible and the stories so detailed that many readers will not need to go further to be convinced. But anecdotal evidence alone, no matter how powerful or plausible, will not shift our cultural convictions on this issue, not in the age of science. Anecdotal evidence is the weakest form of evidence, and there is simply too much at stake for us to base our judgment on testimony alone. If psi is going to get traction in our culture, it's going to have to be proven in the laboratory. And it is.

Like all scientific research, the methodological and interpretive issues surrounding this research are complex and challenging for the layperson to navigate. Fortunately there are several excellent books that summarize this research and carefully analyze these issues while still managing to be reader friendly. To my mind, the best of these are Rupert Sheldrake's *The Sense of Being Stared At* (2003) and Dean Radin's *The Conscious Universe* (1997) and *Entangled Minds* (2006). While these authors are pro-psi in their conclusions, they evaluate the evidence in the best tradition of critical inquiry. Radin's *Entangled Minds* presents a particularly useful overview of the current research, and I am indebted to Radin for much that follows here. I also recommend Robert Kenny's very useful seed paper "What Can Science Tell Us about Collective Consciousness?" sponsored by the Fetzer Institute and published on their Web site.[13]

These sources boil down thousands of experiments and publications in their narrative, and boiling them down further runs the risk of oversimplifying their findings. In what follows, I will give thumbnail sketches of representative experiments that indicate the high caliber of evidence that has been collected for psi and point out certain patterns in the data. My intention is simply to highlight the fact that current research on psi and collective consciousness supports the existence of the kind of collective dynamics I am alleging here on experiential grounds. Echoing the holism found in quantum theory, psi appears to reflect an inherent connectivity operating in nature beneath physical appearances. I will focus on three areas of research: (1) classic psi experiments, (2) animal psi, and (3) field consciousness studies.

Classic Psi Experiments

Consider the following four experiments.

1. Ganzfeld studies. Ganzfeld experiments (meaning "whole field") are a successor to J. B. Rhine's early card-guessing experiments at Duke University in the 1930s. A woman—we'll call her Jill, following Radin's lead—is sitting in a comfortable reclining chair with halved Ping-Pong balls covering her eyes, listening to pink noise on headphones. A soft red light shines on her face. The combination produces a dreamlike reverie. After fifteen minutes, she is asked to report aloud anything that comes to her mind for the next thirty minutes. Meanwhile, a second person we'll call Jack is located in a nearby building and tries to send Jill an image that has been randomly selected from four possible images. An independent panel judges whether Jill accurately received the image that Jack tried to send her.

Originally developed in the 1970s, the ganzfeld tests have repeatedly generated positive evidence of psi. They have also generated more debate than any other form of modern psi experiment. As a result, says Radin, the ganzfeld test has been refined until it has become "as close to the perfect psi experiment as anyone knows how to conduct." How perfect is it? In 1994, psychologist Daryl Bem from Cornell University and Charles Honorton from the University of Edinburgh published a meta-analysis of a large collection of ganzfeld studies in *Psychological Bulletin*. Their review of just the newer, fully automated experiments that were specifically designed to overcome all known criticisms of previous studies showed significant results with odds against chance of 517 to 1.[14]

2. *Remote viewing studies.* In these experiments, Jill (the "agent") travels to a randomly selected distant location while Jack remains behind in a lab, isolated from contact with anyone who knows where Jill has gone. At a designated time, Jack tries to describe where Jill is, what she is seeing. An independent panel of judges evaluates the results. These experiments were pioneered by physicists Harold Puthoff and Russell Targ at SRI International in the 1970s and were later refined and replicated by other scientists. The Princeton University Engineering Anomalies Research (PEAR) Lab conducted 653 formal remote viewing trials between 1976 and 1999. Robert Jahn, the former Dean of Engineering at Princeton, and psychologist Brenda Dunne calculated that these experiments generated positive evidence for psi with odds against chance of 33 million to 1.[15]

3. *Dream studies.* A series of experiments conducted at the Maimonides Medical Center in Brooklyn, New York, from 1966 to 1973 demonstrated that psi can register even in our sleep. In these experiments, Jack goes to sleep in a soundproof and electromagnetically shielded room. He is wired with electrodes to monitor his brain waves and eye movements. When a technician in the next room observes rapid eye movement (REM), indicating that Jack has begun to dream, he buzzes Jill, who is located in a separate room anywhere from 32 feet to 45 miles away. Jill has with her a sealed envelope that has been randomly selected from eight to twelve envelopes, each

containing a different picture. She opens the envelope and tries to send the dreaming Jack an image of the picture she is holding. When the technician sees that Jack's REM has stopped, he wakes him and asks him to record his dream, while buzzing Jill to stop sending. Then Jack goes back to sleep. When he begins to dream again, the process is repeated, with Jill trying to send the same image to Jack throughout the night. In the morning, an independent panel of judges compares the narrative of Jack's dreams to all the pictures, not knowing which one was used in the experiment. The pictures are ranked 1 to 8 (or 12) in terms of how well each picture matched the recorded dream. If the picture actually used makes it in the top half—that is, above fifty/fifty-chance—it is considered a hit.

In 1993, British psychologists Simon Sherwood and Chris Roe from University College Northampton, England, did a meta-analysis of all existing dream psi research beginning with the original Maimonides series (379 sessions) and continuing through later automated, in-home dream experiments—a total of forty-seven separate experiments involving 1,270 trials. The results were a successful hit rate with odds against chance of 22 billion to 1.[16]

4. DMILS studies. DMILS is an acronym for "direct mental interaction with living systems." These studies are designed to test the mind's ability to influence living systems directly, bypassing the conscious awareness of the recipient. DMILS studies take many forms. In one study, Jill is placed in a room that looks like a walk-in freezer. She is completely shielded from electromagnetic signals and acoustic noise, as isolated from the outside world as you can possibly get. Inside she sits in a chair and relaxes while her skin conductance is continuously monitored and recorded. Meanwhile, Jack is taken to a distant, soundproof room and is told to follow the instructions that appear on a computer monitor.

When the experiment begins, the monitor signals him to either *calm* or *activate* Jill. If a *calm* order comes up, he imagines her in a relaxing, calming setting (like sun tanning beside a pool). If *activate* comes up, he imagines her engaged in some form of dynamic activity (like running up a hill). A computer program chooses which instruction pops up and the entire operation is automated. Each sequence lasts 20 seconds, between which Jack withdraws his attention from Jill altogether. Over the course of the 30-minute experiment, the computer will generate a random sequence of approximately twenty calm and twenty activate instructions. Jill does not know when or in what way Jack is trying to influence her.

After the session ends, the researcher compares the automated record of the *calm* and *activate* messages with Jill's skin conductance. It turns out that when Jack was sending Jill calming thoughts, her body showed lower skin conductance activity—indicating greater relaxation. When Jack was sending Jill activating thoughts, her skin conductance was elevated.

This extraordinary result suggests that our *bodies* can register and respond to thoughts directed toward us from a distance by another person without our conscious mind necessarily participating. In 2004, psychologist Stefan Schmidt and his colleagues at the University of Freiburg Hospital, Germany, published a meta-analysis of forty DMILS studies like this in the *British Journal of Psychology*. The overall results were significant with odds against chance of 1,000 to 1.[17]

A subset of DMILS studies have even demonstrated a correlation in the brain wave patterns of paired subjects when one of them is subjected to a stimulus. This is almost like pinching one person and having the other person say ouch. This result has been replicated in numerous experiments. In one study published in 2004 by Leanna Standish of Bastyr University and her colleagues, researchers took the additional step of putting the receiver in an fMRI (functional magnetic resonance imaging) scanner, allowing them to identify the precise location in the brain of the psi-mediated influence. When the sender, who was in a distant room, was viewing a flickering light, the receiver registered a highly significant increase in brain activity *in their visual cortex*. The odds against this happening by chance were calculated to be 14,000 to 1.[18]

These DMILS studies are supported by research on *distant healing*, first brought to public attention in Larry Dossey's best-selling book *Healing Words* (1993). In these studies, persons who are prayed for by other persons showed improved health as measured by shorter hospital stays, faster recovery after surgery, less pain medication, and so on. Over the past forty years, there have been more than 150 controlled studies of distant healing intention. Over two-thirds of these studies demonstrated statistically significant healing effects.[19] Of the more than fifty of these studies that were rated to be of excellent methodological quality, 74 percent produced statistically significant results.[20]

Summarizing the findings from these four sets of experiments, we return to our original question. Does the human tendency to mingle with those around us extend to the psyche? Despite the cry from the conservative mainstream, the answer from science seems to be a clear—YES. Atkins's contention that "there is no known effect that cannot be explained by conventional science" turns out to be a statement of faith, not science.

Under controlled studies that have been replicated in peer reviewed journals, science has demonstrated that *people register the thoughts directed to them from physically distant persons.* This influence registers not only when we are awake but also when we are asleep. Even when we are not paying it conscious attention, our bodies respond to it. Our biochemistry shifts, our brains "pulse in synchrony" with other brains.

At a level beneath conscious awareness, our mental borders appear to be porous, our minds in *continuous* subtle exchange with minds around us. Rather than interpret psi as an unnatural, "paranormal" bridging of ontologically separate minds, the cumulative evidence, some of which is still to come, suggests that it is better thought of as the local activation of a latent, organic, nonlocal consciousness, a collective knowing that is always present beneath our conscious awareness.

Animal Psi

My reason for looking at animal psi is simply to make the point that this capacity for mental communion with those around us is not a "higher capacity" restricted to human beings but a trait we appear to share with other members of the animal kingdom. Indeed, animals often seem to be better at it than humans. Recognizing the psychic ability of animals suggests that psi is simply part of our evolutionary pedigree. As Rupert Sheldrake emphasizes, psi, or what he calls the "extended mind," is part of our *biological* nature.

Like the anecdotal evidence for human psi, the anecdotal evidence for animal psi is quite strong. Barbara Woodhouse, a well-known British dog trainer, has observed that, among dog trainers, telepathic abilities are usually taken for granted. "No one in their senses disputes them," she says. The staff at Sandringham, the country retreat of the Queen of England, concurs. Apparently the staff do not need to be told when the Queen, who is a serious dog enthusiast, is about to arrive. "All the dogs in the kennels start barking the moment she reaches the gate," says Bill Meldrum, the head game keeper, "and that is half a mile away. We don't know how they can tell and they don't do that with anyone else."[21]

Or consider the following case reported by J. Allen Boone in his book *Kinship with All Life.* Boone was in an Asian jungle where he had spent several hours watching monkeys playing in a clearing. Suddenly everything changed.

With startling abruptness, every monkey quit whatever he happened to be doing and then looked in the same southerly direction. And then, motivated by obvious fear and panic, they went stampeding out of the clearing in a northerly direction. . . . What had caused this sudden exodus I couldn't remotely imagine. I decided to remain where I was . . . and see what was going to happen next. . . . Three puzzling hours went ticking by. Then into the clearing from the south came five men walking in single file. The first two were carrying rifles, and other three were attendants. They were as surprised to see me as I was to see them. We introduced ourselves. . . . In the midst of this a most illuminating fact was revealed. At the precise moment those two hunters had picked up their rifles and headed for the clearing, three hours' walking distance away, every monkey in the clearing had fled from the place.[22]

Rupert Sheldrake has compiled a large collection of such reports documenting the existence of animal psi in his book *Dogs That Know When Their Owners Are Coming Home* (1999). The centerpiece of the book is his analysis of dogs and cats that appear to know with uncanny accuracy when their owners are on their way home—at odd hours and unscheduled times, after short or long absences, and often in unusual circumstances. After ruling out cases that might be explained by possible sensory input—hearing or smell or signal—many of the remaining cases strongly suggest that the animals were responding to their owner's *intention* to return home, not just their action in doing so.

From here, Sheldrake moves on to survey a wide range of unusual animal behavior that contributes to the case for animal psi. He reports on dogs who have made journeys of hundreds of miles to get back home or to find their master. In one case, a dog crossed the English channel to track down his owner in the trenches of World War I, becoming the hero of the regiment in the process. He reports on the Chinese program for using unusual animal behavior to predict earthquakes, studies of the migratory feats of birds and butterflies, and pets who are able to anticipate their masters' epileptic seizures or who know when their masters have died. The cumulative effect of all this critically sifted testimony is powerful indeed, but Sheldrake goes beyond interesting anecdotes to test the psychic sensitivity of animals scientifically. Consider the case of Jaytee.

In order to test the apparent ability of a mixed-breed terrier named Jaytee to anticipate the arrival home of his mistress, Pamela Smart, Sheldrake carried out a series of experiments—thirty trials over a 14-month period. Making a long story short, he videotaped the window perch where Jaytee would wait for Pam. The camera was left running continuously in long-play mode while Pam was away and was time coded. Pam would return home without notice and on no schedule.

An independent analysis of the video showed that Jaytee waited at the window much more frequently while Pam was on her way home, and he began waiting when she *decided* to return, before she actually began her trip. The differences in the time Jaytee spent at the window throughout the day and shortly before her return was statistically highly significant ($p < 0.000001$). The data suggest that Jaytee's emotional tie to Pamela activates a latent collective intelligence that connects her to Pamela, allowing her to sense Pamela's decision to come home. The potential for this transspecies connection must be an innate feature of consciousness itself.[23]

We take one step closer to the issue of collective intelligence if we consider the remarkable accomplishments of flocks of birds, schools of fish, and colonies of insects.

Flocks of birds flying in tight formation seem to pivot as one, changing directions so quickly that scientists have puzzled over how they manage to do it. Wayne Potts, a biologist now at the University of Utah, studied the banking movements of dunlins in Puget Sound in the 1980s. Using high-speed photography, he found that the birds were responding to maneuver waves that could start anywhere in the formation, radiating through the flock incredibly fast, taking only 15 milliseconds to pass from neighbor to neighbor. This was more than twice as fast as the startle response dunlins in captivity showed to a sudden stimulus (38 milliseconds).

Potts concluded that the birds were not responding to their immediate neighbors but to the maneuver wave as a whole. He assumed that the birds were using vision to detect the approaching wave, but Sheldrake has pointed out that this would require continuous, unblinking, 360-degree visual attention and would not explain how the birds were detecting waves that approached them from behind, outside their visual field.[24]

Similarly, schools of fish swimming in tight formation change their direction frequently and effortlessly as though they were a single organism. When they are attacked by a predator, each fish darts away from the center of the school in a dramatic maneuver called a flash expansion. The entire expansion can take place in 20 milliseconds with fish accelerating to a speed of ten to twenty body lengths per second, yet they do not collide. It is as though each fish knows where its neighbors are going to flee. Attempting to figure out how they accomplish this remarkable feat, scientists have rendered fish blind with opaque contacts and severed the nerves they use to sense small shifts in water pressure on their sides—all to no avail. The blind and aquatically "deaf" fish continue to flash with their school just as before.[25] (I report this treatment of fish with a shudder for the lives we maim in the name of understanding their complex beauty.)

Lastly, consider the architectural feats of the humble termite. Working separately, termites first make columns, then bend them toward each other, joining them at a midpoint—an extraordinary feat considering that termites are blind. Nor do they accomplish this engineering marvel by smell or shuttling back and forth checking out each other's work. Researchers have shoved large steel plates down the middle of the mounds, completely isolating workers into two separate groups, and yet they continue to construct columns and tunnels that are perfectly aligned.[26]

In his book *The Social Insects*, Harvard biologist E. O. Wilson highlights science's complete failure to solve this riddle within any conventional frame of reference: "The total simulation of construction of complex nests from a knowledge of the summed behaviors of the individual insects has not been accomplished and stands as a challenge to both biologists and mathematicians."[27] The question, he says, is "Who has the blueprint of the nest?"

Sheldrake believes that all three of these examples of closely coordinated social behavior can be explained in terms of his concept of morphic fields. Birds fly "as one," fish swim "as one," and termites build "as one" because each is participating in a collective mental field, a living form of collective intelligence. His answer to Wilson's question is that the termite colony as a whole has the blueprint: "I suggest that this plan is embodied in the organizing field of the colony. This field is not inside the individual insects; rather, they are inside the collective field."[28]

Similarly, the behavior of birds and fish begins to make more sense if we see them as operating inside a group mental field, reflecting a kind of group intelligence. Sheldrake writes: "To make models without taking such fields into account is rather like trying to explain the behavior of iron filings around a magnet ignoring the field, as if the patterns somehow 'emerged' from programs within the individual iron particles."[29] Such social mental fields and collective telepathic abilities would have considerable survival value, and therefore the genes associated with these abilities would be favored in the push–pull of evolution.

I do not want to oversimplify the complex issues generated by research into animal psi or to sidestep challenges raised by skeptics. I personally find Sheldrake's arguments convincing, but readers will want to examine the evidence for themselves and draw their own conclusions. Even this brief excursion into his work, however, has shown us something important. It suggests that the human tendency to enter into subtle mental communion with each other is a trait that is shared with other species and, as such, is a feature of our minds that is rooted in our evolutionary ancestry. It fits into a larger pattern running throughout the animal kingdom. Simply put, psi and collective intelligence are part of the tissue of nature's web.[30]

Field Consciousness Studies

While much psi research studies how consciousness behaves between pairs of subjects, a more recent line of inquiry attempts to study larger fields of consciousness. The goal in field consciousness experiments is to explore whether and how consciousness permeates and influences entire groups. As such, this line of inquiry is particularly relevant to teachers and to the thesis being put forward in this book. The term "field consciousness studies" was coined by Roger Nelson at the Princeton Engineering Anomalies Research Laboratory (PEAR) for research they were doing at Princeton starting in the mid-1990s, but the precursor to that work goes back to research started in the 1970s that attempted to document the impact of meditation on society at large.

The "Maharishi Effect"

It is widely recognized today that meditation is beneficial for those who practice it. Hundreds of studies have documented its positive effects including improved health, improved social skills, higher resistance to illness, and greater sense of psychological well-being. Through meditation, persons have been able to lower their blood pressure and their cholesterol levels, and have even slowed or reversed biological aging. More recent research has begun to identify some of the neurological mechanisms through which meditation produces these effects. Few people today doubt that meditation is good for you.

Many spiritual traditions, however, have also held that meditation is good for people who simply happen to be living near meditators, that the effects of meditation radiate outward through a field of consciousness that unites all beings and all existence. In traditional cultures, it was considered a boon for a community to have a contemplative living and practicing nearby—better still, a group of contemplatives as there is always greater strength in numbers. Likewise, Christianity has long held that the effects of spiritual practice radiate beyond the walls of monasteries and convents and benefit the community in subtle but tangible ways.

This conviction about the collective impact of meditation is so strongly held that it is often taught that the first "false view" that must be put aside in one's meditation practice is the illusion that one is practicing for one's individual transformation alone. In Buddhism, for example, one begins each meditation session by cultivating *bodhichitta*, the intention to help all sentient beings, and finishes each session by distributing the benefits of the practice to all beings. Practitioners of Transcendental Meditation (TM) share this conviction that meditation has a collective beneficial impact, which they have dubbed the "Maharishi effect" in deference to their founder Maharishi Mahesh Yogi. The difference with TM, however, is that its practitioners have gone to considerable trouble to provide scientific evidence for this claim.

The hypothesis is simple enough. Maharishi teaches that all individual consciousness is embedded in a collective consciousness that is itself ultimately rooted in the "Unified Field" of the universe. From his perspective, which derives from India's Vedantic tradition, forms of social pathology such as crime, drug abuse, and violence are seen not only as personal problems but as symptoms of stress in the collective consciousness of humanity. Maharishi has proposed that if just 1 percent of the population in a geographic area practices TM, it will have an ameliorating effect on the surrounding society via the Unified Field—less than 1 percent if a more advanced meditation technique called TM-Sidhi is practiced. His contention is that the coherence achieved by a group of meditators is more powerful than the incoherence of the larger system they are part of. By merging with the Unified Field and entering into states of deep peace and internal coherence, meditators create coherence in the collective psyche, resulting in lower levels of social pathology and higher indicators of social well-being.

The test conditions for this hypothesis are simple in theory, but tricky in practice: identify the target area, bring in the meditators, establish the parameters you want to track (violent crime, automobile accidents, robberies, etc.), measure them before, during, and after the test period, control for the extraneous variables, and statistically evaluate the results. Of these, the trickiest part is controlling for the extraneous variables. Obviously we do not want accidental conditions such as good weather, an improved economy, or other urban initiatives to skew the data.

Because scientists are naturally suspicious of any group of researchers who have a vested interested in the outcome, such as promoters of TM or those who work for the Maharishi University of Management, it will be critical that the research is completely transparent and meets the highest professional standards. It must be subject to the peer review process and any positive results must be replicated. In addition, it would be ideal if the research were reviewed by an independent blue ribbon panel of experts to further protect against bias.

Supporters of TM believe they have met all these conditions and have successfully made the case for the Maharishi effect; critics are not so sure. Mainstream scientists have tended to discount their research due to the vested interest of the sponsoring organization in promoting its brand of meditation. Everyone is aware that bias can influence scientific research, as we have seen in the tobacco and pharmaceutical industries, and the concern is that the same thing could be happening here. Nevertheless, the sheer volume of the evidence collected and the fact that many of these studies have been published in respected journals with stringent peer review procedures such as *Journal of Conflict Resolution, Journal of Mind and Behavior,* and *Social Indicators Research* suggests that this body of research cannot be dismissed out of hand.

For example, a two-month study conducted in Washington, D.C., in 1993, demonstrated that violent crime, which had been steadily increasing during the previous five months, fell 23 percent during the experiment, reaching its lowest point at the end of the study when the greatest number of meditators were practicing (4,000 persons). As soon as the group disbanded, the crime rate rose again. The study showed that the results were not due to variables such as weather, increased police presence, or any special anticrime campaign.[31]

In another study, twenty-four cities with 1 percent meditators were matched with twenty-four control cities on total population, college population, and geographic region. Stepwise discriminate analysis showed that the control cities were similar on per capita income, percentage of persons aged fifteen to twenty-nine, stability of residence, percentage unemployed, and percentage of families with incomes below poverty level. The results showed a 22 percent reduction in crime for the cities with meditators compared to an increase in crime by 2 percent in control cities (p < .005). Furthermore, the analysis showed an 89 percent reduction in the crime rate trend compared to an increase of 53 percent in the control cities (p < .05).[32] These results have been replicated in over forty studies carried out around the globe, including in war-torn countries.[33]

Despite these remarkable outcomes, questions have lingered. The indicators of social order being studied are obviously influenced by many factors. Even when the most obvious ones have been taken into account, the question remains whether all the relevant causal factors have been isolated and controlled for. There is always the possibility that something other than meditation, something hidden or overlooked, is causing these shifts.

On the other hand, the more this pattern is replicated in studies carried out in different cities and in different years, the more one cannot help suspecting that meditation may be the key variable responsible for the change. At this point, the debate remains open. If we had an instrument that could give us a *purely objective measure* of the presence of the influence of group intention, it might tip the argument. It may be that scientists have created precisely such an instrument.

Global Consciousness Project

Field consciousness studies is an exciting line of research begun by Princeton psychologist Roger Nelson and centered in the PEAR lab. Dean Radin at the Institute of Noetic Sciences (IONS) is also a key researcher in this field, and it was he who introduced me to this research while I was Director of Transformative Learning at IONS from 2000 to 2002.

The essence of this research is to determine whether the behavior of a group can influence the output of a random number generator (RNG) and in what circumstances it may do so. Today's technology has allowed scientists to design compact, portable, and extremely accurate RNGs that produce a purely random output, known as entropy. These RNGs can be connected to computer networks allowing a continuous, second-by-second recording and compiling of their output. Statistical procedures can then be used to determine whether their randomness has been disturbed and the exact time at which any such anomalies occurred. One might think of these RNGs as thermometers monitoring the ambient temperature of chance in a room.

Field consciousness experiments ask the following question: When an RNG is placed near a group engaged in an activity calling for highly focused attention, such as meditation or group dialogue, will the behavior of the group influence the random output of a nearby RNG? If the recorded randomness significantly decreases during these exercises and other variables have been eliminated, we can reasonably infer that something the group is doing is influencing the RNG. The suggestion is that the presence of coherent minds acting in concert is infusing the environment with an ordering field that reduces entropy. As Dean Radin puts it in *Entangled Minds*, "[I]f we assume that mind and matter are related, then when one side of the mind ⟷ matter relationship changes by becoming highly ordered, the other side of the equation should show unusual forms of order as well."[34]

Being only a decade old, field consciousness studies is still in its infancy. Nevertheless, Radin reports that, by 2005, more than a hundred field consciousness experiments have been carried out in the United States, Europe, and Japan, and many of these provided documentation that groups do in fact appear to be capable of influencing nearby RNGs. These experiments were conducted at theatrical performances, scientific conferences, psychotherapy sessions, Native American rituals, Japanese festivals, sports competitions, and live television broadcasts.[35]

These studies suggest that when persons engage in collective activities involving focused intention and high psychological arousal, something they are doing influences the ambient randomness of their environment. By comparing test conditions that did and did not produce positive results, Nelson came up with a recipe for the conditions that were likely to produce positive results. These included: circumstances that evoke warm feelings of togetherness, emotional content that draws people together, strong personal involvement focused on a group goal involving a deeply engrossing theme, creative or humorous moments, and activities enlivened with a sense of novelty and located at uplifting physical sites. This list reads like a recipe for good teaching.

Demonstrating a correlation between a human activity and the anomalous behavior of a RNG does not itself prove a causal influence, of course, but it is highly suggestive of one. In order to determine whether these correlations were indicating a true causal relationship, Radin and colleagues from the California Pacific Medical Center carried out an experiment in which they incorporated RNGs into an experiment on intentional healing.

They tested the ability of practitioners of *Johrei*—a Japanese spiritual healing practice—to influence the growth of human brain cells under controlled laboratory conditions over a three day period with RNGs running in the background. They hypothesized that if the *Johrei* practitioners were influencing two physical systems simultaneously—one living (the brain cells) and one nonliving (the RNGs)—it would strengthen the conclusion that something they were doing was actually causing the RNGs to behave differently. In this experiment not only were the healers able to positively influence the growth of cells (with odds against chance at 1,100 to 1), but the RNGs registered the event, producing a peak response at the very time when the peak healing took place (with odds against chance of 1.3 million to 1).[36]

The finding that persons engaged in group activities involving focused attention, heightened emotions, and group goals were actually able to influence a piece of machinery operating in the room was so striking that it led Nelson in 1997 to begin an ambitious international research project called the *Global Consciousness Project*. Working with colleagues in the high-tech sector, Nelson created an Internet-based, worldwide network of RNGs. By 2005, sixty-five RNGs located around the world were engaged in a continuously running field consciousness experiment. Their output is being continuously collected and funneled via the Internet to computers in which the data is stored and analyzed.

Radin compares the RNG network to a global system of buoys, each with a bell that rings as the buoy dances on the waves of the ocean. Usually the ringing of all the bells is random because the action of the waves is random and uncoordinated. But if the bells suddenly started ringing together, as though synchronized in a swelling harmonic chord, we would be justified in thinking that they were all being influenced by some common underwater event rising from the deep.

Today a network of worldwide media outlets and the Internet generate a nearly instantaneous distribution of news around the planet, thus allowing historically unprecedented numbers of people in multiple countries to pay attention to the same event at the same moment in time. Never before have so many eyes, ears, and minds been pointed in the same direction at the same time.

Nelson and an international consortium of scientists have been exploring whether a global network of RNGs might actually be able to register the focused attention of these millions, even billions of people. By April 2005, they had analyzed 198 events of global interest, including natural disasters, new year celebrations, terrorist activity, massive meditations, sports events, outbreaks of war, tragic deaths of celebrities, and so on. Many of these showed the predicted influence registering on the network.

The untimely death of Princess Diana on August 31, 1997, for example, riveted world attention, leading the Global Consciousness Project team to predict that her funeral, which was to be broadcast worldwide a week later, would register on the GCP network as millions watched the proceedings live. Compiling the feedback from twelve RNGs scattered across the United States and Europe (the total number of RNGs operational at that time), they found a significant deviation from chance in their output, with odds against chance of 100 to 1.

Similarly, the funeral of Pope John Paul II on April 8, 2005, captured the attention of millions of viewers around the planet. It too produced a predicted statistically significant shift in the GCP data with odds against chance of 42 to 1. The network returned to chance within hours of the funeral.[37]

The most dramatic event analyzed by the project thus far, however, occurred on September 11, 2001, when terrorists flew two planes into the World Trade Center in New York. On that day, the GCP network deviated wildly and registered the single largest drop for any day in 2001. As Radin puts it, "In metaphorical terms, it means the GCP bell rang loudest on that day." The GCP team published their study of the statistical anomalies associated with the event in the journal *Foundation of Physics Letters*. According to their analysis, on September 11, the GCP network showed an extremely unlikely and persistent structure called an autocorrelation, with odds against chance of a million to one. Something caused the network of RNGs to behave in a dramatically nonrandom manner. The GCP team believes that the most likely candidate was the change in humanity's collective attention.[38]

Between 1998 and 2005, 185 such events were evaluated. The overall results show a clear deviation from chance, with odds against chance of 36,400 to 1, leading Radin to conclude: "This suggests that when millions to billions of people become coherently focused that the amount of *physical* coherence or order in the world also increases."[39] Roger Nelson concurs:

We do not have a theoretical understanding of the sort that must underlie robust interpretations ... but I would like to describe a speculation ... that the instruments have captured the reaction of a global consciousness. ... The results from this scientific study are an apparent manifestation of the ancient idea that we are all interconnected, and that what we think and feel has an effect on others.[40]

Conclusions

I want to emphasize again that the evidence cited in this chapter does not prove the full range of observations or proposals that I am making in this book, but one takes support where one finds it and in this case science is lending significant support to my general thesis.

Lists are sometimes useful, so, in the interest of clarity, let me list seven conclusions about the properties of consciousness that seem warranted, given this research. I have adapted this list from Radin's book *The Conscious Universe* while adding one item from Sheldrake's research on animal psi.

Consciousness and Individuals

1. Consciousness extends beyond the individual and has quantum field-like qualities.
2. Consciousness injects order (coherence) into systems in proportion to the strength of consciousness present.
3. The strength of consciousness in an individual fluctuates continuously and is regulated by one's focus of attention. (Ordinary perception is generally thought to have a relatively low focus of attention compared to meditation, peak experiences, and other nonordinary states.)
4. Animals show some of the same psychic capacities as humans, suggesting that psi is rooted in our evolutionary ancestry.

Consciousness and Groups

5. A group of individuals can be said to have a group consciousness and thus possess a collective intelligence.
6. When a group's attention is scattered, its mental coherence is weaker and group consciousness is reduced to effectively zero, approximating background noise. When a group's focus of attention is strong, group coherence is increased and group

consciousness is stronger. The strength of the group field is also influenced by the number of individuals present in the group.

7. Strong group fields can influence surrounding systems, both animate and inanimate. The stronger and more coherent the field of consciousness, the greater the influence and the higher the collective intelligence of the group.[41]

Evidence for these conclusions has been published in such prestigious journals as *Nature, Physics Essays, Neuroscience Letters, Science, Behavioral Neuroscience, Psychological Bulletin, British Journal of Psychology,* and *Foundation of Physics Letters.* Given that fact, one wonders how such fine scientists as those mentioned at the beginning of this chapter can continue to dismiss psi out of hand as "bunk."

Explaining the resistance of mainstream thinkers to psi is certainly beyond the scope of this chapter and will in the end be the job of cultural historians. When that story is finally told, I think it will point out that many scientists for a time confused method with metaphysics. That is, they conflated the scientific method with the metaphysical worldview that prevailed at the time science was being birthed— reductive materialism.

Perhaps in its early years science needed the postulate that matter was all that existed in order to achieve its breakthroughs and establish itself, but this is no longer the case. As already noted, the philosopher of science Karl Popper has observed that, in the twentieth century, materialism "transcended itself." In that pivotal century, science began to move beyond the metaphysical assumptions of its early formative years and to posit a much more complex, multi-dimensional universe laced with patterns of influence beyond anything envisioned a century ago. When string theorists are postulating a universe of eleven dimensions and physicists are estimating that 96 percent of the total energy of the universe is invisible "dark matter" and "dark energy," traditional materialism has lost its footing. But shifts of metaphysical paradigms take time, and cultural perceptions lag behind discovery. In the interval, there is a growing divide between what science is *actually* showing us about consciousness and what academics *think* science demands that we believe about consciousness. This disparity has led Thomas Etter of the Boundary Institute to make the following observation:

When a belief is widely held in the face of overwhelming evidence to the contrary, we call it superstition. By that criterion, the most egregious superstition of modern times, perhaps of all time, is the "scientific" belief in the nonexistence of psi.[42]

I would like to conclude this chapter by underscoring again the deep compatibility of the insights emerging from research into the nature of consciousness and insights emerging in quantum theory into the nature of physical reality. This is a complex topic that bears more extended treatment than I can give it here. Instead I will simply draw a few points from Radin's thoughtful discussion in *Entangled Minds* and close by mentioning the seminal work of Ervin Laszlo.

"It is within physics that the principal puzzle of psi resides," says Radin. "If physics prohibits information from transcending the ordinary boundaries of space and time, then from a scientific point of view psi is simply impossible." But contemporary physics does *not* carry this prohibition; in fact, just the opposite has been emerging. Those who follow developments in quantum theory even from the sidelines know that physics has demonstrated the existence of a profound interconnectivity and holism underlying the physical world. Einstein called this nonlocal interconnectivity "spooky action at a distance." Erwin Schrödinger coined the term "entanglement" for it, saying, "I would not call that *one* but *the* characteristic trait of quantum mechanics."[43]

Originally predicted on the basis of the mathematics of quantum theory, quantum entanglement has been repeatedly demonstrated in laboratories since 1972. Once thought to be a feature of only the microscopic world of subatomic particles, leaving the macroscopic world we walk around in operating according to the rules of Newtonian physics, scientists are now finding that the effects of quantum entanglement "scale up" into our macroscopic world. Reviewing the research on entanglement for *New Scientist* in 2004, Michael Brooks concluded: "Physicists now believe that entanglement between particles exists everywhere, all the time, and have recently found shocking evidence that it affects the wider, 'macroscopic' world that we inhabit."[44] That is, the world we walk around in, the world we perceive with our senses, the world we think and feel in is showing itself to be saturated with interconnectivity.

Virtually everything in our physical environment is composed of quanta that have been interacting with other quanta from the big bang to the present, leading some theorists to describe the universe as a single, giant quantum system. In their book *The Nonlocal Universe*, the historian of science Robert Nadeau and physicist Menas Kafatos from George Mason University write:

Quantum entanglement grows exponentially with the number of particles involved in the original quantum state and ... there is no
theoretical limit on the number of these entangled particles. If this is the
case, the universe on a very basic level could be a vast web of particles,
which remain in contact with one another over any distance in "no
time" in the absence of the transfer of energy or information. This
suggests, however strange or bizarre it might seem, *that all of physical
reality is a single quantum system* that responds together to further
interactions.[45]

If all of physical reality is an integrated quantum system, this is a very
different theoretical framework within which to view psi and collective intelligence than the world described by Newtonian physics.
Newtonian physics reinforced our "commonsense" perception that
our minds are fundamentally isolated entities and encouraged the
atomistic psychology that emerged in the nineteenth and early twentieth century. Quantum theory invites a more holistic, integral
psychology to emerge, one that is more receptive to psi and collective
intelligence.

There are many steps to the argument that would link quantum
theory and psi, too many to repeat the discussion here. Radin gives a
useful account that ends with his concluding that "psi is—literally—the
human experience of quantum interconnectedness."[46] Whether or not
one wants to draw this specific conclusion, one cannot help being
struck by the coherence of quantum theory's demonstration of an
entangled universe and psi's demonstration of entangled consciousness.

The discovery that the physical universe is a quantum system
points to a participatory epistemology in which the boundaries
between self and other are not erased but rendered more permeable.
It recontextualizes all individual, local cognition within the deeper
nonlocal potentials of the universe. It encourages an interpretation of
psi that sees psi as the activation of a preexisting connectivity that is
rooted in the permeable and communal nature of reality itself. Thus,
it permits and might even predict the patterns of collective intelligence
I am pointing to in this volume. Radin concludes:

At a level of reality deeper than the ordinary senses can grasp, our
brains and minds are in intimate communion with the universe....
[Because of this communion]we can get glimpses of information about
other people's minds, distant objects, or the future or past. We get this
not through the ordinary senses and not because signals from those

other minds and objects travel to our brain. But because at some level our mind/brain is *already coexistent* with other people's minds, distant objects, and everything else.... From this perspective, psychic experiences are reframed not as mysterious "powers of the mind" but as momentary glimpses of the entangled fabric of reality.[47]

In this chapter, I have kept the discussion close to experimental research rather than address attempts to formulate a grand synthesis of theory, but at its close I want to highlight Ervin Laszlo's accomplishment in formulating just such a comprehensive synthesis of physical science and consciousness research. In an important series of books—*The Interconnected Universe* (1999a), *The Connectivity Hypothesis* (2003), and *Science and the Akashic Field* (2004), and *Science and the Reenchantment of the Cosmos* (2006)—Laszlo has formulated a comprehensive metatheory that represents a significant advance in scientific vision while providing an expanded context for conceptualizing psi and collective consciousness.

Laszlo weaves together findings from quantum physics, post-Darwinian biology, cosmology, and consciousness research to propose the existence of a fundamental field he calls the A-field. The A-field is a manifestation of the quantum vacuum, the superimplicate order behind our explicate world. It is a field in which nonlocality and superconductivity are the norm, the generative matrix of the big bang and the receiver of the possible big crunch. In Laszlo's hands, the A-field becomes a Metaverse that stands behind our universe.

According to Laszlo, this Metaverse explains how our universe functions nonlocally as one organism across vast distances; it illumines the statistically improbable first conditions that have impelled our universe on such a fruitful evolutionary journey (because it holds and uses the learning gleaned from previous evolutionary cycles); and it provides a conceptual framework that honors reports of transpersonal states of consciousness (because it is the Mind that embraces all other minds). In creating this bridge between the hard sciences and transpersonal psychology, Laszlo shows us a universe where psi is expected and intelligence is inherently collective from the very start.

part ii.

Working with Fields of Consciousness

CHAPTER 4

Working with Fields

The outer work can never be small
if the inner work is great.
And the outer work can never be great
if the inner work is small.
—Meister Eckhart

Working with students every day has changed my perception of the depth and dynamics of the mind, and this in turn has changed how I engage my students. As my understanding of consciousness has deepened, my approach to teaching has gone through a parallel deepening, leading me to do things I would never have imagined doing when I began my career thirty years ago. If anyone had told me then what I'm about to tell you now, I probably wouldn't have believed them. This is the great gift my students have given me.

In this chapter, I want to lay out some of the strategies I've developed through the years for working with fields of consciousness as they emerge in the classroom. There are many ways of working with these fields, and the suggestions that follow only scratch the surface. We are just beginning to grasp the significance of collective consciousness and its implications for how we teach. As we learn more about the collective dynamics of consciousness, new pedagogical strategies will emerge. This is a time of exploration and innovation.

In writing this chapter, I have wrestled with how candid to be about how I work with these fields. Part of me wants to describe just the bare bones of the principles involved. I'm a private person by nature, and it's not easy for me to expose this much of my inner world to public scrutiny. Moreover, if I speak the language that is most natural to me, it will combine consciousness discourse with spiritual discourse. Readers who are spirituality-friendly will not be put off by this language, but others may prefer a more spiritually neutral language. I understand and sympathize with this position, especially given the superficiality of much new age spirituality on the left and the socially conservative agenda of the religious right. On the other hand, if I distance myself from what I am and how I truly operate, the danger is that the abstracted discussion will not have the juice that lived experience brings to the table.

In the end, I have decided to take the risk of candidly describing how I actually work with these fields. I will describe the specific techniques that I use and the assumptions I am making about how the universe works that I bring to these techniques. This is a risky game because I will not argue for these assumptions here or give all the reasons and research that went into their formation. That would be an interesting conversation, but it belongs to a different time and place. I am going to trust that readers will recognize the larger intellectual context for many of these convictions or at the very least will be willing to give them a tentative hearing here.

What follows, therefore, reflects a spiritual view of existence. I embrace a multidimensional universe alive with multiple forms of life, but I do not accept any one culture's description of this multiverse as definitive or adequate. I also want to own my limitations and make it clear that the phenomena I'm addressing are larger than any one discipline can encompass and certainly larger than I can encompass. I therefore encourage readers to critique my positions as they see fit and to experiment with these fields in ways that are most meaningful to them.[1]

Fields of Consciousness

In the new perspective that is emerging in consciousness research today, our personal minds can be thought of as fields and fields have porous boundaries. Fields are open systems. Being porous and open, mental fields seem to be particularly susceptible to *coupling*, to forming spontaneous connections with other minds. As Dean Radin puts it, "individual minds may combine into networks of entangled minds, giving rise to more complex 'mind circuits.'"

We must twist language to describe the undulations and currents of the resulting patterns of consciousness. While not losing their individual integrity, human minds "flow" and "merge" with other minds to form larger wholes—group fields. Though generated by individual minds, these fields have a life of their own that persists even after the minds that contributed to them have moved on to other activities. They have "sinews" and "fibers." They have "pockets" and "circles" and "eddies." This capacity to couple with other minds, when combined with developments in contemporary physics, suggests that there is a preexisting wholeness underlying individual consciousness, an innate collective potential that can be activated and brought forward.

The class field is a form of collective consciousness that holds our individual minds in communal embrace. It is the instructor's silent partner in the room, a field of consciousness that connects this present group of students to all the students who have previously taken this course with him or her. Through this field, present learning is quickened by previous learning. Just as the prior learning of others has set the stage for these students, their learning will create a slightly stronger and richer platform for those who follow. This is the nature of fields, to become stronger with repetition and gather momentum over time.

The learning fields that develop around teachers are the unregistered student in our courses. Though they do not show up on any roster, they are nonetheless tangibly present in the room. Once you recognize the existence of these fields, it is a natural step to begin working with them *directly*—not just indirectly by working with your students, but directly by engaging the fields themselves.

As the instructor, you can work with these fields because you are already part of them, already woven into their fabric. As the teacher of the course, you have been part of the course field from the beginning, and so your mark on it is deep. This is an important point. The teacher is the constant in the long development of the course mind. He or she has been the thread of continuity in the constant turnover of students through the years. These fields, while composed of the energy of many minds, have gathered around *this* person's repeated actions in the world. They are inherently collective fields with many roots and tendrils, but the instructor is their center. If anyone can influence these fields directly, the instructor is in the best position to do so.

Working with these fields is a natural and logical extension of our role as educators. If you understand the model of consciousness that is emerging today, if you grasp the significance of the themes of connectivity, wholeness, superconductivity, resonance, and emergence in contemporary thought, then working with these fields becomes a natural extension of your love of teaching and your desire to do it well. It is simply the "next step" in developing a more conscious pedagogy.

I've broken my strategies for working with these fields into four categories: preparing the field, nourishing the field, visualization exercises, and closing the field. A fifth category, connecting the field through conversation, will be discussed separately in the next chapter.

Preparing the Class Field

Preparing the class field is a process of engaging the learning field being created by the students who are about to take a course with you *before* the course actually begins. *As an intentional field, the class field begins to form when students first decide to take a course and gets stronger as they go through the various steps of enacting that decision.* Because the class field or class mind begins to form before a course begins, I begin working with it before classes start, usually as soon as registration begins.

In preparing the class field, my intention is to remove obstacles to the learning that is about to take place, both my obstacles and those of my students. In doing this, I am making a number of assumptions. In addition to assuming the existence of this field, I assume that I can communicate with it and enter into conscious communion with it. Because this is an intentional field, I assume that my intention can influence it in some way. This may be a bold presumption, but both research and a long line of meditation masters support this belief.

I also assume that, as the instructor for the course, my intention is in certain respects the *seed catalyst* of this field, calling it into existence, so to speak. For this reason, I believe it is important for me to clarify my intention for my course and my students before we begin our work together. Clarifying and focusing my intention is the first step toward having a productive semester, and this involves reconnecting with the ideals that guide my professional life.

Before the semester begins, I take some time to *review my commitments*. I remind myself why I am doing what I do for a living and ask myself if I am prepared to do it again. I review my beliefs about humanity, the role of education in changing people's lives, and the critical point we have come to in history. Placing my course in this larger context, I recommit myself to serving my students to the best of my ability.

If I find that I am not ready to give them my best effort or if I am distracted by other things going on in my life, frustrated with departmental politics or just plain tired, I stay with it as long as it takes until I can reconnect with my deeper commitments. Sometimes this realignment takes days or even weeks of attention. Teaching consciously—by which I mean bringing my *full* consciousness with all its levels to the act of teaching and engaging my students with all their levels—is demanding work. I don't deserve the privilege unless I am ready to give it my best effort.

Next, I *screen the field*. In the weeks during registration, I bring my soon-to-be students to mind and hold them in my awareness. I reach out to them mentally and ask that our time together be beneficial and productive. Because of my respect for the power of the forces that may be triggered by our coming together, I ask that the right students show up in my classes. Speaking to their unconscious, I ask that those who are ready to do this work come forward and that those who are not be guided to choose other courses. I project my intentions for the course that they may choose in the deep mystery that surrounds us what best serves their purpose, and then I surrender to the larger wisdom that brings us together.

I don't pretend that I can control these processes, of course, and would not try to calculate the impact of this exercise, but *given what we already know about the power of conscious thought*, I would not be acting responsibly as an educator if I did not clarify my intention and project it outwardly as clearly and powerfully as I know how. I repeat this process several times before a course begins. As soon as I have a tentative roster for the course, I include it in the exercise.

If this sounds suspiciously like prayer, you may be right. Prayer is such a loaded word in our post-9/11, neoconservative, Christian-ascendancy culture that I hesitate to use it. Academics are not supposed to pray, or at least not talk publicly about praying lest they appear less rigorous, less academic. It would be safer to use more neutral language, to speak here only about "projected intention," but this strikes me as playing word games. The fact is, I do pray for my students, not in the name of God and not prayer in any conventional sense, but it feels like prayer. And yet it is motivated not by religion or faith but by my growing respect for the power of conscious intention. It reflects not premodern sentiment but postmodern research.

Let me put on the table another assumption that I make in preparing the class field. I assume that I am not doing this by myself, but am entering into relationship with existing forces, powers, or beings that are willing to help me in this work. I assume that these forces include at the very minimum the souls of my students. By *soul* I mean the consciousness that is larger than their egoic personality, that is the source of their personality (mediated by their genetic matrix). In addition to the souls of my students, I assume that there are *guardians*, for want of a better term, that are interested in what we are doing here on Earth and in this classroom.

This may sound like a monstrously arrogant assumption that gives undue status to human beings, making us the narcissistic center of too much spiritual attention, but it seems to me even more arrogant to assume that the only intelligent beings in the entire Cosmos are we physical beings. For a variety of reasons, I have joined the ranks of those who believe that the Cosmos includes many nonphysical dimensions and beings who live in these dimensions as we live in space-time. I believe that there is a world of saints and bodhisattvas, wearing different names in different cultures, "higher beings" of goodness and liberated consciousness that support our activities on this planet.[2]

In preparing the class field, therefore, I ask for the help and assistance of these beings who can see the larger landscape more clearly than I and can do things that I cannot. I call to them without knowing their names and ask them to help me serve the highest good of my students. Thus, my posture in preparing the field is essentially one of *collaboration and cooperation.* I also invoke the guardians of the place where I work, the institution I am part of, and my discipline, because I assume that where there is organization in the physical world, there is a kind of parallel organization in the spiritual world. By entering into a respectful, open, and receptive relationship with these powers, we open ourselves to their help and assistance.

If I'm going to describe how I actually work with these fields, I must put one more assumption on the table, yet I hesitate to do so because it's a complex topic in its own right and one that may trigger alarms for some readers. Furthermore, it's not absolutely necessary to include it because it is not essential to the concept of fields in the narrowest sense. Learning fields exist in the present moment, and reincarnation introduces the larger horizon of time. It addresses how the past influences and shapes the present in ways that go beyond Sheldrake's discussion.

The positive reason for including the concept of reincarnation is this. Because reincarnation deepens our understanding of the history that goes into the making of each human being, it also deepens our understanding of the texture of the fields that are generated when human beings come together in groups. Thus, it influences how I work with the fields my students and I are generating when we meet in this lifetime. In the end, I have decided to include it here because it is a concept that has profoundly influenced how I see life and how I relate to my students. Let me interrupt this discussion, then, to take a short detour into the topic of rebirth.

To reincarnate or not to reincarnate

As a philosopher of religion, my conviction is that reincarnation is in the process of becoming an empirically demonstrated fact of nature. A bold assertion, perhaps, but warranted. If it were simply a tenet of faith as it has been in centuries past, I would leave it out of the discussion, but because a large body of critical evidence for rebirth has now been collected by scientifically trained researchers, I think it is appropriate to include it here. In fact, one of the best kept secrets in the academic community is the overwhelming strength of the evidence for reincarnation.

Many laypersons are not aware of this body of research, but it is making inroads in professional circles, kicking up resistance but slowly melting our cultural resistance to the concept. As a natural phenomenon, reincarnation is compatible with science, though we do not yet have a complete understanding of the precise mechanisms involved or a model that integrates the concept with known scientific principles. Even without such a model, however, I think we have sufficient evidence to recognize that reincarnation is one of the ways our universe is growing itself into increasingly complex forms, just as we accept evolution on the basis of the fossil record even without a complete understanding of the processes that produced this record.

For most of our evolutionary history, life could only express its creativity through the burgeoning diversity of entire species. Thus, evolution has largely been seen as shaping groups rather than individuals within these groups. At some point along the way, however, nature appears to have found a way to also evolve individuals within certain groups by preserving their learning and folding it into new expressions of their mind-stream. This appears to have taken place within the human species, and we'll leave the question of other species alone for now.

From this perspective, the emergence of reincarnation is closely associated with the emergence of *individuality.* I believe that the compounding of learning that rebirth enacts as it folds more and more experience into successive incarnations is responsible for the extraordinary differentiation, diversification, and self-empowerment that has been taking place in human history. From my perspective, reincarnation is a natural continuation of evolution and emergence.[3]

Gallup polls taken in 1990 and 2001 revealed the surprising fact that approximately 25 percent of the adult American public believes in reincarnation, and I suspect that the percentage will be higher for those who pick up this book. Even so, some readers may be uncomfortable with this concept because they may think that it is incompatible with Christian theology on the one hand or with our scientific scruples on the other—incorrectly, I might add, on both counts.

I have deep roots in the Christian tradition and I am convinced, together with the Scottish theologian Geddes MacGregor, that Christianity can incorporate reincarnation into its theology without diluting its identity or mission. Historically, mainstream Christian theology has shown itself willing to embrace any fact of nature for which there is sufficient evidence to convince us that it truly is a fact. Evolution was once thought to be irreconcilable with Christian faith, but many theologians have demonstrated that this is no longer the case. I think that the same thing will eventually happen for reincarnation.[4]

As for science, the matter hinges on the question: How credible is the evidence for rebirth? While I think that the evidence is currently very strong, this is not the place to argue its merits. I have outlined this evidence in my book *Lifecycles* and discussed it further in *Dark Night, Early Dawn*. Here I will only list some sources that readers can consult if they want to examine this evidence for themselves.

The nucleus of the evidence for rebirth comes from three sources. First and foremost is Ian Stevenson's meticulous study of thousands of young children from around the globe who appear to have spontaneous memories of their most recently concluded life. For thirty-four years (1967–2001), Stevenson was the Carlson Professor of Psychiatry in the Department of Psychiatric Medicine at the University of Virginia. The striking body of evidence that he collected and evaluated over this period is the foundation of the empirical case for reincarnation today, and many consider Stevenson the Charles Darwin of reincarnation theory.[5]

A second area of research is the clinical evidence coming from past-life therapy. There are hundreds of cases in print of patients who have reconnected with their former life memories in ways that produced striking and beneficial results for their therapeutic process, accounts that have been carefully screened and analyzed by responsible therapists.[6]

A third source of data is the unsought appearance of past-life memories in forms of experiential psychotherapy that do not particularly focus on reincarnation. When people open to deep levels of their unconscious, past-life memories often surface spontaneously even when the client is not specifically looking for them, and in some cases when the client has previously rejected the notion of reincarnation.[7]

To these three bodies of contemporary evidence we can add the cross-cultural testimony of many ancient spiritual traditions, both Eastern and Western, which have systematically explored the deep psyche through meditation and concluded that understanding the cycle of death and rebirth is the starting point of wisdom. Without this key insight, they contend, the deeper order and logic of human existence cannot be recognized.[8]

By itself, Stevenson's evidence is sufficient to justify a strong reincarnation hypothesis, but when all these sources are taken into account, the cumulative case gets stronger still. Readers may choose to reject or accept this evidence as they see fit, but since I've already published a book endorsing it, it would be disingenuous of me to hide the fact that rebirth has been an important part of my thinking for many years. To me, reincarnation illumines the great depth of the human personality and the historical forces that have produced this depth. Thus it leads me to see my students as beings of great depth and to relate to them accordingly.

In this chapter, I am not asking the reader to take my word for the evidence cited but only to consider the following hypothetical with me. *If* one were convinced that reincarnation is a fact of life, how would it influence the task of working with the class field? How might it change one's perception of the student–teacher relationship? If readers will go this far with me, they can return to consider the evidence for rebirth on their own and decide whether this view of life deserves their assent. Now let us return to the discussion of preparing the class field.

I mentioned previously that, in screening the field, I address the souls of my students. With reincarnation now on the table, I can say more straightforwardly that for me the soul is the consciousness that integrates *all one's lives*, both one's present life and one's past lives. It holds all our experience, integrating everything we have learned into a meta-identity that underpins our egoic identity.

If we are living in a reincarnating universe, I assume it is likely that I have had dealings with at least some of my students in previous life-times—or, to put it more carefully, that my soul has had dealings with their souls. It also seems to be a safe assumption that because life is the messy business it is, some of these earlier encounters probably went well while others probably didn't. With some students, our previous contact probably left behind the blessings that friendship brings while with others it probably left bruises. When we meet again in this lifetime, therefore, this deeper history may be activated as our present contact brings forward the residue of our past from the unconscious.

In a universe that weaves human beings in and out of time over thousands of years in complex cycles of cause and effect, we are constantly picking up where we left off in previous lifetimes, renewing relationships and the feelings associated with those relationships and hopefully moving them forward. We could make ourselves dizzy trying to figure out all the details, and that would largely be a waste of time, I think. To live our lives well, we do not need to see everything that created the circumstances in which we now find ourselves; we need only live those circumstances well.

With all this in mind, as I prepare the class field I open myself to the souls of my students and I ask them to forgive me any injury I may have caused them in the past, either directly or indirectly, intentionally or unintentionally. I also actively forgive them any injury they may have caused me and commit myself to managing as consciously as I can any negative feelings that our present contact may stir in me. My intention is to let bygones be bygones that we may meet in this lifetime with clean slates. Reincarnation is not just about healing the past, of course, but also working together to create a positive present and future. In this lifetime, my students and I meet in the role of teacher and student. As I prepare the class field, therefore, I commit myself to fulfilling my side of this role as best I can and to helping my students achieve their personal goals in this lifetime.

Specific Ritual Forms

I have described the basic intentions involved in preparing the class field rather than specific rituals or procedures because I think these core intentions can be expressed in a variety of intellectual, philosophical, and spiritual frameworks. I encourage readers to experiment with the tools that their specific traditions make available to them to embody these intentions. In the end, the specific rituals may be less important than the power of focused intention itself. Rituals may open the door, but heartfelt intention may carry the greater weight.

Having said this, I also do not want to underestimate the power of ritual. Intention needs to be focused to have its greatest impact and ritual does this. Furthermore, the power of ritual is augmented if one works with rituals that have a long history. Sheldrake's concept of formative causation and morphic resonance supports the time-honored view that powerful fields develop around spiritual practices that have been used for many generations. The longer people have performed a particular practice through history, the stronger its field will be. *When one aligns one's present intention with such a field, it amplifies the power of that intention.*

With both these considerations in mind, let me mention one practice that I have used to prepare my class fields. I will not describe it in sufficient detail for persons to perform it themselves because that would not be appropriate. This practice must be learned from those trained and empowered to transmit it. I mention it here only to give an example of the kind of practices one might use for this purpose.

For the past ten years, I have been using a Tibetan Buddhist practice called *Chöd* to work with class fields. *Chöd* means "to cut" and refers to cutting the cords of karmic cause and effect that keep us repeating the patterns of the past in the present. It also refers to cutting the cords that bind us to the illusion that we are a private self separate from the larger whole of life. *Chöd* is a powerful practice that derives from the Tibetan saint Machig Labdrön, a spiritually realized woman who lived in twelfth-century Tibet. It is a practice taught by many teachers of Vajrayana Buddhism today. I received it from Tsultrim Allione, founder of Tara Mandala, a Buddhist retreat center in Colorado.

The essence of the *Chöd* practice lies in symbolically sacrificing one's egoic self, receiving spiritual nourishment from a deeper reality in return, and then sharing that spiritual nourishment with others—in this case with my students—thus canceling old debts. By "feeding the demons" of our self-cherishing, one cuts through that which keeps us small in order to awaken both ourselves and others to that pristine consciousness that encompasses and permeates all existence. This practice does not require that the other parties know that they are being included in this ritual to receive its benefit. The basic idea is that karma is like a cord held by two people. If one person drops the cord, the other person will feel it at some level and respond.[9]

My subjective perception is that when I began to include my students in my *Chöd* practice, it had an immediate and beneficial impact on my classes. Teaching went more smoothly and productively. I encountered fewer obstacles in the classroom and the students seemed to have an easier time learning on many levels. In my more advanced courses where the more involved students gathered, the disruptive effects described in chapter 1 seemed to be ameliorated, allowing these fields to rise with fewer disturbances and greater transformative impact. These are entirely subjective impressions, of course, without any objective assessment to support them. There are several dissertations here waiting for the right graduate students. (Can Dean Radin and Roger Nelson's random number generators detect the presence of learning fields in a classroom? Can we use this technology to assess the comparative effectiveness of different strategies for working with these fields?)

The positive impact of including my students in this practice was so striking that I now include my students in my daily practice as soon as registration begins, weeks before classes actually start. I shudder sometimes at what my colleagues would think if they could see me performing the *Chöd* ritual in front of a student roster for a course that has not yet begun, but to my mind this is simply an extension of my responsibilities as a teacher. It is the logical consequence of recognizing the fields generated by my activities and discovering that I can influence these fields directly. It is simply being efficient as an educator.

Like most rituals, the *Chöd* practice takes some time and a quiet place to perform, but the intention of mutual forgiveness and blessing can be cultivated in short exercises throughout the day. One can, for example, bring this intention to mind while driving to work or walking across campus. It's simply a matter of being conscious of the energetic field we are continuously creating with our thoughts and remembering to choose the thoughts of forgiveness and reconciliation.

Again, I encourage readers to explore the specific spiritual and psychological traditions they feel most comfortable with and to adopt or construct the meditations, rituals, or intentional exercises they feel most aligned with. One can be an atheist, I think, and still work with these fields in a powerful and effective manner—though an unusual atheist to be sure. The key lies in recognizing that our intention is the seed of our behavior, and our behavior generates patterns of contact with others that cumulatively create energetic fields. The more consciousness we bring to our teaching, the more we will generate strong and positive learning fields.

Nourishing the Field

The same practices that are used to prepare the class field before a course begins can be used *to purify and elevate the field* as the semester proceeds. These practices do not require the participation of the students. The basic exercise is essentially the same as for preparing the field. One brings the class field into one's conscious awareness and works with it in some way. The difference is that now the students have become known entities to you. They have become real people who challenge you in specific ways, and this gives you more specific content to work with. The same practices that were used to prepare the field can be used to address this content once a course has begun. Let me give an example, this time focusing on a meditation practice.

Teaching is exhilarating work on the good days, but it's also exhausting work, with many ups and downs. After a frustrating day when the students were uncommunicative or did not complete their assignments or when we were not up to snuff ourselves, meditation can help us regroup and reset our personal thermostat. It can also become a platform for engaging the class mind. If we consciously incorporate the class field into our meditation practice, we can sometimes melt obstacles when they are still in their early stages or gently lift the baseline of the room.

There are many meditation practices in different traditions for working with other persons. I am going to assume that readers who meditate regularly are already familiar with these practices or that they can learn them from qualified teachers. When using these practices to support one's teaching, one simply enlarges the "target" of one's meditation to include one's class fields. Where the practice instructs you to engage a particular person, you substitute the class field. One may think that including so many people in one's practice would dilute its effect, diminishing its impact to near-zero, but this is an older way of thinking that does not reflect current insights into the dynamics of nonlinear systems. For what it's worth, my experience has been that when I am working with a field that is rooted in my work in the world, I can engage this field with positive results.

One practice that I have used to do so is the Buddhist practice of *tonlin*—the practice of exchanging self and other. *Tonlin* is a compassion practice in which you seek not only to expand your own awareness but also to have a positive impact on another person. In this practice, you enter into meditative quiet and bring a particular person to mind. Then you consciously take on their suffering, drawing into yourself any problems they may be carrying, and send them joy and happiness in return. You visualize yourself drawing dark clouds from them representing their pain and conflict and sending them bright light in return.

A teacher can use the practice of *tonlin* to purify and uplift their class fields. Once you have established yourself in the calm of meditation, you bring your students to mind and do the practice of exchanging self and other with the class field, drawing in the stresses and resistances of the entire class and nourishing the field by flooding it with white light. Some may fear that taking on this much darkness may be harmful, but this turns out to be an unfounded worry. Besides, are we not already engaged in this kind of give-and-take with our students? We are taking on their ignorance to a degree by entering into dialogue with them and sharing with them our understanding in the hope that it will be helpful to them. The practice of *tonlin* simply takes this exchange to a deeper energetic level.

Another reason for working with the class field during the semester is to *skillfully manage the explosive energies of accelerated learning*. Once a course begins and the class field has congealed, it begins to come under the influence of the course field, the cumulative learning field surrounding a course. As I see it, the course field is the older, more powerful core of the field. As the course field begins to penetrate the class field, it begins to touch individual students. If the course field is strong, it can unleash powerful influences in the room, influences so strong they can sometimes be disruptive.

Power is not about nice and it's not always gentle. In fact, the impact of these fields sometimes reminds me of the Hindu goddess Kali. Fierce in continence and form, Kali's compassion expresses itself in ruthlessly tearing away old structures in order to make room for new growth. Stripping away the old is beneficial, but challenging. Students may find themselves grasping a new way of thinking more quickly than they are comfortable with. They may find themselves being drawn into levels of existential self-scrutiny they had not anticipated or feel disoriented by rapidly changing their minds around convictions they've held for a long time. Sometimes the sudden opening of intellectual doors may lead them to consider changing their major or even bring a new career path into view. All of this can be dizzying for students.

As their instructor, it is not our place, of course, to think that we can know what our students should believe or what they should do with their lives. Our job is simply to present options. But sometimes the simple act of presenting options compounded with the influence of these group fields and the resonance of lived experience provokes deep changes in our students, and we should not ignore the challenges these changes generate for them. For all these reasons, if we are meditators, it is beneficial to hold our students in the open, nonjudgmental, and supportive field of our meditative awareness throughout the semester. If one teaches to change lives, as I think most educators do, one naturally uses all the resources at one's disposal. For me, this includes holding my students in my contemplative awareness as long as I am engaged with them in a course.

The class field can also be tapped to *diagnose problems* that come up during the semester. Sometimes when I have finished a lecture and am packing up my books for the walk back to my office, I get a nagging sense that something is not right. If I look objectively at the lecture I've just given, at the facts I presented and how the students seemed to take them in, everything appears fine on the surface. And yet there is a gnawing feeling in the pit of my stomach that all is not well. Sometimes it works the other way round too. Viewed from the outside, everything may have gone wrong in class, but in the middle of the chaos my gut is telling me that everything is OK.

When I get back to my office and my thoughts have settled or sometimes when I'm sitting in meditation the following morning, if I bring my students to mind and hold them in my awareness, the reason for the discomfort will often show itself. What the rational mind cannot always catch on the fly, the deeper mind registers more clearly. I may have them at one level, but I'm losing them at another. Once I see what the problem is, I can decide what changes to make. Alternatively, I may see more clearly what's behind the fruitful chaos. Disruptive days sometimes signal new voices coming forward in the room or new lines of thought surfacing. Falling apart is an important part of the cycle of learning. I may need to fan the flames of dissent rather than drown them with answers.

Every teacher has had these moments of insight as we try to read what's happening in our courses, and we interpret them in different ways. One of the ways I understand them is by drawing on the concept of the class field. When I'm trying to discern what's going on beneath the surface in my classroom—the significance of a look, the meaning of a casual remark, the reaction of the room to a new concept—I try to tune into the class field. This field is not outside me; I am part of it. My mind is a fractal participant in its complex patterns. If we think of the field as having holographic properties—the whole registering in every part—then as part of that field I am already registering the dynamics of the entire room at a very subtle level. It's only a matter of whether I am able to tune into that level of consciousness where this awareness is already registering and take the time to do so.

Some may suggest that this is simply another language for tuning into personal intuition, and it may be. Certainly, intuition is involved.

And yet, as I think about Roger Nelson's random number generators responding to shifting patterns of collective attention, I think there is more going on than just personal intuition. The back door of the personal opens to the collective domain. The class field is an extraordinarily subtle phenomenon. It is an information-rich pond that collects and reflects the experiences of all its participants. If one practices the art of tuning into this pond, it will register more clearly in our awareness. This is a skill that can be cultivated. The collective mind of our class will speak to us, awaken in us a sense of what's going wrong and what's going right in our classroom. Intuitions will become more articulate. Options for new interventions will present themselves.

I want to underscore in closing that an important part of nourishing the field is being willing to confront our students' disappointment with something we've done or failed to do in class. Of all the challenges teaching presents us with, this is perhaps the hardest and for that reason one of the most productive. It hurts when you are explaining a concept that you find beautiful and your students just yawn. It's confusing when a lecture you've used effectively for years suddenly stops working. Ideas that had previously opened doors begin to fall flat. Why? What's happening? Our ego panics. The temptation is to blame the students. If they would just pay better attention or if they cared more about their education, perhaps the old flame would catch. But sometimes its not the students' fault at all. Sometimes something deeper is afoot—the field is speaking.

My students' disappointment with a lecture that has been a consistent winner in the past often signals that a shift has taken place in our collective field. A commitment to nourishing the field challenges me to follow these shifts where they lead. My experience is that this shift consistently serves my needs as well as my students' needs. Something about how I have been approaching this subject has outlived its usefulness. No matter that it worked before; it's now time to experiment again, to enter the unknown again, to find a new approach. The students need me to do this; something in me needs me to do this. Nourishing the field calls me to be constantly realigning myself with the energy generated by our coming together. Parker Palmer put it well when he said, "Teaching is a daily exercise in vulnerability."

When I take the time to step back and open myself to this realignment, I often discover that the time has come for me to change something about how I think or feel about a subject. Life is about growth, not fixed success. How I approached a subject in the past may have been an honest expression of my person then and it therefore ignited a positive response in my students, but now something more is called for. It's time for me to embrace a larger horizon, to become more than I was.

My students' disappointment often points the way forward in this process. If I delay or defer the task, things will only get worse. If I stay on automatic pilot and try to maintain the past trajectory, my teaching will slowly lose its vitality. Week by week, semester by semester, the gap between me and my students will get wider. But if I am willing to sit with the discomfort of their disappointment and wrestle with the task at hand, something new presents itself. Finding the right pivot always triggers an immediate response in the room. Heads lift, eyes light up, the energy shifts. Nourishing the field, therefore, is not simply about delivering something to the students. It's also about being willing to receive feedback and follow it where it leads. It's about allowing not only the students but you yourself to be nourished by the ever-changing course field.

Visualization Exercises

Most of the preceding suggestions have involved strategies for working with the class field outside of the classroom and without the students participating. It is also possible to work with the class field inside the classroom with the students actively participating in the exercise. Visualization exercises can activate the latent potential of the class field and strengthen its influence in the room. Usually I use these exercises only in my upper division courses where the students can be made aware of the theory behind the exercise. Using them in introductory classes, at my university at least, would probably be seen as just too "weird." (Singing is also a potent way to strengthen group fields, as many religious orders have recognized, but that too would be a hard sell in a university classroom. I have used both visualization and simple tonal singing in workshops when I want to accelerate and deepen the emergence of a group field as quickly as possible.)

The key to visualization lies in the perception that our thoughts can influence reality, that seeing something clearly in our mind can actually influence the subtle processes that pulse through a room. This notion makes absolutely no sense in the mind-reduces-to-brain model of consciousness, but the Tibetan Buddhist tradition and many other sophisticated contemplative traditions have long emphasized the transformative power of skillful visualization. Moreover, this concept has been taken over today by Olympic coaches working with their athletes and mainstream physicians working with their patients. The insight that the mind can shape our experience in profound and subtle ways seems to be gaining ground in our pragmatic culture.

When I do a visualization exercise with my students or workshop participants, I let the images emerge out of my immediate, intuitive awareness rather than use a preplanned exercise. I wasn't comfortable taking these kinds of risks in the beginning, but experience has taught me that a visualization sequence that arises from the energetic field of a specific group will be more powerful for that group than a one-size-fits-all, cookie-cutter exercise. To bring this exercise forward, I clear my mind as best I can, tune into the people present, and trust the images that emerge in my awareness from this subtle communion. Using this approach, I don't know where a visualization exercise is going to go, but it has always gone in a good direction, touching people in ways that I could never have anticipated or consciously planned. I am continually amazed by what these exercises evoke in people.

Even in these intuitively guided exercises there are patterns, however, and the core project in the beginning is to strengthen the awareness that, by acting together, we create a collective energy that nourishes everyone present and helps our shared work. Let me give one example of a visualization sequence just to suggest the general tenor of the images that can emerge. I will present this as a verbatim transcript of an exercise that would take between ten and fifteen minutes.

- Preliminary instructions to relax . . . clear your mind . . . focus on your breathing . . . settle into the present moment.
- See our group arranged in a circle. (This suggestion works surprisingly well even when the students are all facing forward in a conventional classroom arrangement.)
- Begin to feel an energy . . . a warm golden light moving through you . . . around the circle from left to right . . . it enters your left arm . . . moves through your body . . . exits through your right arm . . . passing to the person on your right.
- Golden light . . . like warm steam . . . brighter . . . stronger . . . faster . . . very strong now . . . the energy is flowing through you.
- Now . . . from either your heart or your forehead (whichever feels more natural to you) . . . project a beam of this golden light to the center of the circle . . . where it joins with the other beams . . . to become . . . a bright flame . . . the resulting image . . . resembling a wagon wheel made of light . . . light moves around the circle . . . and projects through us to the center . . . where it becomes a bright fire.

- In the center ... the flame grows brighter ... stronger ...
- As the golden fire grows brighter ... warmer ... it begins to rise higher.
- The fire at the center ... now expands to become a canopy of light ... that comes down around all of us ... surrounding all of us.
- The light moves around our circle ... into the raised center ... and now it envelops all of us ... we are held by this canopy of light ... nourished by it.
- Rest and let this energy flow through us.
- Now ... as we begin to come back to our bodily awareness ... we can leave this thought form intact ... it can remain intact ... even as, at another level ... we bring our attention back to our individual awareness.
- Wiggle your toes and fingers ... stretch your arms ... when you're ready open your eyes.

This exercise strengthens the field by making what is already taking place at a subtle energetic level more conscious. In a course, the actions of individuals combine to form a whole that influences everyone in the room. The visualization exercise augments this process. By actively visualizing something collective that moves through us, respecting our individuality and yet combining our energy to form something that nourishes everyone in the room, we encourage the emergence of an integrated group awareness that augments the individuals present. By giving conscious visual expression to what is taking place subliminally, we empower the class field.

Closing the Field

Just as it is important to prepare the class field at the beginning of a course and to nourish and purify it during the course, it is also important to close the field well at the end of the course. All cycles have beginnings and endings. If you do not decisively close the class field at the end of the semester, you may have students dribbling into your office for months, feeling strangely unable to let go of the course.

I did not appreciate the importance of closing the field in the early years when these fields were first surfacing in my classroom, and it took me a while to understand what was happening. Initially I took the appearance of these students at my door as a compliment, thinking that they had just really enjoyed the course. Only gradually did I realize that something was amiss. They were having difficulty letting go of the course; they were caught by something. I began to realize that the group field was still dynamically active in their psyche. Because the field had not been closed well, they were stuck, with no physical place to go to express the psychic link they still felt to the class mind.

The more powerfully you invite the group mind to enter your classroom, the more important it is to dissolve that mind at the end of the course and to reempower the students as self-sufficient fields of awareness, whole and complete within themselves. There are several ways in which this can be done.

In courses where one has used a visualization exercise to open and strengthen the field, the same exercise can be run in reverse to close the field at the end of the semester. In the previous exercise, for example, the first step would be to invite the students to bring the original image back to mind. Then I would ask them to visualize the canopy of light retracting back into the bright flame, then let the flame sink lower until it is once again level with the circle of students. Next, I would instruct them to reach into the center of the fire, take out a handful of the flame, place it inside their chest, and seal it inside themselves. When everyone has done this, the fire in the center of the circle has disappeared; the collective fire has been reassimilated. The circle energy moving around the room is then brought to a stop, and everyone draws its energy back into their person.

What we had constructed from our collective intention, we have now reappropriated. Because the fire at the center was a composite of all our energies, each of us now carries a small piece of everyone in the room sealed in our individual person. This exercise honors and empowers what has actually taken place during the semester. Our personal learning in a course is always influenced by other people's learning—by the questions they asked, the opinions they've shared, and the enthusiasm they brought to the project. Now is the time of ending, of separation, integration, and individuation.

In introductory courses in which visualization exercises are not possible or in situations that do not allow me to address these processes this explicitly, the same result can be achieved by a well-choreographed last lecture or final group discussion. Sometimes I will lead a group discussion at the end of a semester in which I invite the students to identify an idea covered during the semester that was particularly meaningful to them. I put these up on the board, both so that we can review what we have accomplished (closure) and see what was meaningful to *other* people in the room (individuation). This often leads to a discussion of what different people are doing with these ideas, once again affirming our individual preferences and predilections.

The integration of the class mind into the course mind at the end of a semester seems to take place naturally, like a tree adding a new ring of growth to its girth, and does not require special handling on a teacher's part. And yet, the course mind is in my thoughts when I remind students that they are now part of a long lineage of students who have completed this course. At the end of the semester, I often collect their recommendations for how I can improve the course for the next group of students, and I do so not only to harvest their valuable feedback but also to reinforce their sense of being part of a larger project of learning that will continue *without them* as they move on in their academic career. I sometimes remind them that they will now carry the new understanding they have acquired here into other courses and eventually into their work in the world where it will combine with still new sources of information to form unpredictable combinations of insight and action, quietly and implicitly reinforcing the theme of self-empowerment and future orientation.

The ritual of a final exam can also be an effective means of closing the class field. The act of demonstrating what one has learned helps bring that cycle of learning to a definitive end. Similarly, giving back the last round of papers provides us with an opportunity to celebrate what has been accomplished. Because saying thanks is an important part of closure, we should create an atmosphere in our last meeting with the students that allows them to express their appreciation for the course if they want to do so, even if it is as simple as a handshake as they turn in their exam. An end of the semester, pizza at the student union or a pot luck dinner at your home should always include a discussion of "What's next?" Here, as elsewhere, what makes for good teaching makes for healthy fields. The instincts are the same and many of the things we do naturally will be the same.

Lastly, all these processes can be reinforced by rituals of closure performed privately. Just as we prepared the class field before the course began through skillful intention, we can similarly close the class field at its end. Through ritual, meditation, and focused intention, we can bring our students into our awareness, affirm their separate journeys, and send them back into the stream of life.

For us too, the end of the semester is a time of closure, and closure asks two things of us. First, it asks that we give thanks—for the privilege of teaching and for the help we have received from visible and invisible sources. It would not be wise to ask for help at the beginning of an enterprise and then fail to give thanks for it at its end. Second, closure asks that we take time to reflect on what we have learned from the semester. If we're not expanding, we've begun to grow rigid and die, so what has life been trying to teach us these past fifteen weeks through these particular students? Where did we fail and why? Where did we succeed? What new idea or awareness has been tapping at our window these past months?

However one chooses to do it, it's important to definitively close the class field at the end of the semester in order to encourage a smooth release of all parties and to empower the students as they move on to new courses where they will join new circles and become part of new learning fields. As in life, so in teaching—the end is implicit in the beginning. In this relentless rhythm of opening and closing, we feel the pulse of the living classroom.

If the suggestions outlined in this chapter seem exotic and a little hard to swallow, I certainly understand. I did not come by them without my own internal struggle. We are not accustomed to thinking of consciousness as a significant force in the world. Our thoughts *feel* fleeting and ephemeral and not this powerful. Here the road divides and everyone must make their own choices. All I can say at this point is that the longer I have explored my own interior depths and observed the dance of consciousness taking place among my students, the more convinced I am that consciousness is a truly active and potent force in the world.

Consciousness seems to be like light. When light is scattered and incoherent, its influence is low, but when it is focused into the coherent light of a laser, it becomes a powerful force of nature. Similarly, consciousness can be scattered or focused. The more integrated our conscious awareness and the more intentional focus we bring to our actions, the more influence our consciousness has on life around us. This is something everyone has to discover for themselves. For those teachers who are engaged in deep transformational practice or who have begun to experience the subtle influence of the collective learning fields that form around them as they work, I hope the strategies outlined here will be helpful.

CHAPTER 5

Café Conversations

All that we humans do, we do in conversation.... As we live in conversation new kinds of objects continue to appear, and as we take these objects and live with them, new domains of existence appear!
—Humberto Maturana and Pille Bunnell

Most of the strategies for working with learning fields outlined in the preceding chapter involve exercises of intention. When one works with fields of consciousness directly, one uses consciousness to influence consciousness. Various spiritual practices and mental protocols focus and empower our intention in this undertaking, but ultimately we are using our consciousness to engage and influence the fields of consciousness we are part of. The strategies presented were primarily ones that teachers could use by themselves without involving their students. Now it's time to look at a different way of working with these fields, one that is less direct but quite powerful, less mental and more social. And this is conversation.

Skillful conversation encourages *collective resonance* with what are inherently collective fields of consciousness. When this collective resonance occurs, it can feel like a fresh breeze blowing through the room, a collective rippling of awakening to new possibilities, a contagious insight that breeds more insights. A room in conversation is more likely to trigger collective resonances with the course field—and here I deliberately shift to the larger, more potent field—than a room in which learning is taking place individually. In short, *conversation connects the field.*

I did not always recognize or appreciate the power of conversation to stimulate group contact with these fields. My initiation into this understanding took place after I had been teaching for many years when I took a two-year leave of absence from my university position in 2000–2002 to work as the Director of Transformative Learning at the Institute of Noetic Sciences (IONS) in northern California, a nonprofit organization involved in consciousness research and education. In that capacity, I had the privilege of meeting and working with Juanita Brown, David Isaacs, and Meg Wheatley. Through them and other contacts in the Noetic community, I was introduced to the dialogic movement, a social movement that is refining the art of conversation into a powerful vehicle of social transformation and intellectual discovery.

The dialogic movement weaves together a complex strand of influences with roots in Humberto Maturana, David Bohm, and Krishnamurti's work. It has generated a host of organizations that in one way or another seek to harvest the power of dialogue to change lives—the Co-Intelligence Institute, the National Coalition for Dialogue and Deliberation, America Speaks, the Appreciative Inquiry Commons, the Berkana Institute, the Center for Nonviolent Communication, the Commonway Institute, Conversation Cafés, CoVision, Global Renaissance Alliance, the Heartland Circle, Pioneers of Change, the Socrates Café, and the Society for Organizational Learning. Through these organizations, strategic dialogue is influencing the personal growth movement, the social activist network, and the corridors of corporate power.

Here was a group of social pioneers and cultural entrepreneurs who were using strategic dialogue to tap the same collective fields that I had already come to recognize operating inside in my classroom. In this movement, dialogue was being consciously scripted to evoke contact with that "something larger" that "lives in the middle" between people, something that comes into being only when people gather in groups. They too were talking about the "magic" of unanticipated leaps of thought, but they were using conversation to evoke it.

The World Café

While there are numerous schools of conversation, in this chapter I want to focus on the work of Juanita Brown, David Isaacs, and the World Café Community. Their recent book, *The World Café*, is an excellent and pragmatic guide to creating collaborative conversation written by persons sensitive to the working of group fields. From Juanita Brown, I learned that the electricity and illumination that I and my students had felt when our minds were sparked by the animating presence of learning fields also flowed through large groups when they are engaged in skillful dialogue. She convinced me that the quickening of insight that some of my students had spontaneously experienced could be cultivated as a *group experience* through dialogue. As the director of IONS' international conference in 2001, I worked with Juanita to integrate the World Café into our conference program. In a striking demonstration of the power of conversation, at that conference over 1,200 conference-goers participated in simultaneous Cafés on the main ballroom floor.

Since returning to my university position, I've been working to bring the World Café back to my classroom. Having seen its power demonstrated in the nonprofit sector, I wanted to try to harness that power in my classes. This chapter is an interim report on this ongoing project. I will summarize my attempt to adapt the seven principles of the World Café to the academic setting and share some preliminary feedback from the students. I will also offer some speculative observations on Cafés and learning fields. Before getting started, however, I want to emphasize that I'm still a novice at the Café game. My pedagogical strength has been as a lecturer—setting out a vision, provoking strong give-and-take with the students, and following this dialogue where it leads. But even old dogs can learn new tricks, and this is a trick worth learning if you take fields of consciousness seriously.

In a number of my courses I've instituted what I call *Friday Cafés*. In a course that meets three days a week, I will often spend two days lecturing followed by a Café on Friday. A Café is not just a glitzy name for the same old class discussion but a distinctive kind of conversation that is carefully choreographed and harvested. The essence of the Café model is deceptively simple—small, intimate conversations around well-framed questions. In these conversations, participants periodically rotate around the room, allowing ideas to cross-pollinate and new combinations of insights to emerge. The gold of the process is in the details, and *The World Café* is filled with practical suggestions for interrupting old conversation habits and seeding new ones. It outlines a "conversational architecture" that allows large numbers of people to engage in conversations that make the group more receptive to the amplifying power of the learning fields surrounding a course. Peter Senge, author of *The Fifth Discipline* and founding chair of the Society for Organizational Learning, writes: "Café conversations are the most reliable way I have yet encountered for all of us to tap into collective creating."[1]

Differences of Set and Setting

Like any host, I have had to adapt the Café model to my situation. Because the academic environment is different from the one that birthed the World Café, I've had to make some adjustments to the Café model. Before I describe these adaptations, let me summarize two basic differences between the set and setting I work in as an educator and the set and setting of most of the Cafés described in *The World Café*.

The first difference centers on the *goal* of the Café. The emphasis in *The World Café* is on using Cafés to enhance creativity and evoke new insights. Cafés are convened around questions that are open-ended in nature. They are not primarily about implementation or traditional problem-solving but discovery and innovation. Cafés are about exploring unknown possibilities.

While this certainly applies to some of the conversations I want my students to have, it does not apply to all of them. Often I have more modest expectations for a Friday Café. I want to use some Cafés, for example, to deepen the students' integration of ideas they have covered in the week's reading, and this smacks of implementation more than discovery. I need to make sure my students understand a certain body of thought before I launch them into exploring its implications, and this consolidation process can be accelerated by chewing on the reading in a Café setting. They may find that other students interpreted the reading differently or drew different conclusions from it, and this will deepen their understanding of the author's points.

Rather than being open-ended inquiries, therefore, our Friday Cafés are structured around our course agenda and class assignments. A Café can become a forum in which students discuss their plans for a paper they are working on or debrief after their papers are completed, sharing their results with other students and pooling their learning. While these projects may diverge from the original Café protocol, they have benefited greatly from *The World Café*'s insights into what makes for skillful dialogue. Rather than reserve the Café approach for only those conversations in which the questions being asked are truly open-ended, I have adapted the Café model to my educational needs. Sometimes Friday Cafés do sound the philosophical waters in ways that are genuinely exploratory and discovery-oriented. On other days, they will have a more modest agenda.

> Dialogue is the central aspect of co-intelligence. We can only generate higher levels of intelligence among us if we are doing some high quality talking with one another.
>
> —Tom Atlee, *The Tao of Democracy*

A second difference centers on *motivation*. People participating in a World Café in the nonprofit or business sector usually come together because they want to talk about a question they care deeply about. Participants are "stakeholders" who feel called to participate in the undertaking. Such a high-level motivation often cannot be assumed in the academic setting, especially at an open-enrollment university and in courses that lie outside one's major.

Let's be honest. There are volunteers and there are conscripts. The World Café draws primarily volunteers, but my courses are often filled with conscripts. Much of my initial work lies in converting conscripts into stakeholders. Getting students to care deeply about the material they are studying is often half the challenge. So, in designing my Friday Cafés, I have to work with human nature as it comes to me and within the constraints of the system I am part of, as do all Café hosts. This sometimes calls for incorporating measures that may seem odd in community Cafés but which work well in educational settings. My students, for example, are graded on their participation in their Cafés.

When I design a course that commits up to one-third of our class time to conversation, this represents an enormous investment of pedagogical resources. Our time together is precious, so I want the students to take these conversations seriously and to come prepared to use them productively. Students understand that if something does not count toward their final grade, it isn't being treated as a significant part of the course, and they don't take it as seriously. Therefore, I want to give students the incentive of an honest day's pay for an honest day's labor, and this means grading their participation in the Café. However odd this may sound to Café hosts outside of academia, the students understand that this is the system we live within. They understand the rules of the academic game, and I find that they respond well to any system that is imaginative, rewards genuine participation, and helps them succeed. Bottom line: well-organized Cafés stimulate student interest.

Friday Cafés: Adapting the Principles of the World Café

My primary objective in this chapter is to entice educators who are interested in learning fields to pick up a copy of *The World Café* and see for themselves whether the Café model might be useful to their teaching. I cannot do justice to the creative manner in which Cafés are presented there but will settle for summarizing the seven principles of the World Café followed by a few observations on how I have adapted these principles to my university setting.

In addition to the differences in set and setting already mentioned, the most important point to keep in mind is that *the entire semester is really one long conversation*. If you take a semester approach to planning one's Cafés, you will find that principles that cannot be realized in every Café can be realized over a semester of Cafés. The goal is to design a semester-long conversation that will take place in a series of installments.

> Developing meaningful dialogue is about creating conceptual fields that deepen or shift thinking.
> —Linda Lambert and others, *The Constructivist Leader*

The seven principles of the World Café are:
1. Set the context
2. Create hospitable space
3. Explore questions that matter
4. Encourage everyone's contribution
5. Cross-pollinate and connect diverse perspectives
6. Listen together for patterns, insights, and deeper questions
7. Harvest and share collective discoveries[2]

Set the Context

Setting the context is about clarifying the procedures the Café will use and its agenda. Why are we here? Why are we doing things this way? What is the expected outcome? Who's here? What do we hope to accomplish today? Once the methodological preliminaries are handled, setting the context shifts to clarifying the topic and context of each week's conversation.

I find that it takes about two class periods of going over the Café principles for students to understand and internalize how Cafés work, what is unique about this approach to conversation, and what the possible outcomes are. In the beginning of the semester, therefore, we have Cafés about Cafés while introducing ourselves to each other, going over the protocol and whetting our appetite for the first "real" Café that usually takes place in the third week. Once the students understand the rules of the game, setting the context shifts to clarifying the topic for that week's conversation. This is handled in the lectures leading up to Friday's Café. Monday and Wednesday's lectures set the framework for Friday's conversation. In ways small and large, they will clarify the purpose of the Café, explain the issues behind the question we are asking, and place the conversation into larger intellectual context.

Create Hospitable Space

This is the most difficult principle to honor in a conventional classroom, which sadly is not designed for conversation. The World Café is modeled on the French café—small tables seating four people, checkered tablecloths, a flower in the center of each table and a cup holding colored markers, and plenty of paper for drawing and scribbling down thoughts and insights that surface in the dialogue. The seminal insight is that hospitable settings encourage deeper conversations, and therefore you want to create as warm and inviting a setting as possible.

Pulling this off in a classroom can be a challenge, but students can be quite resourceful when given the opportunity. Sometimes desks gets pushed back and we sit on the floor. Book bags and shoes can be lined up along a wall. Attempting to create space that supports good conversation has led me to pay more attention to small details. For example, I don't allow students to gather in jumbled arrangements, but get them to form carefully arranged clusters. At the very minimum, our Cafés are neat, small circles where people sit face to face. When we have to settle for simply turning desks to face each other, they do so at 90 degrees. In short, we try to bring as much order and warmth into the room as possible.

Explore Questions That Matter

Finding the right question for the Friday Café is the most challenging part of the exercise for me, and here the seasoned advice in *The World Café* can be particularly helpful. Clarify what work I want the question to accomplish. Find the question that, if explored thoroughly, could lead to breakthrough. What question will surface hidden assumptions while leaving room for new questions to emerge? What is the big question that lies underneath the smaller questions? What question is the author not asking? Are we not asking? My job is to bring these considerations to the content we are working with that week and find a conversation question that will tease out the deepest learning possible for these particular students.

Sometimes I set the question for the Café because I want to aim the conversation in a direction that will connect with work we will be doing several weeks down the road. At other times I let the students set the question after they have developed a sense of what makes for a good question. In the early weeks, I coach them on how to identify and shape powerful questions. After this, we sometimes take a collaborative approach. On Monday, when they are responsible for having completed the reading assignment, the students will turn in questions they would like to see us discuss. By Wednesday's class I will have sorted through their proposals and identified questions that I think have the most promise, sometimes merging pieces of different questions into one or sharpening an edge here or there. Ideally, I want to offer students the final choice, and so I try to give them several questions to choose from and let them make the final decision. The more participation and buy-in I can get on Monday and Wednesday, the stronger Friday's Café likely will be.

Side Topic: Grading

It's important that the students know the question before Friday so they can prepare for the conversation because they will usually be graded on their participation. This may not be necessary or even desirable in some academic settings, but it adds an edge that can be useful in others. Friday Cafés are centered on questions that are specific to the material we're covering that week. Even when the students are exploring the farther-reaching implications of this material or their interpretation of its significance, they are starting from a shared body of knowledge that they must control if they are to participate meaningfully in the conversation. They are accountable to each other for a good exchange of ideas, and grades reflect this accountability.

There are many ways to handle grading and I'm still experimenting with options. One strategy I have used with success is to have students evaluate each other. My preference is to have them grade each other on only one thing—their level of preparedness for the conversation. Students are more comfortable assessing degree of preparedness than performance, and they can usually tell whether another student has done the necessary prep work or is just bluffing. I find that if a student is well prepared, he or she will likely participate robustly in the conversation, and therefore assessing preparedness is usually a good way of indirectly assessing performance.

As for the mechanics, if there are four persons in a group, I pass out three index cards to each student. At the end of the Café, each student will write down the name of each of their group partners on a separate card and beside it put down a number from 1 to 4 following a clearly defined assessment scale. Thus, each student will receive three separate grades that I will then average. Sometimes I will pass out a fourth card—it's easier if it's a different color—to collect the student's self-assessment, which I will make note of but not include in the final grade tabulation. How others see us can be a helpful corrective to how we see ourselves, and comparing other-assessment grades with self-assessment grades can sometimes be useful in giving students feedback.

In general, I've found that students take the responsibility of grading seriously and are fair judges of each other. Because the groups are rotated frequently throughout the semester, everyone is looked at by many eyes, and this discourages exchanging grading "favors." On the whole, I have found that the task of grading does not get in the way of good dialogue. Students understand the necessity of grades; they only ask that they be assigned fairly and be associated with meaningful and reasonable tasks.

Encourage Everyone's Participation

In Cafés, everyone talks; no one is allowed to hide. Several techniques apply here. First, each person speaks briefly during the preliminary check-in before the conversation begins. Once the conversation starts, it can be interrupted periodically with a short silence during which we take stock to make sure everyone has been speaking. Sometimes we use a "talking stone" (or a "talking pen"). Whoever has the talking stone is the only one speaking. To slow things down further, a 15-second pause can be inserted between putting the stone down and another student picking it up. Another way to encourage everyone's participation is covered later under "slicing the room."

Cross-Pollinate and Connect Diverse Perspectives

In a World Café, participants periodically rotate among the tables to form new groups, thus mixing perspectives and sewing threads of one conversation into another. One person will stay at their table and take responsibility for summarizing to newcomers the highlights of the previous conversation while the other three mix with other groups. Sometimes it's the ideas themselves that travel, as when key insights are written down on cards and floated around the room to be read by other groups.

It is cross-pollination more than any other feature of the Café that is responsible for creating powerful resonances with the course field. Mixing and combining perspectives connects the field. Juanita Brown lays out the theory clearly:

> By intentionally inviting diverse participants and encouraging each person's unique contribution, we bring more variety to the "ecology" of conversation. As participants then move from table to table, carrying seed ideas from one Café table to another, they link and connect their thoughts, ideas, and questions, mirroring Maturana and Varela's iterating networks of conversation.
>
> The introduction of powerful questions seems to function as an attractor that focuses attention in the "synapses of the group mind," thus activating the conversational network's self-organizing capacity. The new connections simultaneously create a space of novelty ... in which new opportunities and spaces of possibility can be explored with the opportunity to "bring forth a world" together.
>
> ... [I]t is the creative cross-pollination of people and ideas combined with the disciplined use of questions as attractors that is perhaps the World Café's defining contribution to dialogic learning and collective intelligence.[3]

A room that is in conversation is connecting itself. Cross-pollination folds conversations into new conversations. Ideas developed in one context seed new ideas in other contexts. This interweaving of conversation streams generates a fruitful chaos that sometimes leads to breakthroughs in thinking. Something new emerges, something no one present has ever thought before or would likely have thought had they worked just on their own. In this way Café dialogue and the group itself become a vehicle of learning and discovery.

Once a class has experienced this collective activation of insight, they suddenly "get it" and realize the true power of the Café. Without my having to explain any of the theoretical parameters, they have discovered for themselves that *a kind of learning becomes possible when we learn together that does not occur when we learn separately.* Such an experience signals the emergence of what David Marsing, former senior executive at Intel, calls a "higher fusion of thinking." Tom Atlee, author of *The Tao of Democracy,* calls it "co-intelligence." When co-intelligence enters the room, it can trigger what I call *great learning.*

In the academic setting, I have only short blocks of time to work with—usually 50 minutes. Sometimes this allows us to do the "Café shuffle," changing groups and "stirring the room," but not always. Sometimes the question chosen for the week's Café would be disrupted by this much discontinuity. What may not be realized in one Café, however, can be realized for the semester-long conversation as a whole.

In the Friday Cafés, we rotate our groups regularly throughout the semester, usually every two to three weeks. I try to coordinate this rotation of groups with the natural break points in the syllabus, giving the course a social pulse that accompanies its intellectual pulse. The cross-pollination described in *The World Café* also takes place in these rolling turnovers, at a slower pace but with similar impact. Taking in many perspectives over weeks and months activates the "synapses of the group mind," but it's a long-term simmer rather than a feverish boil. Persons who participate in a series of Cafés with different partners find themselves shifting their perspectives faster than if they had studied the material in isolation or in fixed groups all semester long.

Listen Together for Patterns, Insights, and Deeper Questions

I find that this is the trickiest part of the Café model to convey to students. It sounds easy, but it's a slippery fish, hard to hold on to. Old listening habits are difficult to break, and this one takes a lot of coaching and reminding.

For the Café to work, students have to learn a new way of listening. Usually we listen from our personal reference point—what do I think about what someone is saying? We tend to judge what someone else says in terms of how compatible it is with our own convictions. Sometimes we manage to listen from the other person's reference point, as when we try to see the world through their eyes. What the Café calls us to develop, however, is a third way of listening. Juanita calls it "listening for the middle." I sometimes call it "listening with the third ear," which is usually good for a chuckle among students who are familiar with the Eastern concept of the "third eye." When one listens with the third ear, one is trying to listen free of self-reference, free of ego.

The task is to listen to the *whole conversation* in order to recognize the larger patterns emerging in it. In listening for the middle, one tries to hear the "voice of the conversation" rather than the voices of its individual members. This can be challenging when you're cross-pollinating the room and the ideas are getting layered on top of each other. Having a large common sheet of paper to write on can bring the emerging themes of a conversation into focus.

Sometimes it helps to designate one person in each group to track the conversation as a whole. It's their job to keep one foot out of the circle of talkers and observe the *patterns* of the conversation. When one does this, one sometimes spots new ideas popping through the flow. Sometimes seeing a pattern allows one to ask new questions that reach "underneath" those patterns. "What is the group not asking?" "What assumptions are we making to say this or that?" Opening the third ear can be tricky, but some students seem to have a knack for it. Once students see it done, it gets easier to replicate.

Listening together for the deeper patterns in a conversation is an essential skill students need to develop for the Café to really "take" in the classroom. It is the cognitive partner of cross-pollinating, the psychological skill that complements that social skill. Neither one by itself would get us very far, but the two together make a powerful combination. When you create a complex web of thought-patterns in the room, you must learn to recognize what is emerging in those patterns. Learning to listen in this multimodal, chaos-friendly way is a skill that can be practiced. It is a valuable skill that students will take away from the Café exercise, one that will serve them well in their future careers.

Once students learn how to listen in this more expansive way, they sometimes become highly sensitive to more conventional, restrictive ways of listening. It's as if they suddenly see an invisible disease that infects ordinary conversations, a disease one student called "narrow-listening." Another called it "listening small." One occasionally hears above the din in the room a raised voice saying, "You're listening in the old way. Loosen up!"

Once students get this new way of listening, it sometimes blossoms into other forms of expansive awareness. They begin to see how narrow our habitual cognitive focus usually is, not just in listening but in how we speak, how we think, and how we pay attention. The cognitive habits that keep us small are just that—habits. When students learn to drop one of these habits, it sometimes leads to their seeing and dropping other forms of the same habit. They learn that *narrowness itself is a habit*. Expansiveness can also become a habit, a natural way of being in the world. The World Café teaches us to listen expansively.

Harvest and Share Collective Discoveries

For a class to have a *whole-system* conversation, the students must become aware of themselves as a whole system, and this means that they must learn what the other groups in the room have been talking about. This is important for the highest synthesis of thinking to take place. Frankly, however, it's hard to pull off in a 50-minute class. When the Café is cooking, students can feel the buzz in the room. They *know* they're part of a larger conversation. But it takes time to harvest that larger conversation and to put its patterns in front of everyone's eyes. Rather than try to accomplish this in every Café, I take a multipronged approach, using different strategies within different time frames.

The quickest way to harvest a room is to collect short reports from the different groups at the end of a Café—the most important insight to emerge, the major conflict that came up, questions left unanswered. Five minutes of pulling the pieces together at the end of a class are a good investment, but this quick overview is just the beginning of whole-system self-awareness. While useful, it tends to seed an awareness that we don't have time to cultivate further on that day.

Periodically, therefore, we do a larger harvest, dedicating a larger portion of the Café to collecting discoveries—putting ideas on the board, posting sheets of table notes on the wall, and so on. If we spend several weeks digesting a book, for example, on the last Café, we will spend extra time harvesting our cumulative assessment of the book. As the semester moves toward its close, we begin to harvest the larger ideas and themes that have been emerging over the semester. Because the semester is one long conversation, harvesting our collective discoveries becomes a more significant part of the Cafés in the final weeks of the course.

Student Responses to Cafés

Let me be candid and say that I initially turned to the Café to dilute my presence in the classroom. My upper division courses regularly push students to their edges by inviting them to rethink some of their fundamental philosophical convictions. This is good, honest work, but sometimes you can have too much of a good thing. Whether it was something about the content of the material, or how I worked with it, or something about the resonances carried over from my spiritual practice, whatever the combination of circumstances, I began to realize that the students needed less of me in the room. Without intending it, I could move too quickly through their mental defenses, either because I had seen them so many times or because I was spontaneously reading them more deeply. The learning process became "too hot," taking them too far too fast. I needed to slow things down.

The Friday Cafés did this, but they did much more. The Cafés began to create community in the classroom. Students began to comment on how helpful it was to be able to talk with other students about the challenging topics we were studying. Given the fact that many of the ideas we investigate in my courses fall outside conventional Western thought, the Cafés were the only places many of my students had to process this information socially, to try it on for size, to test out their thinking on other people. (I might mention that the university where I teach is largely a commuter campus, making our students a more transient population than on residential campuses and Cafés therefore even more important.) Cafés build relationships and relationships build community. The conversations students were having in class began to spill over outside the classroom. Fueled by the common act of inquiry, students began to form nodes of community outside of class, meeting with their friends to continue the conversation.

I began to realize that in addition to everything else, the Cafés were deepening learning by sewing the ideas we were engaging in the course into the larger conversational life of the students. The students were learning not only to think in a new way but to speak in a new way, and speaking was deepening their absorption of new ideas.

I came to appreciate at a deeper level that Maturana and Bunnell really were right when they said "All that we humans do, we do in conversation." When new concepts are sewn into the conversational life of our students, they root themselves more deeply in their intellectual lives, and isn't this the goal of education? We may cover less material than if I lectured for all three days, but the Cafés were helping students keep more of what they we did cover, *and* they had the experience of participating in a collective creative endeavor. This is the deepest contribution of the Café to the living classroom. When all goes well and the conditions are right, collective inspiration rises in our midst.

I also began to realize that giving the students a collective vehicle for digesting the ideas they were absorbing from my lectures did more than dilute my voice in the room. Interestingly enough, it also strengthened my voice. A strong Café balances a strong lecturing presence. By giving the students more space to absorb impactful ideas, the Cafés made it possible for me to safely bring strong ideas forward.

A few last observations on working with Cafés before moving to closing thoughts. Because the semester can be treated as one long conversation, the Café trajectory arches over fifteen weeks. The early Cafés are typically spent introducing ourselves to each other, internalizing the rules of Café, and raising people's expectations for what we might accomplish by using this approach to collaborative learning. Once the Cafés begin to focus on course content, the structure of the Cafés can be made more complicated as the semester progresses.

In the beginning, for example, we usually start with one-question Cafés—Cafés in which all the groups are exploring the same question. Later we progress to multiple-question Cafés—Cafés in which different groups are discussing different questions and we bring the results together at the end. Or, to give another example, we typically begin with Cafés where the students do not rotate inside the hour, but once the students get the knack of having pithy, to-the-point conversations, we may experiment with rotating tables during class. Student input on setting the question can likewise begin slowly and increase with experience. Harvesting the conversations can also become more complex as the semester moves along. In all these areas, the general strategy is to keep it simple in the beginning and initiate students into the full potential of the Café protocol as the course develops, taking them in step-by-step as they are ready.

One more advanced technique is what I call *slicing the room*. The Café is designed to bring forward as many voices into the room as possible. Sometimes this is facilitated by pulling together certain clusters of voices that have something in common. When we slice the room, we are deliberately putting certain groups of students together to see whether new points of view will emerge from these clusters. We may slice the room along gender lines, for example, gathering men and women into separate groups. We may slice it by race, age, year in school, or major (sciences vs. humanities vs. fine arts). The goal is ultimately not to divide the room but to reinforce what may be its minority voices in order to bring their full contribution forward.

When you have energized the learning fields and deepened their influence in the room through conversation, it's important to close these fields well at the end of the semester. This means that the last Café should always be focused on "wrapping up" the semester-long conversation. Now is the time to look back and remind ourselves where we started and where we've come. We are drawing the conversation to a close. This is the Café to take stock of where we are now, individually and collectively. It's a good time to say thanks to your partners, to count our takeaways, and look to the future.

Cafés and Learning Fields

When we talk and listen together, we create the conditions for something new to enter the room. The theoretical question I'd like to consider in this last section is: How does this happen and why? More specifically, how are we to integrate the creativity that conversation can unleash into the theory of learning fields developed in earlier chapters?

There seem to be several levels to the answer. At the first level, creativity is enhanced because the Café more effectively taps the full potential of all the people present. By seeking *everyone's* input to thought-provoking questions and by systematically *cross-fertilizing* streams of input and making the room self-aware of its thought processes, the Café increases the likelihood that something new will emerge in the room. This much is relatively straightforward. By throwing out the biggest net, we catch the most fish.

From the perspective of learning fields, however, deeper dynamics are also at play. Here the inquiry pivots to ask, "While the room is being tapped and shuffled and brought forward at the physical level, what is happening at the level of its learning fields?" The short answer I've given is that Café conversations *connect the field*. Now it's time to go deeper into what this actually means and to explore what mechanisms may be at play. Here are a few speculative suggestions.

When we enter into meaningful, reciprocal, and cross-pollinating conversations, I think we energize not only each other but the subtle fields we are part of. I like to imagine that good Cafés push linear systems into nonlinear conditions. Looking first at just the individual, when we interrupt our old thought patterns by taking in new ideas and connecting old concepts in novel ways, we are deliberately creating instabilities in our thinking. When we challenge the certainty of what we already "know," we push our egos into what we might think of as the nonlinear condition of uncertainty. If our previous belief system cannot integrate all the new information we are taking in, pressure builds in the system. Something must change; some revision of our thinking is demanded.

Turning now to groups, when we push all the individual egos in a room into this fruitful chaos, we are pushing the *class ego* into chaos. The class ego, in this instance, is the collective persona of the class. It is the intellectual consensus that the students share simply by virtue of growing up and being enculturated in the same culture. It's the collective judgments implicit in the room, the implicit paradigms and truths they collectively assume. Largely unconscious in the beginning, the class ego becomes exposed when the class begins to speak and listen to itself as it takes in new concepts. When the class ego is pushed into the nonlinear conditions of uncertainty, the students *as a group* may become less confident about the assumptions they had previously been making, less clear about how A connects to B in their inherited maps of the world. The *group* begins to ask new questions, to seek new answers. The organized chaos of collective learning has begun.

My suspicion is that when the *class mind* is highly aroused in this manner and is able to sustain a high level of self-awareness, it becomes more susceptible to the influence of the surrounding *course mind*. This influence allows the learning that had taken place in the past to accelerate and deepen the learning taking place in the present. *By driving the class mind into the nonlinear conditions of organized chaos, communion with the underlying course mind is deepened.* When this happens, the thought processes of the present generation of students become more transparent to the learning that has taken place around these issues by prior generations of students. Students tend to become more susceptible to the stream of learning from previous semesters, as though all the classes year after year were having one, gigantic meta-conversation. Underneath the cross-fertilization occurring within the present class, therefore, a deeper cross-fertilization is taking place between earlier classes and this present group of students. The momentum of discovery carries forward. Collectively, the students move more quickly through the preliminaries and to the present cutting edge of learning and discovery.

This brings me to the primary difference between the perspective presented in *The World Café* and the theoretical framework I've been developing in this book. I think that it's fair to say that the World Café focuses on empowering and accessing the *class mind*, and it does so brilliantly, but it does not extend its theoretical discussion to include what I have called the *course mind*. It focuses on actualizing the collective potential of the people who are present in the room today, on skillfully linking them to one another to facilitate creative break-throughs in their thinking. To this important work, I think we should add the perspective of history and appreciate the *deepening effect that past conversations have on our present conversation*. In short, we need to expand our theoretical framework to take into account the psychic momentum that builds around conversations that are repeated many times.

For example, if a group were to hold a World Café every week for many years, gathering repeatedly to pursue an evolving set of ques-tions, I think something like a "Café mind" would develop around it. Even if some members of the group left and others joined, as long as there were continuity of theme and project, a Café mind would grow, becoming more powerful over time. From a theoretical perspective, we would eventually want to distinguish *various levels of this Café mind*, and here some distinction like the one I've drawn between the class mind and the course mind might be useful. This distinction would help us explain, for example, why groups that have been meeting for many years often have a certain power that newer groups do not have, however fresh they may be in other respects. It gives us a deeper theoretical framework for understanding *and harnessing* the forces that are driving the breakthroughs that occur in an ongoing Café—inviting us to look beyond those who are present in the room to participants in earlier Cafés.

The World Café community is open to this perspective and I know Juanita Brown honors the deepening effect of experience on psychic fields. I suggested earlier that there are many different types of fields reflecting the different types of activities people engage in—learning fields for teachers, healing fields for doctors, human performance fields for coaches, and so on. By this same logic, persons who repeat-edly lead people into conversation would develop *dialogic fields* around them. The more often they engaged in strategic conversations, the more powerful the dialogic fields around them would become. From this perspective, an experienced Café host could be seen as bringing to a conversation not only their conscious Café skills but also the influence of their cumulative dialogic fields. Eventually just their presence would tend to support good dialogue in the room. This subtle influence would flow from all the prior experiences of learning that their field now embodied.

This is the rationale behind the practice of inviting certain elders into meetings where they are not necessarily familiar with the issues being discussed or expected to make any contribution to the content of the discussion. They are there because their very presence is seen as energetically contributing to productive conversation. Anne Dosher is such an person. Juanita Brown describes Anne as the "elder, mentor and 'guardian of the soul' of the World Café." Because I have experienced firsthand how Anne's presence can deepen a conversation circle, I understand what Juanita means.

Having said all this, I want to remind the reader that, from my perspective at least, neither the class mind nor the course mind is the ultimate source of the creativity that emerges in a Café. As a repository of past learning, the course mind may explain how students "catch up" with the learning of earlier students, but by itself it does not explain how they take the next step of adding still new layers of insight and understanding to the course field. This is the theoretical limitation that Rupert Sheldrake ran up against in his theory of morphic fields. As a theoretical construct, morphic fields can explain the momentum of the past into the present, but they cannot explain where the new actually comes from. They cannot explain creativity and novelty.[4] For this we must develop a deeper metaphysical vision.

As I mentioned in a previous chapter, from the perspective of transpersonal psychology, the course field is an *intermediate field* that lies between the class field and still deeper fields of consciousness that exist in the universe. The course field is not itself the source of the creativity that breaks forth when a room is in dynamic conversation, but a *mediating field* through which those in the room connect with still deeper pools of intelligence and knowing.

I think that when the course mind is activated by a dynamically integrated class mind, the two congeal to form something like a *collective lens* that focuses a flow of energy and insight between those present in the room and deeper fields of transpersonal intelligence. We might think of these deeper fields as analogous to Jung's concept of the collective unconscious, or James Lovelock's concept of Gaia consciousness, or still deeper vistas of archetypal awareness. Without attempting to chart all the possibilities, the transpersonal perspective suggests that we live surrounded by a multilayered cosmic intelligence, the force responsible for birthing and growing the extraordinary universe we are part of.

When we use the Café protocols to connect students in skillful conversation, I think it amplifies the strength of the group's collective lens. If we energize the collective lens of a course field semester after semester, we increase its sensitivity to this larger cosmic intelligence. Repetition deepens the groove of access. When new students align themselves with a learning project that has been going on for many years, the group becomes a more sensitive *collective receiver* of this intelligence's ongoing influence. Centered in such a highly energized course field, the signals that reach their awareness come from deeper within the Universal Mind than would otherwise take place. The unexpected rises more easily; the new enters the room more often. Lightning strikes. The magic happens.

part iii.

Teaching in a
Living Universe

CHAPTER 6

Waking Up in the Classroom

We have a mission to create, for we are evolution incarnate. We are her self-awareness, her frontal lobes and fingertips. We are second-generation star stuff come alive. We are parts of something 3.5 billion years old, but pubertal in cosmic time. We are neurons of this planet's interspecies mind.

—Howard Bloom, *Global Brain*

Imagine what educators might accomplish in a culture that recognized and embraced the inherent connectivity of consciousness and the field dynamics of mind. Imagine how different our lives as teachers would be if our students *expected* us to support their alignment with group fields, if it were *assumed* on the first day of class that we would lead them in exercises of attunement. I think of such a future. I think of a time when we will take our students into these exercises as a matter of course, when our students will choose to tune themselves to the collective fields they are part of because they will have learned from their own experience that it quickens and deepens their learning. I look to a tomorrow when teachers will balance their outer preparation of course content with an inner preparation in which they hold their students in contemplation and heartfelt communion.

That future is now. It is time for us to bring the quantum vision, the ecological vision, the participatory vision into not only *what* we teach but *how*. It is time for our academic disciplines to move beyond the fragmentation of the atomistic model of consciousness and embrace an integral model that is more coherent with both our scientific research and the best of our spiritual traditions. Instead of seeing our minds as locked inside separate boxes, it is time for us to give birth to a holistic vision in which individual consciousness is seen as a field embedded in living fields of collective awareness.

The Living Intelligence of Self-Organizing Systems

The line of thought outlined in this volume describes a classroom that is profoundly alive. It describes a depth and breadth of aliveness so astonishing that it ruptures earlier models of consciousness and signals a fresh starting point for how educators might see themselves. It is rooted in an "unrepentant holism," to borrow a phrase from Stuart Kaufman's book *At Home in the Universe*. Kaufman is a leading thinker at the Santa Fe Institute on self-organization and the science of complexity, and his book explores the origins of order in biological organisms. In contrast to traditional Darwinians who suppose that the order we see in organisms is due to the "grinding away of a molecular Rube Goldberg machine," Kaufman argues that order in nature arises *spontaneously*. "We appear to have been profoundly wrong," he writes. "Order, vast and generative, arises naturally.... I propose that much of the order in organisms may not be the result of selection at all, but of the spontaneous order of self-organized systems." [1] "Order for free," he calls it.

In a similar fashion, I see the emergence of collective intelligence in groups as the spontaneous expression of self-organization, applied here to networks of consciousness rather than biological networks. I do not want to hijack Kaufman's words and make them serve ends he may not endorse, but it seems to me that we are both pointing to a fundamental feature of living systems. The resonances that spring up between minds in a classroom appear to reflect an *innate* intelligence emergent in the room, a *living* intelligence that expresses itself in the spontaneous ordering of self-organizing systems.[2] Order for free. Nature's wisdom arising in groups.

As a culture, we have been slow to recognize the presence of this order-generating intelligence in human affairs. Trained since Descartes to see the universe as a machine, we often dismiss the symptoms of this living intelligence as mere coincidence. But you could not convince a young woman who was in one of my classes recently that the "coincidence" that rippled through her life two years ago was devoid of intelligence. It was too sharply defined, too perfectly shaped to be mere accident. Here's her story.

During her freshman year in college, a family emergency required that she take legal custody of her two younger brothers. This sudden and unexpected turn of events pushed her to her limits as she struggled to stay in school while juggling these new responsibilities. Describing that year, she wrote:

It seemed like an impossible undertaking in the beginning. However, when the time came and I was living in the midst of it, everything fell into place. People came forward to help that I would have never expected and most of whom I haven't really made contact with since. When I no longer needed to have custody of my brothers, they exited my life silently. Their job was done.

The really striking thing, however, is what happened next.

After it was all over and I went back to college my sophomore year, my new roommate, who had been randomly assigned to me, was also in the process of getting custody of her younger two brothers. It had to be more than a coincidence that I would be randomly paired to share a room with another teenage girl who was struggling with the idea of being the sole caretaker of her two younger siblings! Because of my experience, I was able to help her through it. I am thoroughly convinced that everything is connected in some way and we are here to help each other to grow and learn.

How many such "coincidences" does it take before we recognize that there is a living intelligence expressing itself in the fabric of circumstance, a distributed intelligence not housed in one life, but registering in the coming together of many lives? Perhaps one more example may help. This one comes from the distinguished author Alex Haley and was originally published in an article he wrote for *PARADE* magazine. There he wrote:

While shopping in a Knoxville supermarket recently, I was startled when a smiling, personable clerk came up and grasped my hand. "My tutor just assigned me an article about you that's in my study book," he exclaimed. "Sir, I'm studying to learn to read."

The young man, who identified himself as Joseph Rivera, said he'd bluffed his way through high school until he finally dropped out to work full-time because he saw no pressing need for reading and writing.

The coincidence struck me as remarkable, since *PARADE* had just asked me to write an article about the critical nationwide need for a higher level of literacy and reading.[3]

This meeting gave Haley the perfect starting point for his article, and he addressed the problem of illiteracy in America by telling

Joseph Rivera's story. One suspects, of course, that this encounter wasn't a "remarkable coincidence" at all but the workings of a deeper order of intelligence that was located not in Alex Haley alone or in Joseph Rivera but in *both* of them together (*and* Rivera's tutor *and PARADE*'s editors). This intelligence resides in the deeper folds of the universe, not in any one place but in the living whole of it. It is a *distributed* intelligence that sparks and makes connections.

It is not simply that something in Haley drew Rivera to him that he might fulfill his publishing obligation, but rather that something both of them were already participating in brought them together to realize a greater action. Haley's intention to address the problem of illiteracy and Rivera's determination to overcome his own illiteracy combined to become a vessel of a larger intelligence seeking to uplift the whole, not pulling on life from some outside position but sparking up *inside* the potential of circumstance. By showcasing Rivera's life in his article, Haley was able to bring his courage and determination to public awareness where it could become seeds of hope for thousands of other persons burdened by illiteracy. Through these semihidden processes the collective nourishes itself, grows itself, develops itself.

The Circle of Learning

I have seen similar patterns of synchronistic collaboration surface in my classroom many times through the years. Sometimes it happens, for example, that I read a book or have an experience that gives me a new understanding of a concept or idea. Not long thereafter, a student shows up in one of my classes and asks me a question that is deeply significant to them personally, and I am able to help them with it only because of my own recent breakthrough. Had they come on the scene the previous semester, I could not have been of much use to them, but, arriving when they did, the information was available and the transfer was made.

When this had happened more than a few times, it became clear to me that there was an invisible connection between the timing of my personal discovery and the appearance of this student asking for this specific knowledge. A larger intelligence seemed to be expressing itself in this synergistic play of circumstance. To observe how the universe brings people together at the right moment to encourage the growth of a larger system is a humbling experience and awakens a sense of the numinous whole operating inside the rhythms of everyday life.

Having made this jump in thinking, however, I found that I was still underestimating the scale of the processes involved. I thought that the universe was capable of using the knowledge that I was acquiring to address questions fermenting inside my students. Only gradually did I realize that I was still missing half of the picture because I was still thinking too self-referentially. As my experience of the class mind deepened, I began to realize that in some cases I had it backwards, that I was putting the cart before the horse. If students were sometimes drawn to me because of my recent discoveries, at other times my discoveries themselves were being driven not by my personal need to know but *by my students' need to know*.

I slowly began to realize that the hunger fermenting within my students to understand some aspect of reality seemed to be creating a *field of need* around them that was actually influencing my interest in studying these things. What I had previously thought of as "my" desire to understand something was in fact the registering in my personal awareness of a larger desire that was rooted in a collective field generated by my present and future students, and perhaps even by those people whom my students would in turn influence. I came to see that the *circle of learning between student and teacher is a flow that has no clearly defined beginning*. My students' desire to understand and my capacity to articulate were two sides of a synaptic bridge in a larger mind, and only when we came together and combined our resources did we fulfill our respective roles in this larger dance.

This was such a radical shift in perspective that it initially left me feeling disoriented, and only slowly did I get my bearings in this new world. If my students' need to understand certain things could actually "enter" me and either seed or merge with my need to understand these same things, then my courses were a collective project from the very start. Even my career as a teacher is not my private affair any longer, but is itself embedded in a larger process of collective human discovery.

If this is so, my students and I are deeply implicated in each other's destinies. Each of us has a role to play in this drama, but there is a higher perspective that sometimes breaks through. One sometimes senses the presence of a hidden playwright inside the scene even as we are acting it out. In the play's most transparent moments, one gets the acute sense that our individual roles contribute to the self-actualization of a *single* intelligence, a *single* aspiration seeking expression in the world. It is not some ghost in the machine operating "behind" the veil of matter, but an innate intelligence that is rising *inside* life itself.

It is a shattering moment when one realizes that the roots of one's life do not begin in oneself. The supposed privacy of our person suddenly dissolves as a larger landscape of cause and effect comes into view. As the shock of resistance fades, an exquisite beauty emerges. One cannot help but surrender to this larger tapestry that weaves our hopes and ambitions together with those around us so elegantly, intertwining the development of the one and the development of the many so exquisitely. This is how the world truly is, how it lives beneath the surface—not cancelling our individuality but grounding it in a vast tapestry of time and opportunity.

Being used by an intelligent universe in service of others is one of the sweetest experiences I have known in life, and I'm sure many teachers will recognize the sensation. The experience brings with it a delicious nectar that dissolves one's habitual fixations and for a moment releases one into a transparency that erases the world of separate parts and catches you in a seamless totality that takes your breath away. At one level all the "selves" in the room are still present, our separate identities are still in play—the students there, me here—and yet at another level, the bubble pops and there stands naked the breath of some larger awareness that dwarfs us, a crystalline clarity against which our personal minds appear as but shadows. What can we say about this mysterious aliveness except that it is *collective* for it involves many of us, it is *conscious* for it sees and knows, it is *intelligent* for its actions inform, coordinate, and illumine, and it is *one*, seamless in itself, nondual in manifestation. Suddenly the aliveness of the universe has made itself felt again. Suddenly we are not isolated after all again. Suddenly we are never alone again.

Teaching as Transmission

In this circle of learning, personal experience carries great weight. I think every teacher has had the experience that when we are speaking about something we have experienced personally, our words have greater impact than when we are describing something that we know only intellectually, from a distance. At one level, it's not hard to understand why this happens, to identify the subtle cues that signal the difference to our students. And yet I think something more than subtle cues is operating here. If you are a skillful presenter, you've learned to package your delivery in persuasive rhetoric. A decent showman can make almost anything come alive, even things we have little firsthand knowledge of. But somehow our students can sense the difference. What is it exactly that strips our words of power in one instance and gives them power in another?

Time and again I have carefully watched as I approach a topic in my lectures where my personal experience reaches its limits. My presentation is just as animated, my organization of information just as complete, and yet it is as though my words now fall off 6 feet in front of me, barely reaching the front row. In my particular field of discourse, this shift has been most apparent when the concepts I am trying to convey reflect subtle existential capacities such as the experience of *nirvana*, emptiness, no-self, non-duality, and Original Mind. For years, no matter how much I tried to compensate for my lack of firsthand experience by supplementing with knowledge borrowed from others, my ability to awaken insight in my students seemed constrained by the degree to which these insights had truly awakened inside me. Ideas may seed conceptual understanding, but experience seems to open opportunities to actually participate in the reality being described to some degree.

As I have pondered these things, I have taken a page from Vajrayana Buddhism, the form of Buddhism that emerged in Tibet. In this tradition, it is said that there are three levels at which a spiritual practice is taught. The first level is the description of the *mechanics* of the practice—the explanation of the words and gestures that make up the body of the practice. The second level is the communication of the *meaning* of the practice, its deeper intention and purpose. Both these levels can be taught by persons who have only intellectual knowledge of the practice. The third level, the deepest level, is the transmission of the *essence* of the practice, and this can be given only by one who has mastered the practice experientially. This transference of essence is called the *lung*, meaning "transmission."

The vision here is that when a person has performed a practice hundreds of thousands of times, reciting the prayers associated with it hundreds of thousands of times, an energy builds in them that is the fruition of this particular practice. Only when they have brought the practice to fruition in this way are they empowered to give transmission of the practice to others. When they do so, they literally transmit into the recipient the seed energy of the practice as it now lives inside them, an energy that the recipient will then nourish and grow through performing the same practice themselves. I think of transmission as being conferred through skillful resonance, as when a vibrating tuning fork is brought near a quiescent tuning fork until something of the energy of the one is transferred to the other.

Over the years, I've come to believe that *all powerful teaching involves transmission* in this technical sense of the term. When teachers who have the gift of inspiring others ply their craft, there is an alchemy at work that is deeper than mere intellectual exchange. Increasingly I am convinced that underneath the flow of ideas a deeper energetic exchange is taking place. As our words go out into the room, something of us goes with them, underneath them, silently and invisibly. Beneath the exchange of verbal information a deeper commerce is at work *where consciousness engages consciousness directly*, and it is this deeper commerce that hinges on experience.

When we have firsthand knowledge of what we are speaking about, it creates an energetic bridge across which our words travel, allowing them to land with greater impact. When experience is not there, the bridge is not formed, and the same words delivered with the same skill do not have the same impact. In this situation, we deliver only ideas. I think that this deeper engagement takes place inside all our disciplines. A lecturer on art who actually creates art, a professor of poetry who fashions verse, a business professor who lives the marketplace all bring themselves into the room with their lecture notes and give of themselves as they speak in ways beyond their conscious awareness.

Teaching is an extremely personal venture that draws on all our inner resources. Parker Palmer describes this well when he writes:

> Face to face with my students, only one resource is at my immediate command: my identity, my selfhood, my sense of this "I" who teaches—without which I have no sense of the "Thou" who learns.... This book builds on a simple premise: *good teaching cannot be reduced to technique; good teaching comes from the identity and integrity of the teacher.*[4]

I could not agree more. When we teach, what we *are* enters the room. Of course, our words and ideas always flow from what we are, but I'm suggesting that there is something deeper at work as well. Something of our *presence* enters the room and there it reaches out to join with the *presence* of receptive students. Fields couple with fields. Energetic bridges form spontaneously around us that reflect less what we think than what we have experienced. If our words are coherent with what we are, their power is amplified; but when our words outstrip our experience, as sometimes they must, their power diminishes at some square of the difference and they rapidly lose their ability to influence. This happens, even if our intentions are the best, because we cannot cheat nature and these energetic bridges are simply nature in action.

In another telling passage, Palmer writes, "Deep speaks to deep, and when we have not sounded our own depths, we cannot sound the depths of our students' lives."[5] I believe that the inverse of this principle also holds. When we *have* sounded our depths, we cannot help sounding the depths of our students. Deep does speak to deep—involuntarily, automatically, silently, energetically. When depth has awakened within us, it reaches into the room without need of our conscious direction. Whatever we do, whatever we say, everything dances on this deeper movement.

This is the pith of the lesson that emerged in the chapter on resonance. Underneath the conscious scripting of our lectures, our being reaches into the room and touches our students. There it mingles and merges with their being, sometimes siphoning into the room *their* experiences, bringing forward the truths *they* need to hear. When the right conditions are present, this is a natural and unstoppable effect. It is put into action not just by subliminal physical cues folded into our delivery but by an invisible living energy that is present in the room.

States of consciousness are contagious. This contagion is true for teachers in every discipline. Experience awakens experience; depth triggers depth. When we are distracted and teach from the edges of our being instead of from our center, as we sometimes do when our schedule is crowded or the day is long, our capacity to initiate others will be diminished. But when we are aligned with our center and teach from that alignment, it is more likely that our teaching will exhibit the initiating power of transmission. It does so because consciousness is a living power in the room, and our consciousness is rooted in what we are. It cannot be faked—but neither can it be contained.

A Preexisting Wholeness

The habit of thinking in terms of the private mind is so strong in our culture that to consider another alternative pushes not only the boundaries of our thinking but the boundaries of our experience as well. It asks us to go beyond how we usually experience the world and look more deeply into the subtle fabric of our lives. What do all these experiences of connectivity in life and in different laboratory settings sum to? What do they suggest is true about our minds, our consciousness, and the universe we live in?

I think we should begin by affirming the historic importance of our extraordinary individuality. Like great prisms, each of us embodies a unique experience of the world. The longer we simmer in the caldron of time, the more distinctive our cut and polish.

But then a second truth emerges. We have seen that when unique human beings come together to pursue common projects, spontaneous bonds are forged. As we connect with each other through words and signs, we also couple together at deeper energetic levels, reinforcing and building on each other in compounding formations.

What fascinates and intimidates me is the depth of what sometimes rises in me in the company of my students. Something invisible inside me senses and responds to something unspoken inside them. Where does this awareness come from? How does it know what is needed? Surely this knowing is not located in me in any conventional sense of "me." The "I" I am busy being on a daily basis cannot keep track of this much information, yet something seems to. Something riffles my memory banks and pulls out the right piece of information for the situation, something the student needs to hear, something they are ready to hear. When this happens, it is the most natural feeling in the world, truly effortless yet completely beyond my customary reach. Where do these sparks of connection come from? What are they telling us about ourselves?

The language I have used to describe these things starts with our everyday experience of being separate persons. I have spoken of "sparks jumping" and this image assumes the reality of separate beings. The same is true for words like "coupling" and other phrases I've used. And yet I think the emergence of these sparks and couplings points to the existence of a deeper underlying wholeness operating beneath the surface of life. These spontaneous connections take place because the potential for connectivity is an inherent feature of our universe, and this potential appears to reflect the fact that at a more subtle level of reality *we already are one*. The potential for connecting with others is rooted in a wholeness that already exists.

Seen in this light, *all* the variations of connectivity described in this book took place inside a preexisting wholeness of consciousness and oneness of being. At core the universe lives and moves as One. When our minds couple with other minds, it appears to activate some aspect of this underlying wholeness and bring it forward into localized expression. Though this wholeness may come into conscious focus during these brief episodes, it is the ever-present background reality.

Thus, the language I have used of sparks "jumping" between separate lives is an accurate description of these things up to a point, but, seen from a deeper perspective, it is also an incomplete and possibly misleading description. Underneath the diversity of relative reality is a *preexisting wholeness* that is inherent in nature itself.

This interpretation of the metaphysics of connectivity in human experience is deeply congruent with the holistic vision that emerged in contemporary physics during the last century. Among scientists, the discussion of nonlocality, superconductivity, and super-coherence has pointed to the existence of a primary holism operating in nature. One of the first to draw the public's attention to this shift in thinking was Fritjof Capra. In his early study, *The Tao of Physics*, published in 1975, he wrote:

> In modern physics, the universe as a machine has been transcended by a view of it as one indivisible, dynamic whole whose parts are essentially interrelated and can be understood only as patterns of a cosmic process.[6]

Similarly, when the Nobel Laureate Erwin Schrödinger applied the insights of physics to the task of understanding the nature of consciousness, he concluded that consciousness was fundamentally a unified phenomenon, writing:

> In all the world there is no kind of framework within which we can find consciousness in the plural; this is simply something we construct because of the spatio-temporal plurality of individuals, but it is a false construction.

David Bohm concurs:

> Deep down the consciousness of mankind is one. This is a virtual certainty because even in the [quantum] vacuum matter is one.

Henry Stapp adds another voice to the emerging chorus, emphasizing that nature and consciousness are connected through nonlocality:

> The new physics presents prima facie evidence that our human thoughts are linked to nature by nonlocal connections: what a person chooses to do in one region seems immediately to affect what is true elsewhere in the universe.[7]

When we combine these trends in physics with the "new story" emerging in cosmology, the evidence mounts that we are living in a *living universe*, a universe that is alive as a whole in more ways than we had suspected even a few short decades ago.[8] After summarizing a large body of scientific evidence that supports this interpretation of the universe, Erwin Laszlo concludes:

> A new concept of the universe is emerging.... In this concept the universe is a highly integrated, coherent system, much like a living organism. Its crucial feature is information that is generated, conserved, and conveyed by and among all its parts. This feature is entirely fundamental.[9]

In his book *Promise Ahead*, Duane Elgin reviews a similar body of evidence and draws essentially the same conclusion:

> Our universe is revealing itself to be a profoundly *unified system* in which the interrelations of all the parts, moment-by-moment, determine the condition of the whole. Our universe is infused with an immense amount of energy, and is being continuously regenerated in its entirety, while making use of a reflective capacity or consciousness throughout.[10]

In the universe physicists are describing today—unified, self-coherent, saturated with consciousness, regenerative, and creative—reports of living resonance and collective mental functioning appear to be completely natural and even expected events. The fact that our interactions in the classroom reflect a collective intelligence not housed in one person but distributed throughout seems to be coherent with the underlying holism that scientists are discovering in other quarters. It is too early to connect all the dots, but where these trends are heading seems clear. One conclusion beckons: *The classroom is alive because the universe itself is alive.* Our classrooms are teaming with intelligent connectivity because at a deeper level the universe itself is teaming with intelligent connectivity.

In pointing to this living wholeness, scientific theory and personal experience affirm each other's conclusions. When the spark of connection jumps in my classroom, it *feels* as if a living consciousness that I am part of uses my knowledge to accomplish a purpose that lies beyond my personal horizon. The experience brings with it a sense of awe and wonder, but above all a sense of *transparency*—in the technical Buddhist sense of *sunyata*. A state of awareness rises that is "empty-of-self" and "transparent" to a larger wholeness operating in the room. Everything is as it was before, but the usual membranes of life are for a moment dissolved. A preexisting, living wholeness absorbs all relative partitions. An innate, *ever*-present, *ever*-self-manifesting Totality reveals itself within its garden of semiseparate beings.

These thoughts echo the conclusion that William James came to at the end of his distinguished career at Harvard. In the last year of his life, James wrote an article in which he tried to pull together some summary judgment from his lifelong study of consciousness. There he wrote:

> We with our lives are like islands in the sea, or like trees in the forest. The maple and the pine ... commingle their roots in the darkness underground, and the islands also hang together through the ocean's bottom, just so there is a continuum of cosmic consciousness, against which our individuality builds but accidental fences, and into which our several minds plunge as into a mother-sea or reservoir.[11]

As the paradigm of connectivity and wholeness takes deeper root in the twenty-first century, it is inevitable that many changes will take place in educational theory and practice. This is not just a shift in theory but a shift in *paradigm,* a shift in the core vision that informs many theories. As we begin to recognize the human potential we are presently wasting and to harness the potential of our collective consciousness, self-reinforcing cycles of discovery will be set in motion. Just as the habits of separation reinforce separation, the habits of connection will reinforce connection. Consciously tuning into group fields will strengthen those fields and thus increase their influence in our classrooms. As we begin to recognize more clearly the threads that weave our lives into a larger mosaic of intentionality and opportunity, the intelligence of this mosaic will be able to express itself more robustly. Subtle feedback networks will become stronger. Latent pathways of communion will manifest more demonstrably.

Ponds and Nets

When I have searched for an image to convey the understanding of consciousness that has been emerging in this study, I see a pond at dawn's first light. A small lake in glassy repose, absolutely still, sun breaking the horizon, morning mist rising, wooded shoreline, insects buzzing. Any movement pings its mirror surface. A wing touches down, a fish rises, a bug dances—instantly the pond responds, ripples cascading out in circles. Mind is something like this. Exquisitely sensitive to itself, not fragmented but whole. If stirred, waves radiate through it rhythmically, carrying information and energy. Our individual minds are distinct, but not private. They rise within and continuously commune with a larger field of Mind.

Tap the water once and the ripples quickly fade, absorbed by the inertia of the whole. But tap it repeatedly and the ripples reinforce each other and combine to form standing waves in the water. Consciousness is something like this. Actions done once quickly fade, but actions repeated many times gather momentum, especially shared actions enacted with emotional and intellectual intensity. The same inquiry repeated over many years, engaging hundreds, eventually thousands of minds in the same dance builds momentum. If the topic is deserving and engagement is strong, if minds and hearts are energized, the repercussions are felt even far away, as Stapp suggests.

Like waterbugs dancing on the pond's surface, human beings dance in life, and as we dance, different patterns emerge around us. Sometimes a spark jumps between two poles. Lightning strikes and suddenly a possibility seems closer for someone in the room. There is a pinging in the pond, a strike of heartfelt exchange, a truth transmitted. Unpremeditated and uncontrolled, it is guided by its own radar, advances its own agenda. Why the spark jumps to one and not to another, I don't know. Why sometimes and not always, I don't know. But it happens.

Sometimes instead of a spark there is a pulse that radiates through the room, a deep, slow-moving wave rippling out in circles. Students respond to this pulse differently. Some barely notice it. Perhaps they sense that something is different, but don't know what it is. The course ends and they quickly forget it. Others feel the pulse more strongly and respond. They want to feel this energy again, to be present when these unpremeditated waves move through the room, so they come back for another course the following semester. What the students don't realize is that these sparks and pulses arise not from the teacher alone but from *all of us* acting in concert. They are the sparks and pulses of our *collective* consciousness. They express the learning of our *collective* intelligence. Order for free.

In the class mind, my personal mind is sometimes animated and sometimes burdened. All teachers know this experience. When my students are aroused, my mind is aroused. When they are enlivened, my mind opens and sings. It sees more possibilities, paints with deeper strokes. And when my students are heavy with fatigue, my mind does not sing. When they are comatose, I feel like the walking dead myself. Sometimes all my students will let me give them is information. On those days it feels like I'm just going through the motions of teaching. No matter how hard I try or how fast I dance, I can't get a rise out of them. OK. This time we'll do just information exchange and soon an acceptable but unmemorable lecture will be behind us.

But if I can throw a firecracker here or there, the students may respond and things may shift. If I can push or jostle or joke my way into their attention, if I can find a more authentic place within myself to teach from, new life enters the room. If they begin to want to play with me, sometimes something remarkable happens. Our minds begin to crackle and snap together. Things unusually pertinent come out of our mouths. We collide in ways that are unusually helpful to each other. Something magical rises. The classroom comes alive. The larger aliveness that we always participate in but do not always feel reaches out and blesses us.

Many teachers have had this experience; it is not new. This book only contributes a proposal for how we might understand the underlying dynamic driving these events. I suggest that we are more animated in these situations because the local field of our *collective mind* is aroused. We are for a time more gifted, more insightful, and more effective as teachers because a *collective intelligence* is active with us in the room. Through the sheer force of our assembly, something rises under our feet from the ground of being. The power of assembly amplifies the capacities of those present *if* that assembly is skillfully coordinated, otherwise it is just another crowded room and we all go home disappointed. The potential is *always* present when we congregate, but skillful means must be applied for this collective intelligence to emerge powerfully in the room.

We have invoked numerous scientific insights to support this model of consciousness, but the understanding it embodies is much older than science. The contemplative branches of our spiritual traditions have repeatedly testified to the existence of a pervasive consciousness that saturates our universe, making it a living whole rather than a mechanical assembly of parts. Rather than cite multiple examples here, I will let one passage speak for many.

In the *Garland Scripture* of Mahayana Buddhism, written in the second or third century C.E., there appears a famous passage describing the Net of Indra. This passage is widely revered as a true description of reality as seen through spiritually awakened eyes, a portrait of a holographic universe in which every piece of existence reflects the Totality. It reads:

> Far away in the heavenly abode of the great god Indra, there is a wonderful net which has been hung by some cunning artificer in such a manner that it stretches out indefinitely in all directions. In accordance with the extravagant tastes of deities, the artificer has hung a single glittering jewel at the net's every node, and since the net itself is infinite in dimension, the jewels are infinite in number. There hang the jewels, glittering like stars of the first magnitude, a wonderful sight to behold. If we now arbitrarily select one of these jewels for inspection and look closely at it, we will discover that in its polished surface there are reflected all the other jewels in the net, infinite in number. Not only that, but each of the jewels reflected in this one jewel is also reflecting all the other jewels, so that the process of reflection is infinite.[12]

This passage reminds us that nothing I have been suggesting in this book is new. Energetic resonance and group fields have long been recognized in contemplative circles where it has been common knowledge that spiritual awakening is facilitated by community, psychically as well as physically. This is why *sangha,* the community of committed spiritual seekers, is one of Buddhism's three refuges, and *ecclesia,* the church, is described in Christianity as a boat that carries all safely to the distant shore. If there is any novelty here, it is only the report that these collective dynamics are being detected in the unlikely setting of a university classroom. Even in the cathedrals of the rational enlightenment, in the citadels of secular humanism, the deeper fabric of our collective life shows itself if we allow it.

Sacred Ground

The classroom has always been sacred ground for me, but my appreciation of just how sacred has deepened with time. As the years passed and the living wholeness of the room shattered me again and again, something began to fall apart inside me. Some shell I had been holding onto first softened, then melted. It still comes and goes, trapping me in my silliness and fears, but then, when I'm least expecting it, it suddenly releases me. And there IT is again, absorbing us all in ITS ordinary majesty, thinking inside all our thoughts, desiring inside all our desires. I lose my beginnings and endings in ITS weave. I cannot but surrender to IT, abandon myself entirely to ITS embrace.

In such moments, it is obvious and without need of argument that my mind and the minds of my students participate in a larger ocean of awareness. In these minutes of grace, it is clear that our minds collaborate to bring forward thoughts too large for us to think on our own. In these hours the fragmentation that is my usual condition is healed and an unspeakable delicacy emerges, whispers to me, teasing me beyond my borders, coaxing me to relax, to fear less, to trust more, receive more, share more. Thoughts beyond what I can usually manage tumble through me, sourced in horizons I cannot see, nourished by streams of my brothers' and sisters' knowing. When the walls fall away this completely, I realize clearly that no thought, even our most ordinary thoughts, is one person's creation alone. For better and for worse, we are all implicated in each other's lives. How easy it then appears for the echoes of other minds to show up in our stream of consciousness. How spontaneous the give-and-take of secrets.

But then the walls consolidate again. The partitions rise and I am again a prisoner in my cell. Instead of resting in the innate transparency of being, I am once again reduced to speaking of "bridges" and "sparks" leaping across apparent gaps. The second eye closes and I am again a cyclops in the world of the one-eyed. Was it true? Was it real? Can we trust these fleeting episodes that reveal such depths of wholeness? Doubts return only to give way on yet some other day when the veil again falls away and the splendor returns. The second eye opens and something larger sees through us and calls it good.

In the end, this book is a confession, not of faith but of experience. Those who have had such experiences will understand their elusive nature. Until they become stable, they come and go, reflecting someone else's whim, for we would beg them to stay and continue to bathe us in their grace. But either I am not ready or IT is not ready and the light fades and the lecture continues.

Science confirms the possibilities we glimpse in these transient affairs, but the full flower is hard to catch in the laboratory. One day it may be captured on screen. One day it may be as common as dirt for us to experience this deeply the living weave of hearts and minds, but for now it comes and goes. But while it dances with us, it shows us a great truth about ourselves. It shows us the boundlessness of our *true condition*, the vast expanse of our *complete being*. Our *true heart* reflects the oneness we together are. From this perspective, compassion is not a labor of love but simply the common sap that runs through the entire tree that we already are.

The sacred ground of life is more easily evoked in nature than indoors. Isn't this a truth so obvious that it barely needs saying? The isolation of our egos seems intensified inside the concrete block rooms we teach in, rooms that often lack even windows to remind us that we are part of a larger natural order. It is easier to convey the story of connectivity to my students when I'm sitting with them outside under a tree, on sacred ground itself. The collective mind seems more obvious to everyone when we are nearer living things—inescapable even. For the same reason, students raised on a farm seem to grasp the truth of interpenetration and wholeness more quickly than students raised in suburban igloos. The interdependence of life systems is more obvious to those who have worked the land, and so they more quickly grasp the synergistic coupling of minds as an extension of the same principle.

From this perspective, the philosophy of the separate mind appears to reflect a pathology inherent in our urban existence as much as it does any right championing of our individuality. Our cities bring us together in large numbers, but isolate us in anonymity and social fragmentation. But when we sit quietly in nature, when we slow ourselves down sufficiently to take in the sounds of life buzzing around us or to mark the rhythm of the planets sliding by, the patterns of collective intelligence are easier to grasp. The underlying wholeness of life emerges, the fractal patterns embrace us.

When teachers make nature our classroom, we heal not only the rift between humanity and the other forms of life with whom who share this planet but the rift between ourselves and the Cosmos itself. To see through the second eye, nature is always the better classroom. In her embrace, we come back to our senses. We more easily wake to the truth that we are here *together*, expressions of a hidden and sometimes not-so-hidden Oneness. When we sit under the stars, the words of Chang Tsai, the eleventh century neo-Confucian philosopher, come true again:

> Heaven is my father and Earth is my mother, and even such a small creature as I finds an intimate place in their midst. Therefore that which fills the universe I regard as my body and that which directs the universe I consider as my nature. All people are my brothers and sisters, and all things are my companions.

Postscript: A Calming of the Waters

I would like to conclude with an observation that will illustrate one last time the dynamic quality of the collective mind. In 1999, I made a decision to take my spiritual practice in a gentler direction. After twenty years of exploring deep visionary states of consciousness, I shifted my practice more in the direction of meditation, seeking to integrate that nighttime sky more completely into the sun-drenched world of my everyday consciousness. I had been attending to integration all along, of course, for spiritual experiences that are not integrated leave little lasting impact on the psyche, but now I tilted the balance even more in this direction. The work became less shamanic and more contemplative, more focused on the rhythms of daily awareness. Instead of periodically plunging into the deep interiority of the universe, the focus became more the immediacy of Presence. With this interior shift, the dynamics of my classroom also shifted.

Over time, the waters that had sometimes been so turbulent in my classes seemed to calm down. The change was gradual and I am still monitoring it. It appears that this smoothing of the waters reflects the fact that the practices I am now doing are less cathartic and do not reach as aggressively into the deep psyche. I find that the pointed resonances described in chapters 1 and 2 still occur, but less frequently and at a more subtle level. Whereas previously I had sometimes felt like a lightning rod among my students, triggering energies over which I had little control, now I must consciously cooperate with the process for these connections to manifest. This is not exactly right because lightning still strikes and arrows still hit unseen targets from time to time, but these days it tends to be a more subtle dance that asks for my conscious cooperation.

The fact that my classroom appears to be responding to this shift in my practice demonstrates once again how *sensitive* the fabric of life truly is. We live suspended in a living tissue that is exquisitely subtle and finely tuned. Changes in this tissue do not take place suddenly, but if we watch the larger patterns of our life, there's often an ebb and flow stretching over years that reflects our inner world.

If the web of our life appears to be static and unchanging, to be driven by blind mechanical forces having little to do with us personally, it may be that our inner life has itself become static and repetitious. The fabric of life is responsive to the cumulative power of the choices we are making. If we are choosing to live lives deeply grooved by habit, the surrounding matrix will become similarly flat and seemingly lifeless. On the other hand, if we reach into ourselves and shake up our inner life, the outer world will begin to respond. If we engage the deep psyche in a systematic manner, challenging the limits that hold us in narrow, repetitive cycles of behavior, the repercussions begin to ripple outward and a collective dance begins. If the inner engagement is particularly deep, the dance can become intense. If we slow the inner work down, the dance slows down, but it is always there. That is the point—*the dance is always there.*

> Always we are connected to each other,
> always we are woven into a larger fabric.
> Our personal adventure is part of life's vast odyssey,
> our personal aspirations a fractal embodiment of its
>   vast ambitions.
> In this fact there is great peace.
> We are home even where we stand
> without needing to go anywhere.
> Oneness with life is not acquired
> only recognized.
> Whatever we are becoming,
> whatever we will be ten years from now
> or ten lifetimes from now,
> we will not be more One
> than we are this very moment.
> Still growing from one perspective,
> already whole from another.
> This is the wonder and challenge of the human
>   condition.
> This is the spirit of the living classroom.

Student Stories

Introduction

I generally ask my students to do a lot of writing in my courses. I trust a written essay more than I do objective exams for strengthening the long-term retention of large ideas. Most of the essays my students write address the concepts they are studying, what they understand and don't understand about them, what they like and don't like. They criticize, evaluate, and tabulate—all good grist for the academic mill. Every now and then, however, a student will take the risk of writing something more personal. They show more of who they are inside the educational exercise. Sometimes when I'm presenting a concept in class, it touches a nerve or triggers a memory and students write about it. If I were using only objective exams to evaluate their performance, I would not know what just happened, but in their essays they sometimes show me what's going on inside them at a deeper level or give me a piece of their history.

As a professor of religious studies, it is not my intention to evoke these more personal essays, but I have learned to welcome them as part of the give-and-take of learning. I find that students are more likely to do serious academic work if they are given room to get personal once in a while and to vent when necessary as they explore new ideas. At least this is true for the kinds of ideas I address. For a new concept to have its full impact on students, they have to be able to make it their own. As if following the Buddha's advice 2,500 years ago, they have to test the idea against their own life experience to see if it holds up. When they relate a concept to something that happened to them personally, they are exploring how it applies to real life. In this way these essays become part of their larger intellectual engagement of the course.

Some of the essays my students shared with me over the years were so poignant that I started to collect them. At the time, I didn't know what I wanted to do with them, but I knew that I did not want to be the only person who had the privilege of reading them. If beauty is in the eye of the beholder, what made these stories beautiful to me was the light they threw on consciousness and the deeper workings of life. So I became a collector of stories. After the students had turned in their work for the semester and their grades had been recorded, I would sometimes ask one or two of them if they would consider leaving me a copy of their story for possible use in some future, undefined writing project. I always extended the invitation as gently as I could, giving them ample permission to decline. I've never had a student say no, though many have added, "If you think it would help somebody."

When my third sabbatical gave me the opportunity to write this book, I sifted through the stories I had collected and decided that the time had come for me to give them back to the world. I selected the most striking essays and grouped them into six categories that became the six short chapters that follow. As indicated in the previous introduction, these stories are only *indirectly* related to the primary themes of *The Living Classroom* and should not be read as evidence for its primary assertions. At the same time, they demonstrate the depth of the life-transforming processes that are activated by the magic that sometimes rises when people come together in groups to learn.

Because many of these stories do not fit inside the materialist paradigm that still dominates the modern academic worldview, my students were often hesitant about bringing them forward, even embarrassed. Some had been holding these experiences for years, unable to speak about them to others for fear of ridicule but also unwilling to let them go. In these accounts, we see testimony from ordinary citizens that death is not the end of life, that the universe and what lies behind it are breathtakingly intelligent, and that within each of us lie extraordinary depths of being.

These stories are only anecdotal accounts, of course, and we know that anecdotal evidence is the weakest form of evidence for any hypothesis. And yet if certain experiences keep showing up in peoples' lives and if the persons reporting them are levelheaded, hardworking individuals, it certainly should pique our metaphysical curiosity. If a sufficient number of anecdotal accounts accumulate suggesting that the materialist view of life is a seriously incomplete vision of reality, this should lead us to explore these experiences further or to test the capacities that they imply human beings possess. Our models of reality must accord with the whole of human experience, not simply with an edited subset of experience.

In the end, I share these stories with the reader not to try to prove anything, for that would require a much longer and more detailed argument. I share them because they are fascinating and moving accounts that have been passed to me by honest, intelligent university students who simply wanted to share a private moment in their lives with someone who would listen respectfully.

As we go along, I will provide a rationale for why I think we should treat these stories with intellectual respect, but, for the most part, I will let them speak for themselves. I hope that publishing these accounts will encourage other educators to be more receptive to conversations with their students about their deeper life experiences. Research indicates that college professors usually are not having these kinds of conversations with their students (see chapter 9), but we should be, for they are as much a part of life as other matters we do discuss. I am drawing attention to my students' experiences because if my students are having these experiences, it's likely that your students are too. Taken as a whole, these accounts suggest that we have not yet charted the full scope of the human experience, and this is an exciting thought as we enter the new millennium.

One last observation before we begin. Readers who are looking for confirmation in these accounts of a particular religious creed at the expense of other creeds will probably walk away disappointed, for spirituality is a much wider ocean than religion. Many of the students speaking here come from Christian backgrounds and accordingly interpret their experience in Christian terms. Other students have embraced non-Christian religious traditions that are just as meaningful to them and just as useful for interpreting their experiences. Some have abandoned formal religion altogether and carved out a spiritual worldview for themselves that lies outside religion.

Rather than play one belief system against another, I suggest that the *diversity* of these experiences combined with their *coherence* with one another at a deep structural level points to the existence of a spiritual reality that *no one religion has given us a complete portrait of*. The spiritual domain is simply too vast and complex a reality to be captured by one culture, no matter how great its genius or sensitive its lens. It is only when we put together the teachings and experiences contained in *all* the world's spiritual traditions *and* its sciences that we begin to catch the outline of the larger whole.

At least, this is my suggestion for how we might read these experiences, but it is only a suggestion. In the end, all interpretations are secondary to the experiences themselves, and that's where I would place the greatest emphasis. I want to thank my students for entrusting me with these stories, which I share here in heartfelt gratitude for the time we spent together.

CHAPTER 7

Where We Begin

We don't get to choose our students. They choose us. They come to us as they are, as life has made them. Some have been treated gently by circumstances while others carry deep scars already at an early age. The older our students are, the more life experience they have tucked away and the more they have formed opinions on a variety of topics. As we lecture, we bump into these opinions and experiences. We touch areas of life that they have history with and they react. Sometimes they react strongly because their history is deep or painful.

This chapter is about beginning points. It illustrates the powerful feelings and convictions that students often bring with them into the classroom. Beneath the smooth veneer of good manners and polite etiquette that greets me on the first day of class, there are always pockets of energy hidden in the room. Often they center around pain and disturbance, but sometimes around great beauty or mystery. These pockets of energy can be triggered accidentally or intentionally, skillfully or clumsily, but they're always present, waiting to be activated. If I create a classroom environment that is accepting of these pockets without getting lost or absorbed in them, students will tend to get more involved in the course. The more permission they have to be their true selves in our undertaking, the stronger their participation will be.

Because I teach courses in religious studies, the emotional charges my students bring to my attention usually have something to do with religion and the areas of life religion addresses—meaning and purpose, life and death, suffering and redemption. Students usually have strong feelings on these topics by the time they get to me. Their history colors what they hear me saying in class and shapes their responses to the material I present. When this history is activated, it enters the room, flooding it with memories. These memories are often the starting point of deeper contact between us if the students have the courage to share their experiences with me and I have the openness to receive it. Sharing these memories with me brings their past into the present and in the process opens the door to the possibility of their creating a new future for themselves.

Many of my students come from suburban, middle-class backgrounds, but many don't. Poverty is a serious problem in the city where I teach, and more than a few of my students have struggled financially. This was the case for the nontraditionally aged woman who wrote the following essay about her experience of being poor in America. Her story was provoked by a lecture I gave in a world religions course on the different spiritual paths in Hinduism. What triggered her was my description of *bhakti yoga*, the path to God through loving devotion.

I was strongly repelled by the Hindu concept of *bhakti yoga* because it reminded me of Christianity's burning desire to do everything for the love of God.

I was very poor last year. Our family of 3 lived on $2000 a year plus $100 worth of food stamps a month. It takes a lot out of a person to stand in line for free food and blankets. I can't explain the humbling I had to experience to feed my husband and my child. And the scores of faces I became familiar with ... so hungry, so destitute.

The poor are not rich "in our ways," as the middle class wish to believe. Children abused, wife beaten because she wanted the welfare check to clothe her little ones instead of using it on one of the poor's worst diseases—alcoholism. Teeth rotting because there isn't enough money for proper toothbrushes and paste. They are not lazy. They are crippled by our system of inadequate care! I would wait in lines for hours with these people. Crying for our shame of being the unfortunate and forgotten ones of society.

Then, upon my turn, I was forced to listen to lecture after lecture about Christ and his love and how the Christians of today are following in his footsteps by providing for the needy. I was forced to pray with them. My hungry baby, my depressed husband, waiting at home for me, for cheese and milk and flour so that we might eat that day and these Christians are asking me to pray to a God that has cursed mankind to this kind of destitution because of the ill-called "sin" of two supposed historical figures, Adam and Eve. Some concept of God!

I asked one time why they had this food program and what motivated them to participate. (I almost knocked their socks off by this "intelligent" question. The poor are supposed to be stupid. That's how they got to be poor to begin with.) Their answer lost my individuality. They did this for the love of God, for God loves the poor as well as the rich—and so must they.

They did it out of love. Nice thought, lousy interpretation. If you want to help, help me. Help my baby, help my husband. Don't label me poor and help "the poor." Love me for who I am, not just because I am one of many whom you should love. And the goal of it all burns like indigestion in me. If they don't love me, they'll burn forever. It's a conditional love. They'll love the poor on the condition that they'll enter the pearly gates of heaven. Would they still want to love if it didn't matter to their salvation? I fear not, for the poor smell for lack of soap.

The poor have greasy hair and garbage for clothes. Their house is unswept and cluttered, noisy and decayed. Their food "tastes funny" because it's not made from expensive products or cooked inside the miracle microwave. Their children are whiny from lack of attention and from side effects of their parent's depression. They look funny, smell funny, and even act funny. After all, no one's taught them the rules of social graces. Their name is Legion, for they are many.

And it's not so bad at the day's end, when your stomach is filled and your baby is sleeping and your husband is lying beside you. You at least love each other. That is the nature of "God." To be loved because you're somebody to somebody, not because you're something to somebody.

No, "Christian love" is not for me. I will love on my own accord. If God is there, then he can love as he wishes. I will not do his job for him. I only want to do mine.

This eloquent woman had been wounded by Christianity and by life, making a course in world religions far from just an intellectual exercise for her. In her experience, poverty and Christian love had become tangled in a knot of heartache she describes with breathtaking candor. She's here not just to collect concepts; she's bringing her life experience to the exercise.

How different the next student's experience of Christianity. This essay was written by a young man whose Christian faith had helped him deal with the loss of three close family members. He takes us inside his traditionally religious home and shows us a family struggling to cope with death. At the same time, his essay hints at the seeds of a tension slowly coming to consciousness between his love and respect for his father and questions he has about the faith his father has passed to him.

I was born into a Catholic family and my upbringing was without a doubt that of a Christian. As a child I was always lectured about the importance of the Christian faith and trust in God. My family was large and consisted of four children—three boys and one girl. As children, we were forced to attend church weekly as my parents did. My parents always stressed the importance of saying nightly prayers that would thank God for my family's health and well-being.

When I was seven years old my mom died of cancer. It was the hardest thing for me to handle, for every night I would say my prayers and ask God to watch over my family. Why would he take my mother away? I still remember the night my dad sat all four of us down and tried to explain why God had taken her and where she had gone. To this day I thank my father for that ever comforting speech and even the way he did it. It must have been hard for him as well. Needless to say, it helped get us all over the hump and our lives continued.

At this point in time my dad's mom had come to live with us, for it would have been impossible for him to take care of us and work at the same time. We were still too young to watch over ourselves. Within a span of a few years, my grandmother also became sick and just as we were almost all back on the bike, the Lord decided it was time to take her as well. It was very hard on all of us again as anyone would expect. I again began asking myself—why is God doing this to my family?—and all I could keep thinking about is my dad. The pain he must be enduring, first his wife, now his mother. But once again he stood tall and helped us all through these rough times.

At this time my dad was dating a woman who, while my grandmother was sick, would help out around the house. A short period passed and my dad ended up marrying this woman. A few years after that, when it was least expected, my grandfather on my first mom's side died of a heart attack. He was one of the nicest men in the world. Although I was older, the question of why continued to pass through my mind. Why all at once. Being older and having been through it twice before, we pulled together as a family and once again managed.

Our lives, needless to say, were constantly being forced to change. Every time we began to find security in someone, the Lord thought best to take them. Which, when you're young, is a tough thing to handle, believe me. Fortunately, the Lord chose to grant us a very healthy and strong man for a father, which is something I will always be thankful for, many, many times over.

Why would God take away the loved ones of those who honor and worship Him? The revolution inside this age-old question is held at bay by the affection and respect this student feels for his dad, but it's

there underneath, gnawing at him. Is he ready to engage the contra-
diction he has lived with since he was seven—a loving God who kills
the mothers of young children? Is he ready to take on a more
demanding understanding of God and the universe? Is this why he's
in my class?

When students expose such intimate pieces of their lives in a
course, it raises the dialogue between teacher and student to a more
demanding level. Larger life issues are at play in the exchange. I think
one has to begin such a dialogue by accepting the reality of the
student's experience. It would not do much good to simply tell this
young man that God doesn't "really" take our loved ones from us
while leaving others behind according to some master plan, any more
than it would do much good to say to the woman struggling with
poverty that the depersonalizing love she encountered in the mission
was not the "real" Christian love spoken of in the gospels. This was
their experience at that time in their lives; this is the charged memory
they have brought into the classroom. When they hear me lecture on
a topic that may be emotionally neutral to others, they are provoked,
aroused to agree or disagree. This emotional charge brings energy into
the room. It focuses the mind, sharpens the attention, oils the tongue.
They are engaged.

Death, poverty, and the hardships of life can drive some students
to question whether life itself is a meaningful exercise, as one student
powerfully expressed in the following essay.

You have no idea how I have wrestled with this very thing just recently. I do
agree that negative thinking is a sure ticket to disaster. But the real treat
comes when you have done your best, tried your hardest, followed all the
"rules," played the game according to all of the rules, and you are still
defeated. Even this is acceptable occasionally, but when it keeps
happening time after time you really begin to have serious doubts.

After a long period of time, and I am speaking of years, it is no wonder
depression sets in and becomes a way of life. This is definitely unhealthy.
What I am asking is why! Why can and does this happen to an individual
who is struggling so hard to better himself/herself? Why do some individuals always seem to be the 'victim'?

I have been through the explanation of being chosen for a special
mission; that I am strong and so I was chosen to bear the 'cross,' to be an
example, etc., and none of this washes anymore.

Why can't I have a decent place to live, clothes to wear, enough to eat,
be able to keep warm? Why can't my children have what they need to

develop properly? If I can't have decent health, at least have the proper medical care. I do not expect any of this for nothing. I expect to work very, very hard for these things. But when I do just that and still get pushed deeper into the mire; then I get very angry and begin to have some very serious doubts. I feel very guilty about having these doubts. I feel as if I am insulting God. This is not so. I am simply searching for answers. I simply want a decent, respectful life.

I can understand where this could take a long time as one must work with one's previous experiences. One must align themselves with the pain resistance brings. But there has to be a point where the pain stops if one is to survive at all. *That is what I am searching for at present.* Freedom from emotional pain as well as physical pain and emerging a more complete individual.

Wounds. Every one of our students has a story and some of their stories are about wounds received from parents, friends, society, or life itself. Sometimes the wounds come from religion. Fortunately, most of my students have not been greatly harmed by their experience of religion. Every now and then, however, a student comes along whose experience of religion has been particularly injurious to the human spirit. Subjected to a system that has gone deeply off course, they are victims of what can only be called religious abuse. This was the case for a middle-aged woman who wrote the following account of her religious upbringing.

In the religions I was raised in, God could be a real mean person. I was taught that even if you were very good and did everything God wanted you to do, He was still only going to take a chosen few to heaven. In other words, not everyone was going to make it.

When I was about seven years old, we became Pentecostal. Every Sunday and Wednesday we were told that unless we repented of our sins, we were all going to die and go to Hell, where we would burn forever, that Satan would watch over us and this is where we would spend eternity. Also they would always tell us that the end of the world was coming and would read out of the Book of Revelations, where the world would be destroyed by fire.

Do you have any idea how awful this is to tell a small child? I would go to bed just knowing that sometime in the night I was going to die and end up in Hell, because in this religion everything you liked to do was a sin.

When I was in the fourth grade we moved to Ohio from Pennsylvania and my mother changed religions. This one was worse than the last. Now people spoke in tongues and I was told that because I was a female, it was my fault that there was sin in the world, and if I didn't serve God to the fullest I would have to pay by going to Hell when I died. We were told that the world will come to an end by a horrible war, where people will eat their own children to stay alive. Isn't this a great bedtime story? I lived in fear that this was going to happen at any time, and I knew I wasn't going to Heaven because my mother said so.

When I was about nine or ten years old, I asked the minister where God came from. Trust me, don't ever do this to a minister in a Holy Roller church. You might as well stand up and swear out loud in the middle of the sermon. He had the whole church praying for me because I was possessed by the devil. Well, I learned not to do that again, but this didn't stop me from wondering.

As I grew older we changed churches a lot, but I went along with the flow because I was afraid that maybe they were right about Hell. One thing I could never understand was how God could be a gentle, loving God on one hand and then hear a minister say that vengeance belongs to God. So which is it, love or hate? Does God really punish people?

Despite all this I grew up, married, had children, and divorced. About this time in my life I figured my children needed some sort of religion, so I decided to turn Catholic. I thought this was an easy religion to follow. The kids and I took religion classes and were baptized into the faith, but I just couldn't go to confession. We learned to pray to the Virgin Mary so she could intercede to her son for us for our sins.

All religions preach heaven and hell, salvation. That we need the churches to get to God, that when we die we go into the ground to wait for the coming of Christ, that we will stand before God and be told if we can enter heaven.

All of a sudden this has gotten very hard for me. I just can't seem to say what I feel about God, religion, or anything.

I want to draw attention to the extraordinary shift that takes place at the end of her story. After eloquently describing the litany of horrors she has endured and her heroic struggle for psychological survival, it is as though she suddenly comes to the end of her theological rope. None of the ideas she is summarizing makes sense to her any more. "I just can't seem to say what I feel about God, religion, or anything." When something like this happens to a student, I watch them carefully, for my sense is that life has brought them to a turning point in their lives. Something is about to shift; if one door is closing, another may be opening. Will the pivot ignite a fire that burns her fiercely before it lets her go, or will she make the transition as though she is simply catching up with herself, as though the hard work has already been done?

The experiences people bring into our classrooms are extraordinarily varied, and this is certainly true for their experience of religion. For some students, religion has been a source of inspiration and consolation; for others judgment and misery. For others still, it is simply a vacuum, something they've heard about but never experienced. Consider the following short but poignant description given by a young woman about her home.

I grew up in a house that has known no holidays. Our doorstep was never crowded with clusters of eager trick-or-treaters. Our living room has never sported a jolly Christmas tree, limbs exploding with lights, tinsel, and ornaments. We have never painted even one Easter egg. I grew up in a house, detached.

This student did not tell me what values or family dynamics lay behind such austerity, so I am left wondering as I wait to see what will unfold for her in the course. Clearly, she will bring a completely different set of sensitivities and filters to its themes than the students previously cited, a different set of hopes and expectations.

I have read many essays in which students complain bitterly about religion and essentially hang the entire enterprise out to dry, but I have also read stories of exceptional faith and transformation. One such essay came from a woman I remember well. At a time in my career when my professional neutrality may have been compromised by a tilt toward the East, this woman pulled me back to center by reminding me of the true power of deep Christian faith. She was a quiet, robust middle-aged woman, short but strong, with wavy reddish-blond hair. She carried herself with great dignity, as if she hardly noticed anymore the severe scars from the fire that had melted her skin on one of her arms and her neck. It appeared that the burns covered a large portion of her body.

As the semester progressed, she listened carefully to my description of the beliefs of the world's religions, all the while holding a deep personal faith in the redeeming power of Jesus that she voiced occasionally. It's not easy for someone whose faith has nourished them in important ways to look with an open heart into the beliefs of people who affirm different gods. She struggled to reconcile her faith in the unique salvation offered by Christ with the spiritual depth she intuitively recognized as existing in these other traditions. Eventually she felt moved in one of her essays to tell her story and to explain the roots of her deep convictions.

I was born and raised in a Presbyterian family all my childhood. I was taught that Jesus died on the cross for my sins. I grew up and made my confirmation at the age of thirteen, but it was just something to memorize to me. There was no depth in it for me. It was just like a social gathering for people. There was a scripture or two given, but there was really no meaning or reaching out in God's word.

I have had a lot of tragedies in my life. I was looking for meaning, purpose, and acceptance in me. I came to find my Lord Jesus at the age of thirty, giving all of me to him, finding peace and true joy in my most inner being. I watched him begin healing in my life.

I still had my ups and downs. I had an explosion while working on a van. I was caught under it on fire. They life-flighted me to Akron Burn Center where I was for four and a half months and thirty surgeries. I am still going for more today. I had to learn to walk using my hands and a lot more. I was so angry at God for this. It destroyed all I had and myself. My mental state was gone.

Today I have accepted it—the fire. It was through all of these things that I've learned who I am and where I stand in my religion today.

I am a bound servant to my Lord Jesus. I have a personal relationship with him as one on one. He is my all. The doctors told my family that I wasn't supposed to live, but God has plans for my life—to reach the people who have been down the same road I have. To tell them that there is hope, healing, peace, joy, and unconditional love. If we accept him as our savior and trust no matter what comes my way, he will see me through.

This woman's accident forced her deeper into her being than most of us ever have to go, and she took her faith in Jesus with her. In that terrible descent, the miracle that sometimes happens happened to her. Jesus became the living Christ. She emerged from that hell a different person with a different relationship to life. "I am a bound servant to my Lord Jesus. . . . He is my all." Her words move me deeply even twenty years later. Her faith has the crystalline clarity of radical commitment forged under extreme circumstances. The sheer power of her transformation eclipses knowledge gathered from books alone, the way that experiential knowledge always outshines conceptual knowledge.

There is a tone, a solemnity that students slip into when they present their "statement of faith," as she does in her last paragraph.

These statements are often prefaced by a phrase that signals that these words come from their deepest life experience—"It was through all of these things that I've learned who I am and where I stand in my religion today." Such statements usually come at the end of the story they are sharing and represent the distilled essence of what the person has taken away from their life experience. It is the core they now live by. When a student reveals this core to you, they have taken you into their inner sanctum. You have truly entered sacred ground.

My students have surprised me so many times that I have learned not to make assumptions. A cheery face does not mean a cheery heart; sloppy clothes don't mean a sloppy mind; polite manners in class do not mean that they're not a hellion back in the dorm. I bracket my assumptions again and again, focusing on the here and now and what arises between us surrounded by these four walls. I remind myself that because I can never know what's really going on behind the scenes, the only thing I can do is do my best in the role I've chosen and play the rest by ear.

Behind the usual academic reasons students have for being in our courses, some students are driven by deep personal needs and fierce internal pressures, as this last essay demonstrates. Ideas that other students read from a distance they devour as though it were their last meal. I had such a student in a psychology of religion course a few years back. He was radically invested in the material, attacking the readings and intensely engaging every idea presented. It was only at the end of the course when he turned in his research paper that he gave me a glimpse into what was driving him. He began his paper by narrating a reccurring dream he had had for many years, a dream that indicated that he had been involved in a process of personal transformation for a long time.

In order to help you understand how profoundly this research has affected me personally, I need to relate a dream which has haunted me for the past ten years.

The dream takes place in what I can only describe as the infinite blackness of the Universe. I was present, yet I was not contained in a physical body. In the distance I could hear voices which I knew to be the entire population of the Universe. These voices were softly chanting, begging me over and over, "Give us the answer! Give us the answer!" I could hear one voice over the crowd, much louder and angrier, not begging but demanding me to *"Give them the answer!"* On what I knew to be a superficial level, I kept screaming back to all of them *"I don't know the question!,"* while in the depths of my soul I knew that the answer was desperately trying to break through a barrier which I was trying to maintain between my consciousness and my unconscious. The answer was willing to surface, but I was using all that was within me to keep it buried.

The fear which encompassed me is to this day beyond description. Not only was I overwhelmed with the fear of discovering the answer, but I also knew that once I revealed the answer to myself, it would automatically be revealed to all who asked the question. Once this transference, of which I was in complete control, took place, the masses would not only accept the answer, they would also be satisfied with it. Once they were satisfied, they would be devoured by some force beyond my control and I would be left completely alone in a void of nothingness. I would be in absolute blackness and silence.

The realization of the consequences of my satisfying my own desperate desire for the answer kept me screaming louder and louder, *"I don't know the question!"* I believed that the louder I screamed, the more energy I would produce to prevent the answer from forcing its way into my consciousness and then being transferred and accepted by these voices. I then woke up.

In a course that was "just another course" for other students in the room, this student found the answer he had been searching for all these years. What hidden forces lie behind the convergence of circumstances that empower such a breakthrough? Setting that question aside for the moment, the point I want to make here is that this student brought enormous emotional and mental energy to the course. A room full of such students is energetically different from a room of half-engaged students who are only going through the paces, picking up a few more credits as they move toward graduation. Even a sprinkling of such highly engaged students can shift the energy of a room to a higher register. Energy, attention, and engagement are contagious, and when the energy in a classroom rises, unusual things sometimes happen.

CHAPTER 8

Healing through Writing

Healing is not my work at the university. As a professor of religious studies, my job is to inform, to introduce students to new ideas, and to help them understand and befriend the foreign. Like my colleagues in other departments, I want to help them live a richer intellectual life, to better understand the events taking place in the world around them. I also want them to understand themselves better, not in the narrow sense of the quirks and idiosyncrasies that make them the often charming and sometimes maddening people they are but in the broader sense of the great depths from which their life springs and the enormous potentials that are everywhere trying to rise within them.

Every now and then, however, education spills over into healing. Sometimes the healing is small—an attitude shifted, a grudge surrendered, something old and clinging put aside. Sometimes it reaches deeper into a pain that has shadowed the student for years, a secret life wound. This is what I want to speak about here, when teaching triggers the healing of deep life wounds.

Healing these kinds of wounds requires exposure and exposure requires intimacy, and while I do not cultivate this kind of therapeutic intimacy with my students, they sometimes take the initiative and step forward into exceptionally intimate places in their writing. They often do so knowing that they are going outside the usual boundaries of the course, yet they feel called to do it. They may apologize or send out a feeler to see if it's "OK" to open this door, but sometimes they write as though they had no choice. They simply *must* give voice to the awareness that is rising within them.

As I've watched this happen through the years, I've done my share of soul-searching, asking myself whether this is appropriate, given the courses I teach. What credentials do I have to let my students engage me at this level, to share stories this personal? Am I putting them at risk, letting them open up this deeply without professional support or follow-up? How does this exercise, even if it benefits the student, fit into the project of my course? And yet, as I've watched these episodes come and go, I've come to trust them. I accept them as part of the cycle of growth that sometimes accompanies deep learning. Trying to stop them from happening seems not only counterproductive but pointless.

Sometimes something comes up in class that triggers a memory. Without my intending it, something I say strikes deep and a student responds in writing. They may not anticipate it at the outset, but the act of writing, when courageously followed through to its end, often becomes their way out of a personal hell. The simple act of telling their story and sharing it with a witness sets in motion a process of reconciliation. Such is the power of the written word, as Louise DeSalvo beautifully illustrates in her book *Writing as a Way of Healing: How Telling Our Stories Transforms Our Lives*. If I had had this book sooner in my career, I could have saved myself a lot of worry.

I've thought a lot about what causes students to respond so deeply in a course not designed to elicit this kind of response. I've come to the conclusion that this process is driven by a deep, universal *need to be whole* that lives in all of us. Some natural force is moving inside these students to bring them into a more complete version of themselves, and that means a healed version of themselves. A mysterious process seems to operate behind the scenes to bring the right people together with the right words spoken at the right time to evoke this healing. A student will hear a remark that was just a passing comment to others in the room, but to that student it was a flaming spear thrown directly into their heart, triggering a chain reaction. As their teacher, I may not have intended this consequence, but I dare not get in its way.

When students reach into great personal pain in a course that does not encourage such expeditions, I see it as a spontaneous detoxification process, as one student here notes. Life has lodged a pain in their heart. In response to a felt invitation to live a more complete life, their system moves to rid itself of this pain. They have entered the fire of transformation. They may be only partially aware of what is happening—they simply feel called to write about something painful that happened to them or to relive some painful choice they made. When a student does this, my role is not therapist but witness. As Parker Palmer wisely puts it in *The Courage to Teach*, "the human soul does not want to be fixed, it wants simply to be seen and heard." When the soul is seen and heard, it fixes itself. When we witness a person's story, we are sometimes privileged to be standing beside them when a miracle happens. These miracles come in many shapes and sizes.

In this chapter, I'd like to share with you three stories written by two students. The first comes from a graduating senior and was written in a course on Eastern religions. He was a young man in his early twenties, and in response to a lecture on Hinduism, he chose to write about the death of his father. You never know what will trigger a student. People write about what they need to write about and when the time is right to do so.

Ever since we began talking about the Hindu concept of the soul and karmic stages of development, I began wondering where my soul is and how my soul has matured in the few but very rich 22 years of this life. So I decided the most important thing I can do in the course is to discover my own soul development and spirituality.

I had the rare opportunity to be born into a unique family who showered me with a tremendous amount of love. I remember the ritual my mother and I shared in the evenings after dinner. After the dishes were finished, my mother and I would sit on her rocking chair and rock together, sometimes for hours. We would even sing a song together with the simple words, "I love you" sung over and over.

I remember a Saturday ritual my father and I shared. My father called me his "pal" and despite the age difference (my father was 42 when I was born), he had a special way of communicating with me. I called him "Batman" and he called me "Robin" and we were a team together. We always found something to do on a Saturday morning to get out of the house. He was such a strong man with a kind and terrific heart. By far, *love* was the most important aspect of my life as a young teenager. [He goes on to describe some good memories he had of his siblings and other not so easy experiences he had as a teenager.]

This is the experience I'd like to share with you, Dr. Bache. (A hard experience that's hard to come out.) It was the day after Christmas, 1983, which changed my perception of life, and death. It was about 9:00 A.M. when my father stepped into my room to wake me. At that time I was not yet sober from the drinking I had done at my aunt's house the day before. Everyone saw that I was drunk and it revealed to the entire family just how much growing up I had yet to do. As I got dressed I reflected on my actions the day before. I had embarrassed myself but, more importantly, I had disappointed my father, who had always set a high standard for my conduct. My father wasn't mad at me, though, he simply understood. We set off for the long day ahead of us.

Our first stop was my sister's house. It was bitter cold out and it was important to get my sister's car started. It was so cold I hated being out there for even a few minutes. I was looking under the hood when my father walked into the house. When I saw my father go inside I said to myself, "Thank God." As I walked into the kitchen, I noticed my father was out of breath. He had mucus in his throat and chest so he went into the bathroom to cough some of it out and catch his breath. I followed him. I was standing by the doorway of the bathroom as my father tried to cough some mucus up. He continued and continued coughing. I had no idea that I was watching my father's last struggle for life.

When my father began coughing again, I began to see blood in his spit. I was alarmed but still tremendously confused, I had no idea this was a sure sign of a heart attack. I noticed that when my father saw his own blood, his eyes got bigger and he fell back. It was soon afterwards that I saw my father begin to lose his balance and consciousness. I grabbed him by the waist to hold him up as he tried to spit over the toilet. I screamed for my sister to call the ambulance but they were already on their way. My sister refused to come into the room and I was left holding my father, quickly losing consciousness in my grasp. By the time the ambulance came, my father was unable to hold himself up for he had lost all consciousness. I will always remember the feeling of holding my father during his death. Morbid as it may seem, I was able to show my love for him by holding his body up when he had no strength to do so.

These past two years have been long fought. I had a lot of guilt and a lot of hostility inside me. (Boy did I have a lot of guilt.) But my hostility and guilt ended the next spring when I was sent to stay with a loving priest in Salt Lake City. There I met some interesting people who set my mind on the right path. I met a man who lost both his parents in five months. I stopped feeling sorry for myself and began to take hold of my life. Being a witness to my father's death made me realize how precious life is and how easily it can be snuffed out. I have grown spiritually from this experience because my father's death forced me to grow up and take control of my life. I have worked in school in order to get 21 A's out of my last 23 classes (a big change from a 2.8 student). I now strive to do things that would make my father proud.

My father's death was the result of the natural order of life. Yet his life will be recounted over and over again in my life and in the lives of my children, who will be told of my father's great love for his children.

Writing this essay took a lot out of me emotionally, for I had never sat down and recalled the horrible experience of my father's death in words. For two solid years, Dr. Bache, I had never put to rest this part of my life. I honestly feel that after writing this essay, I have finally released this toxin out of my soul. I'm glad I wrote what I wrote and finally faced this event in my life. I searched a lot, cried a little. I can think of no one I would rather read this than you, Doctor.

I take this student at his word, that, in the act of concretizing his experience in words and sharing it with me, some "toxin" was released from his heart. Clearly, he had already come to terms with the lion's share of his pain, as his improved grade point average shows, but there was still some remnant that troubled him. Perhaps being able to share what happened with his professor was one more step in self-acceptance and bringing himself back into the community of fallible human beings. I hope that remnant has released him now.

The next two essays come from a nontraditionally aged woman in her late twenties, early thirties. She also took a course on Eastern religions with me during which she went through a deep experiential sequence that turned out to be life transforming. It centered on her coming to terms with a would-be abortion of a child from an extramarital pregnancy. Her account of her experience is powerful, and for that reason I want to make it clear that I am not using her story to recommend a position for or against abortion. When called to witness, I do not judge the stories that are shared with me, nor do I judge their authors, and I encourage the reader to do likewise. Please do not insert these stories into your value system and draw conclusions that simply reinforce that system. I ask you instead to witness this story with me and watch what happens as events unfold in her life. She titled the first essay, "An Unwholesome Choosing."

Although the lecture today was invigorating, it hurt. Parts of it were bothersome, like a mosquito I'd like to squash. One part in particular was explosive pain—unbearable and razor sharp. I shall discuss it now. Only a few people know this story and only one other knows all that I am about to say.

You were discussing *karma*, explaining that according to Hindu and Buddhist teaching, its effect was determined by intention and the quality of one's choices—wholesome or unwholesome. Then you used abortion as an example, suggesting that, according to Indian thinking, whether it was "right" or "wrong" depended upon the soul of the person and their stage of development. Right in class, I felt the breath knocked out of me. I felt a stabbing in my gut—and in the very existence of my soul. There was a moment when I thought I couldn't face what you had to say. I wanted to get up and leave. Instead, I hid behind the wall of memories and came out after I knew the subject had been dropped.

In 1982, June 4 [three years before], I lost my first child. Her name was Rebecca or Becky for short. She was 4 months old—in utero. I miscarried her. It's sad, but worse is yet to be spoken. She was illegitimate. I had become pregnant out of wedlock. The man wanted me to have an abortion. I refused, but as time wore on, the more vulnerable I became. He cried shamelessly and his arguments were wisely spoken. I held on as long as I could, but finally reversed my original decision. I wept the tears of bitterness over my own stupidity for getting pregnant to begin with and for taking it out on such a dear sweet child as Becky. I knew her, Dr. Bache, I swear I did.

When we finally came to that decision, I laid in bed alone with her that night and begged her to understand. I told her all of what this life could offer her—the joys, the pleasures, the scrapes and pains. I told her of books and grass, airplanes and love. I shared as much of the world as I could with her, and then asked for her forgiveness. I wanted her to know I was not treating her life lightly. I knew what she was going to lose out on.

That night, in fretful sleep, I met her. This is hard to explain. I knew the soul inside of me, but then I met the eternal soul. She cried with me. She had been looking forward to being my child. She was upset because she didn't think I would have agreed to an abortion—but then, the decision was mine, not hers. You must understand the emotional impact of this meeting. I *knew* my decision was wrong for me, but I was going to do it anyway. And to face this very soul was damn near as close to hell as one can get.

I went for the abortion. Not a moment passed by that I did not sense Becky. She was so compassionate! She'd understood—but she was waiting for me. There was something she was waiting for.

They put me up on the table, legs apart. The indecency of it all hurt even more. Other girls were there, either in the process of having an abortion or about to have one like I was. The sucking machine had blood all over it. It was tubes—long ones. They were attached to what reminded me of an old fashioned glass milk jar. It was see-through. Oh, they had a bit of white paper around it but it too was covered with blood. One girl was crying. Others were stone-faced. All were awake. All were trying not to notice the community horror. There were NO curtains separating us. Stretched out, naked except for paper gown, legs apart, ... civilized human specimens.

I became hysterical. The doctor could not get near me. The nurse and the Cracker Jack counselor tried to hold me down. To no avail—I had lost it. They hoisted me up and put me in an empty room. They brought me my clothes and told me when I was more prepared to come back.

I felt dirty, cheap, betrayed, guilty as hell—but relieved! I was walking on air as I bounced out of there. I hadn't had the abortion!

He tried to talk me back into it. Instead of fighting with him, I merely agreed vocally, but inside I thought "Over my dead body!" I was buying time to get strong again.

But that night, I met her again. I wasn't ready for her—I'd proven that with my choice. She'd come to say goodbye. I tried to argue, but to no avail. I sobbed over what I had lost, I begged her to come again, another time when I'd be more ready. Can you imagine a smile felt but not seen? She smiled, I knew she'd be back someday.

The next day I miscarried. I felt her soul leave me and then a few hours later her body slipped away from mine. The man was grateful. I was more understanding to him—and to me. And I shall never forget my Becky.

She then adds a final paragraph reflecting on her present family in light of the concept of reincarnation, an idea she had independently embraced.

My daughter Samantha is not Becky. She is someone new, someone that I know is adjusted to me. Becky won't come in this life, but in another life. I really blew it, but I am glad for I really did not deserve Becky. I probably would have made this life miserable for her. Samantha, on the other hand, is just right. She really is the perfect daughter for me—and she's here to teach me something. Becky's death as well as Samantha's life are gifts. I treasure them, but the loss of Becky still hurts like hell. That is why I ran from your words in class today. The pain is still so sharp...

Her story does not end here. Later in the course, she wrote a second essay, this one describing an experience she had during the course itself. It recounts a deep release and profound healing that rippled through her world. Taken together, her two essays powerfully illustrate the two sides of the complete *transformational cycle*. First, confrontation, stepping into the fire of memory, reliving a painful event from a greater perspective. Second, release, healing, and the emergence of something new. She called the second story, "Treasures for My Treasure Chest."

One night, I experienced something in my sleep. It was NOT a dream. It was as follows.

I was the only person in the dream. I felt full in the stomach—something was there and great discomfort, but no pain was felt. Yet I felt comfortable with its presence. Though I was myself, my Self changed—altered. And as the alteration was taking place, I felt myself start to miscarry—as though I was aborting another fetus. Oh no, I thought, I'm losing another child! I saw the blood and felt the cramping associated with miscarriage. I reached between my legs and held the thing. I had miscarried.

I brought it up to my face and looked at it. Oh, it's not a child. The physical description was that it was longer than it was wide and consisted of organ-like tissue, wet with blood but smooth in texture. It was warm and softly pulsating. I held it in my two hands and felt an immense amount of loving emotion toward it.

I cradled it in my arms, but not to my breasts as I would a child. I held it instead against my abdomen. And I started to cry. I'd lost something— this thing that I had expelled. It could never go back. It was warm and comforting to me. I needed it. Then my attention fell to my stomach. It was emptied, but not empty. It wasn't full—I could receive into it. I looked down at this thing and realized what it was and what it meant to me.

It was my *dukkha,* my unwholesome choices. [In Buddhism, *dukkha* means "suffering." It refers to the suffering and alienation generated by the ego that keeps us small and spiritually unfulfilled.] Of course it was warm and comforting. It was a part of my life that I relied on! *Dukkha* had become a way of life for me—it had become my friend. I cried when I realized this and held it close to my cheek in a loving manner. I was missing it, but I knew it must go. I held it out in my hands in front of me and lowered it. When my hands returned close to my body, it was gone. I had put down my burden.

The suffering she had been carrying these many years, born from her body and now released, was gone. She then goes on to describe how this experience impacted her life.

I awoke that morning a different kind of person. I talked of my "vision" with my husband. I felt wheels grinding to a halt, altering the steering mechanism. I felt my *karma* change. I came of age. I caught up with myself.

My bitterness is gone. My patience widens. I still have bursts of temper once in a while but that is just my body shell catching up with my soul. My huge peril about sex is now understood. With great pain came great growth. I see my husband in a different light. I *no* longer expect him to see and do things as I do. He is younger, after all [soul-wise]. I appreciate the soul he has and I know I love that soul. It's nice to love someone for who they really are. Even Samantha is loved differently. I always loved her for who she was, but now I love her for herself, not for myself. She had turned into my refuge. If this had continued, I could have suffocated her.

And better yet, I now have a love for myself. Before, I was just a vehicle of purpose. I had many purposes—take care of my husband, child, extended family, school and the world. Now I am me. This me is me, but also part of the whole. (These words are so simple that they cannot contain the true meaning.) I have gained myself at a higher level yet I have not lost myself in turn. I feel I know so much more yet words cannot express it all. And I am only beginning.

In the years that followed when I have had occasion to sit with other students as they agonized over whether all the changes that life was asking them to make were worth it, I have often thought of this brave woman and the blessings that came to her when she answered her call to live a larger life. "I have gained myself at a higher level yet I have not lost myself in turn. . . . And I am only beginning."

CHAPTER 9

Spiritual Experiences

The secular university is not a particularly friendly place for persons who have had life-changing spiritual experiences. You would think that wouldn't be the case in the liberal environment of our campuses, but it often is. The zeitgeist of our times simply doesn't trust great depth of experience, favoring instead the detail of objective measurement. Students who have had deep experiences quickly learn to keep them to themselves, lest they risk subtle forms of censure from their professors. States of consciousness that go beyond ordinary sensate consciousness are seldom addressed in their textbooks except as examples of psychopathology or sometimes as the (questionable) experiences of religious geniuses.

By "spiritual experiences" I mean experiences that appear to reflect a reality that lies beyond space-time as we know it. In an intellectual environment where reason is king and the kingdom is defined by its commitment to the primacy of matter, spiritual experiences are often portrayed as irrational, illusory, illogical, and unsubstantiated. When they are tolerated in the name of diversity, individuals unfortunate enough to actually have one often end up being discretely pointed toward the university counseling center.

And so, many students on our campuses feel they have no alternative but to take what was perhaps the most meaningful, most beautiful experience of their lives and either hide it or set it aside as untrustworthy. "It's just your mind playing tricks on you," they are told or, my favorite, "It's just your unconscious," as if that explained everything. Not given an intellectually respectable conceptual framework by the contemporary academy that can help them make sense of their experiences, they often do let them go and, in so doing, they distance themselves from the truth of their own lives. They separate themselves from something that welled up spontaneously inside them and spoke to them with penetrating insight and authority. And why? Because it did not fit the materialistic, flatlander world that has come to dominate our universities in the last three hundred years.

Research seems to confirm that spirituality is a low priority on our college campuses. In 2003, the Higher Education Research Institute (HERI) at UCLA conducted a pilot survey of 3,680 juniors attending forty-six colleges and universities across the country. Of these, 56 percent reported that their professors "never provide opportunities for them to discuss the meaning and purpose of life," and 62 percent said that their professors "never encourage discussion of spiritual or religious matters." These results were consistent with a separate survey of over 40,000 faculty on 431 campuses conducted that same year by HERI. When faculty were asked whether "colleges should be concerned with facilitating students' spiritual development," only 30 percent answered yes. The lowest responses were found in the biological sciences (22 percent), physical sciences (24 percent), and social sciences (24 percent).[1]

Because some of the courses I teach treat nonordinary experiences with respect while studying them critically, it's not surprising that students sometimes share with me stories of unusual experiences they've had. Sometimes they've been holding these experiences for years, wrestling with them, uncertain what to make of them. I never solicit these stories from my students, yet so many have been thrust upon me over the years that I am truly amazed that my colleagues can continue to pretend that the materialistic worldview they espouse is intact. I honestly wonder how this ideology can continue to stand when confronted with the persistent experience of so many intelligent, healthy citizens that the universe is multidimensional and saturated with more layers of intelligence and agency than register on our physical senses.

But then I remember. My colleagues don't hear these stories because they discourage them from surfacing in their classrooms or in their offices. Students are sharp; they quickly learn what their professors will and will not receive well, and they don't want to end up on their professor's bad side. The tragedy is that many of these same professors pride themselves on being open-minded thinkers and are not aware how much they are suppressing in their students.

Because spirituality is a universal human capacity and not the prerogative of any one culture or religion, the spiritual experiences my students bring to me have taken many forms. Some are compatible with conventional Western religious beliefs, but many seem to draw from other spiritual wells. As indicated in the introduction, I think these experiences, together with those that follow in later chapters, are coherent with one another at a deep structural level. Taken as a group, they appear to be compatible with the perspective of the "perennial tradition" that scholars have identified running through the deepest, most experiential levels of the world's spiritual traditions. In the end, however, I offer these accounts less to draw theological conclusions and more to encourage discussion on our campuses of these kinds of experiences and their implications. I include them because they have been passed to me by thoughtful, honest students who were not trying to curry favor but simply wanted to share a personal experience with someone they trusted.

The first story comes from a middle aged woman and describes an event that happened while her daughter was taking her driver's license test at the bureau of motor vehicles—certainly an odd place to have a spiritual experience. Can we trust this woman? Can we trust what she says is true and not exaggerated? I think there is an integrity and honesty that comes through her writing that the reader can feel, but I leave this for you to decide.

I would like to share with you certain events of my life as they actually happened. My 18 year old son died two years ago in an auto accident out of state. He was totally brain dead upon arrival at the hospital, at which point he was placed on life support systems to preserve body tissue. To be blunt, the doctors wanted his organs. Three days later they pronounced him clinically dead, and his organs were removed.

After it was all over, I returned to Ohio with my 16 year old daughter. The guilt, the hollow ache were consuming. My daughter blamed me and I blamed myself, but I knew that we had to go on. Within four months my daughter had withdrawn into this angry, hateful child, full of violent accidents with me on the receiving end.

It came time for her driver's license test. By this time, I was literally dragging her through the motions of life. I had told her that if she did not pass this test, she would not be able to spend a week's vacation at my parents' lake cottage (her favorite place to be). She coldly informed me that she would unpack as soon as she got home.

We entered the license bureau and she went on one part of the partition and I sat in the waiting area. I sat down, emotionally exhausted and still angry with God for "holding my son hostage." I closed my eyes and prayed to the "Blessed Mother Mary." At that moment I wasn't thinking about my son, only the unhappy young girl who needed so desperately to succeed, to move forward just a little at this point.

As I concentrated, I became aware of a relaxation coming to me. I felt myself welcoming it. I wasn't concentrating at all now. I was sliding into this feeling and very content to be there. I had my eyes closed and my sunglasses on so I wasn't aware of my surroundings. Then "I was" absolute calm and peace. It didn't flow into me or rush through. It was a complete state of being. I didn't hear voices but the message was so real. Again, there are no words to convey this state of being. The message in me said, "You know this calm, this peace, it is you." Then it was not there. It didn't slide out or disappear, it just wasn't there.

The magic to me was that I didn't feel sad, desperate, or hollow. There were no lights or tunnels but I knew the feelings and the message. I know I will be this again. It went beyond feeling calm, feeling peaceful. I *was* that calm, perfect peace, and acceptance. All this took a matter of a minute in human time.

My daughter passed the test with a high score and I congratulated her. She looked at me and said, "I didn't do it, Johnny did [her deceased brother]." When I asked her what she was talking about, she told me that during the test, she felt panicked and was almost ready to turn it back in and forget it. She said the greatest calm and peace came to her. She said it was there in her and then gone all in a matter of seconds but it seemed longer. She said she felt someone was with her at that moment, not standing beside her, not inside her but with her. She said after that she knew it was going to be all right.

I asked her if she felt like Johnny was giving her the answers and she laughed at me and said, "No! I just looked back at the test and it didn't seem that hard anymore."

At that point she said, "I suppose you think I'm crazy now." I had to tell her that I had experienced the same thing. She said, "I can't wait to feel that way again."

Mr. Bache, I have never had that experience again, but I know at some point I will have that state of being. I know and I am willing to wait for it. That moment has made my life worth living again. It took a great deal of counseling to bridge the gaps between my daughter and I. It wasn't until that day that she was even willing to try.

The question that haunts me, though, is, "Will I see my son?" He completed a part of my being. I have had to learn my daughter. I knew my son and he knew me. We completed each other's sentences and knew what each other was feeling without words. We had a total acceptance of each other. Will I know his being again at some point?

An ordinary day lived in the midst of trying circumstances. Nothing unusual about it until the moment her world shifted. As I scrutinize this woman's account looking for signs of its authenticity or contrivance, I am struck by the care she takes to describe her experience as precisely as possible, taxing language in the process. She explains that this experience did not enter or exit gradually like most experiences do. Rather, it was instantly present, whole and intact, and it disappeared all at once, not fading gradually. She was completely unaware that such "wholeness" and "nongradualness" is one of the features meditation teachers look for when they are assessing the genuineness of certain very subtle states of consciousness emerging in their students.

Similarly, she is careful to insist that the experience went beyond feeling calm, for that would suggest that her customary identity was intact throughout the experience, that her ego was "having" an experience of calm. This was something deeper. Unversed in the significance of the distinctions she is drawing, she stretches language beyond its usual boundaries—"'I was' absolute calm and peace," she says, "I *was* that calm." To me, these details speak to the authenticity of her experience. And then there is the confirmation of her daughter's independent experience, leaving us asking—What touched this mother and daughter?

The second story comes from a male senior engineering major. If one pays attention to types, engineers are not supposed to be the "type" to have the kind of experience he describes in this essay. Perhaps that is why he expresses so much relief to have someone to share it with who would not dismiss it. In his story an automobile accident set in motion a series of events that changed his life, completely rearranging his priorities and his understanding of the Divine.

I was really hesitant whether or not I would include this in my journal until your lecture in which you said to write our essays first then edit them later. Well, right then I decided to put it all in and not to edit anything. I feel more confidence in you and I feel that I couldn't tell anyone better in hope that you will pass this on to someone whom it might help.

I was very radical, on drugs and defiant until I had an auto accident. [He describes the accident, a close call but resulting in no serious injuries.] When the accident happened, I realized that if I had been killed, where would I have gone, since I had no rapport at all with God?

After that experience I started to lose friends as fast as I made them. Why? Because the people around me noticed a change that was totally out of character for me. I was finding, searching, and living a life of "Christianity." Therefore, I lost friends who were not really friends. But those that were real friends seemed to follow—as usual.

So, here I am wanting faith so bad and having nothing at all to base it on. I was taking a step to Him. I started reading the Bible and going to church. The more I read, the more I probed my spirituality and the more I came to crave wholesome heartedness. Persistently, I prayed day in and day out for a revelation to be the basis of my lifelong faith. After many, many months of empty results, I kept forging the frontiers of my spirituality and *knowing* that it someday would occur. It did.

While praying one night (under no influences at all) I passed out, so to say, right in the middle of prayer—that is, there was no distinction from my praying consciously to my slipping out of my body—while retaining my consciousness. I could see my body laying there on the bed while I'm a spiritual form and I began to float about. I went out of my window (it was closed I think) and began to rise. The wind was cutting right through me creating a sensation unparalleled in *any* earth-related physical activity.

My spiritual body was definable; that is, it was, as I call it, a loose construction of atoms comprising an outline of my body with some in between. My head was tilted over my left shoulder and my right arm was extended vertically over my head as I rose. During the ascension I could see stars passing me as I felt a magnetism pulling me up accompanied by a strong desire to go up on my part. Tremendously bright light rays hit me and increased the sensation of total life (that is, in all dimensions: mentally, physically, and spiritually). During this journey I had no earthly conceptions of time or space.

I stopped ascending for what was the climax of the journey: For one split instant I was able to lift up my head and look directly at the light, or what was generating the "light of love rays." I saw a white crystalline cube with magnificent radiant power. I don't have any conception of its size because being in space there was no unit of measure which I could compare it to. I can say that it dwarfed me completely. After this split instant I began to descend to Earth feeling 1000 percent contentedness, as though my life was complete. When I reached the ground, I suddenly awoke and noticed it was morning. Then I began to exalt God, and getting out of bed to do this, I almost fell over with fatigue but continued to pray in reverence.

This experience advanced and transformed my ideologies concerning God. Never have I sought a church to give me spirituality, nor any human— just myself. Don't get me wrong, *All* the credit goes to the Almighty but, you see, I independently chose to pursue Him, in my own way. Of course, if it weren't for the accident I had, I wouldn't have evolved to this stage. But I didn't get it in a sermon or from some charismatic preacher.

This student framed his experience in the context of his Christian faith, but one can't help being taken by how unorthodox his experience appears in Christian terms. The peak of the experience is something completely unexpected. The source of the radiant, love-filled rays of light is a giant crystalline cube! Why a cube, of all things? Given his religious background, one would expect to find Christ here or a being of light or some angelic form. Was he even vaguely aware that the psychologist C. G. Jung had years before identified quarternity as a symbol of the archetype of the Divine Self? A cube is a square extended into three dimensions. Was the crystalline cube he encountered in his visionary experience a three dimensional representation of the archetype of the God-within?

While this young man began his spiritual search inside Christianity, his experience "advanced and transformed" his thinking about God in a way that did not send him back in the direction of traditional faith—"Never have I sought a church to give me spirituality, nor any human—just myself." This is a dangerously unorthodox assertion that has gotten more than one Christian mystic into trouble with the ecclesiastical authorities, but he is not exalting himself in any egoic sense. "*All* the credit goes to the Almighty." This student seems to have broken through the personal psyche to touch something profound inside himself, yet transcending himself at the same time, as though the bottom of his bucket had fallen out, spilling everything that was in it into a larger cosmic container. From the encounter he returned completely satiated, "as though my life was complete." This sounds like the real thing to me, even in a world where the real thing is not supposed to happen to engineers.

The next story shares several features with the preceding one. It comes from a male, it seems to involve an out-of-body experience, and it occurred after many months of intense spiritual struggle. This is the only experience in this book that comes from someone other than one of my students; in this case, it's from a close friend of a student. He and this friend, whom I will call Bill, often talked about science, physics, and metaphysics. In the course of those conversations, Bill once spoke about an unusual experience he had in which he had encountered beings of light. After reading some of the literature in my course on near-death episodes in which people reported similar encounters, my student went back to his friend and asked him to describe his experience in greater detail. Bill's words appear in italics, my student's words are in conventional script.

Bill had been meditating and soul-searching for about seven months. He was searching for the very meaning of his existence. He needed to know his purpose. I think we all want to know these things, but Bill was constantly thinking about these things, trying to understand his place in the universe. Then one night he had this experience.

I went to bed that night. As always, the thoughts and questions about the meaning and purpose of my existence were with me. But I thought of these things always, so this night should be no different.

The experience started as a dream, but it was not a dream. It was very real, as real as the conversation we're having right now. I remember being in a steel mill. I was able to see in all directions. I was simply observing and no one knew I was there. I could see a guard at a gate checking people in.

Then I started to rise above everything. I could hear what all the people in the mill were saying, every word. But their words had no meaning. They were just sounds. I felt as if I was going beyond intellect. And I began to realize that I could see all languages of all human races in all of time. All words and all languages had no meaning, they didn't mean anything. I was going someplace that words couldn't describe.

I continued to rise and I felt that I was going out into the universe. I remember seeing a drop of water hit the surface of a huge body of water. And I realized that the water was the universe, and I was the rings spreading out, expanding. I was expanding to fill up the universe. My consciousness was expanding. At the time the feeling was one of bliss.

As I continued to expand, I felt that I was getting in contact with some kind of mind. I just kept expanding, I couldn't stop. I had the feeling that I knew what Jesus knew that gave him the power to heal people.

And I remember thinking that you could expand forever. And suddenly my ego became threatened. I knew that if I kept expanding I would merge with a mind that wasn't individual at all. It didn't have a point of view. It was like a drop of water returning to the ocean; it was no longer a drop of water when it went back into the ocean.

I suddenly became terrified. If I didn't turn around and come back, I was afraid I would dissolve. I felt that there were two alternatives; insanity, because no one would ever believe this happened to me, or if I kept going I would dissolve, die.

I was still expanding. I wanted to go back. I began thinking about all the things that made me who I am. I knew that I better stop or I would go to this thing. I wasn't ready to go.

I started screaming out "MASTERS, HELP!" Suddenly I saw three light beings. They were orbs of light, not like humans, but they had personalities. They said, "If we're going to help you, you must live by this code." They told me the saying and then released me. I woke up immediately. I sat up and then wrote down what they told me. I still carry it in my wallet today.

After Bill told me of his experience, we talked for a while. One of the questions I asked him was where he thought he was during the experience. He said he feels now that he was in another dimension, another plane of consciousness.

I asked him what he meant when he said he knew what Jesus knew that gave him the power to heal. He had a difficult time explaining this, but he said he felt that Jesus was always in contact with this powerful mind. He understood that the mind of God is in every point in the universe and he felt the totality of God within him.

What was the message from the beings of light that he carried in his wallet? Here it is: "*FROM NOW ON, NOW THAT I HAVE PERCEIVED THE LIGHT OF THE INFINITE ALL, I WILL LOVE ALL PEOPLE LIKE NEVER BEFORE AND I WILL LOVE ALL LIFE LIKE NEVER BEFORE.*"

In the past, skeptics have often dismissed experiences like this as hallucinations produced by stress and an overwrought nervous system, but such a cavalier approach to the deep psyche is less likely to succeed in today's more sophisticated, postmodern psychological environment. Significant breakthroughs in many areas of life often take place because people have pushed themselves beyond their limits, and the same is true for spiritual practitioners.

The Rinzai Zen sect in Japan, for example, places great emphasis on a particularly arduous, week-long retreat that takes place in the dead of winter leading up to *Rohatsu*, the day celebrating the Buddha's enlightenment. For seven days, the monks are expected to meditate day and night without stopping, sleeping sitting up on their meditation cushions. It is an ordeal affectionately known as "the monk-killer." We could multiply the examples of extreme spiritual exertion in search of illumination—the Sundance of the Plains Indians, Masai trance dancing, the Tibetan Buddhist three year solitary retreat. Like great Olympic athletes, the dedicated spiritual practitioner is no stranger to pain. We cannot dismiss their results simply because they challenge our everyday sense of reality.

Because this experience started as a dream, some may dismiss it as "just a dream." Perhaps. But Bill insisted that this was "more than a dream," that it was just as real as physical consciousness. His experience begins in a steel mill, that is, it begins where he lives, in Youngstown, a city with a long history of making steel and where steel is still forged. In a quickly escalating series of experiences, he moves beyond his personal perspective into a state where all human languages reside, that is, in a state of collective consciousness. He then moves even deeper, beyond language to a domain words cannot describe, suggesting that he is moving into an even more fundamental and essential state of consciousness.

As he approaches the point of merging with all existence, completely dissolving into the Totality, his ego gets frightened and he pulls back. He is afraid that he is dying. We can certainly understand this reaction; complete merger with the Totality is a frightening prospect that the ego cannot comprehend. How can you become one with the Totality and still exist individually? He is given a reprieve and a set of instructions to help him cultivate the truth of oneness in his daily living. If he lives by these guidelines, the next time Totality beckons, he may be ready to take the final plunge and surrender to that liberation and beatification of the soul that takes place when the ego dies. There is no rush. Eternity will wait a few more years.

One might think that deep spiritual experiences such as these would lead people toward religion if they are "genuine," but this is not always the case. Research into near-death episodes, for example, has shown that persons who have had deep spiritual experiences during an NDE often move *away* from mainstream religion after their recovery rather than toward it. As one student told me, "Once you've tasted the real thing, you can't stand the imitation." This was the case for the following student, a middle aged woman who gave me this short account of a spiritual experience she had had many years before.

In the early 70s I was sitting in a church service when, suddenly a brilliant light captured my focus; warmth and tingling went through my body. I was engulfed in Love that was so powerful that I lost myself, my body, my breath. I came out of it with a feeling of overpowering love for everyone and everything. I wanted to hug the world. Nothing made any sense to me but Love. I could not tolerate watching the news, reading the news, hearing the news. I protected myself from the brutality of war and killing because to take it in caused me untold grief. I sought ways to spread Love and peace through a life of service.

Although she had had this experience in the context of attending a Catholic mass, her experience had the effect of drawing her away from the church. She continues: "I ended up leaving the church because of the atrocities which I saw being done in the name of God. The vision that burned within me was being desecrated, so much so that I got very sick."

The disparity between the purity of the love she experienced in those few minutes and the church's failure to embody that love was so great that it literally made her sick. Living inside the tension of this disparity was wreaking havoc on her body. Her doctors at the Cleveland Clinic advised her to leave her religion, and when she took her spiritual search outside the church, her health began to improve. Her journey subsequently led her in many directions, including back to college, where, like many others these days, she found part of what she was looking for in quantum physics. "When I took a physics course and learned about quantum theory, I was so deeply moved that I thought I was going to burst out of my skin." It was the scientific articulation of the underlying wholeness of life that moved her, for this is what she had experienced sitting in that church years before. "Only in the truth of this powerful quiet LOVE does what I know, what I have experienced, and who I am have meaning. Not only I, but everyone in PERFECT oneness!"

This woman wrestled with her Christianity, but many students, like the engineering student quoted earlier, frame their spiritual experiences in Christian terms, for Christianity is the dominant religious voice of our culture. Some of my students, however, have felt called to embrace Eastern forms of spirituality. The following account comes from one of these, a seasoned man who was in his forties when he wrote this description of a spiritual experience he had had a few years before in the presence of his spiritual teacher.

This nontraditionally aged student had a complex history filled with struggle and alcohol abuse as he had wrestled with his sexual identity, unable to accept himself as the gay man he was. A near-death experience was the turning point in his life. (His NDE appears in chapter 11.) Shortly after that event, he stopped abusing drugs, embraced his sexual identity, and became a licensed counselor specializing in drug dependency, helping hundreds of people lead better lives. As part of his recovery, he had taken up the practice of yoga and meditation, and this is what brought him to the feet of his guru and this experience of God in the form of the Divine Mother.

In early June of 1986 I attended a seminar at Kripalu Center in Eastern Pennsylvania. I was not prepared for this particular roller-coaster ride: I am not certain that I will ever be completely ready. On Sunday morning, the last day of the seminar, my friend Kalyani and I arrived at the outdoor pavilion at 5:15 A.M. for yoga and meditation; it was already crowded. Following practice we decided to skip breakfast so that we could move closer to the front. We managed to get within three rows of the teacher, Gurudev. (Spiritual selfishness raises its ugly head.) The weather was chilly and overcast with a storm threatening any minute. One of the senior staff started the morning chanting, and although it was nearly 7:30, it was dark as night. Kalyani and I wrapped ourselves in a blanket to keep out the chill as we chanted in Sanskrit for about a half hour.

Gurudev arrived at 8:00 along with the storm. After a short centering, our Guru started the morning *darshan* [devotional audience with one's teacher]. I am not certain when it happened. I remember that Gurudev sang softly for a short time, then hesitated for a few moments. I looked directly into his eyes and knew immediately that something out of the ordinary was happening. My Guru was completely, totally open, and a powerful flow of pure energy was connecting us at the chest. I do not know how long this lasted; I cannot be fully certain of anything that happened that morning. I was both receiver and transmitter as I watched Gurudev's normally dark countenance begin to radiate with a light golden glow.

There was a sudden flash of lightning followed immediately by a deafening burst of thunder, then the chant from our group over and over "Shiva-Shakti." The sounds emanated from somewhere deep inside my being. As I again locked my gaze on the beautiful Guru seated directly before me in a flowing white robe, gentle yet powerful hands went to the center of my chest and formed an opening, exposing the heart. I could not believe it, as slowly, imperceptibly my heart was removed and offered to me. I reached forward to receive this gift. In its place I could see the most beautiful flower I had ever seen. I turned to Kalyani who was smiling and nodding to me to take the gift of the Guru. Tears were streaming down my face as I shouted louder than any of the other seekers present, "Shiva-Shakti, Shiva-Shakti." Kalyani joined in and we sang a sacred duet to our teacher who for the moment was the Divine Mother. The power streaming from this inexhaustible source before us surrounded and pierced us as we experienced the most indescribable yoga of our lives. I knew in that instant that the Lord of Death could never have authority over me, even if this body were to die the next moment. I was eminently secure in the Divine Mother's arms and would remain secure in them eternally.

Some time later the experience started to draw to a close, and as it did the sun swept across the green valley to our left. The storm had ended. We finished the morning with the sharing of experiences and insights and 45 minutes of yoga before lunch. Then we loaded our van for the 500 mile trip back to Ohio. I was exhilarated during the long journey home as we shared our experiences over and over again. Later that night back home in my bed, thoughts of the wonderful gifts which had been given to me crowded out any possibility of sleep. I had never until this time felt so totally nurtured and loved. All through the night the subtle energy kept playing along the network of my nerve pathways.

The experience of that Sunday morning faded over the years, but the effects have not. I still feel secure in the Divine Mother's protection and know that my path is clear, even if it is sometimes steep.

All his life this thoughtful man had struggled with how to integrate the masculine and feminine sides of his person. His experience of the Divine Mother emanating from his male guru and embracing him completely was part of his reconciliation of these principles in his life. The man I met was a centered, gentle, and powerful individual, clearly at peace with himself and in service to the world. He had found his way home through an Eastern door.

Some students have shared accounts with me of spiritual experiences that seem to tap religious traditions that are not part of their current landscape at all. It is as though somewhere in their deeper history their souls have participated in these spiritual lineages. This deeper history still lives inside them, giving them a feeling for and sensitivity to these older spiritual currents.

The last story I'd like to share with you is such an account. It was written by a graceful woman in her late twenties who took two courses with me. One of them was a course in transpersonal studies that looked at research on reincarnation and certain types of nonordinary experience. After the course had ended, she sent me the following account of a pivotal experience in her life. In reading it, one cannot help noticing her obvious intelligence and the care with which she sets forth her story. One more person whose courage in confronting extreme circumstances took her where few have traveled.

At the age of 14 (1978), I fell while roller skating, injuring the lower lumbar of my spine. To relieve the pain it was the decision of my mother and an orthopedic surgeon that I have a spinal fusion done. After this surgery, I experienced more intense pain than in the months preceding the fusion. The pain was so severe that it severed the fusion, curving my spine inward to the point where my rib cage literally sat down into my pelvis. I had become a medical wonder and a social outcast all within a year. From this point forward, curious looks, derogatory remarks, and discrimination over-shadowed my life.

At the age of 22 (1986), during my 7th month of pregnancy, I had iden-tical twin girls via emergency Cesarean section. The pregnancy had taken a toll on my spine and I knew that if I did not find a way to correct the situ-ation, I would soon find myself in a wheelchair. After many months of searching, I finally found a doctor with the courage to take on my case at the University of Maryland Hospital, Dr. Charles C. Edwards [actual name]. During the initial examination I was diagnosed with grade 5 spondyloslith-esis (forward slippage of a lumbar vertebra over the one below it). Dr. Edwards informed me that it would take at least 2 to 3 surgeries to correct my spine.

At the age of 24 (1988), I submitted my spine to the knowledgeable hands of Dr. Edwards. The first surgery lasted over 22 hours and it became clear that it would take more than 3 surgeries to correct my spine. This decision finally took me through 2 years of 13 surgeries and 1 1/2 years of rehabilitation. I was opened in the back, front, and left side of my torso. I experienced intensive care, needles ranging from 14 to 22 gauge, blood transfusions, intubations, a chest tube for a collapsed left lung, drainage tubes, bile tubes, tube feedings, catheters, hickmans, decubitus ulcers, Demerol, Tylenol 3 and 4, morphine, morphine addiction, the methadone program, atrophy, hypersensitivity in both legs, loss of dorsiflection in both feet for which I now wear ankle-foot orthotics, physical and occupational therapy with their own set of torture devices, learning to walk again twice and dying twice.

This experience forced me to descend deep within myself to find the love, hope, and strength that would give my pain meaning and the ability to endure. In a sense, I had to rediscover myself to explain the etiology of my pain as a means through which my pain could be accepted and/or tran-scended.

The day after my last surgery, October, 1990, I was given the gift of a vision that would forever change the way I viewed my existence and my relation to the world:

I was lying in my hospital bed when suddenly I felt my being spiraling upwards. When my ascent came to a halt, I found myself sitting on the Earth, in the center of a circle, before a council of Native Americans. Without words they imparted to me that I AM the universe. There is no beyond, only a forgetting of this truth.

The council faded and I felt my spirit wake and a rush of warm air lifted my outstretched wings and tail feathers. I had sight so keen that I could view opposing sides while soaring on the center. I glided over weathered mountains and through lush green valleys. I inhaled air permeated with the woodsy smoke of a fire and heard the dancing bells of a victorious whirling warrior. With every perception I knew and felt quite naturally what it was like to be any of these elements. It was a feeling like I have never known and yet have known all along. I had become a hawk, a warrior, and the environment that surrounded me; one with all that was, is, or ever will be.

This most beautiful part of my vision faded and I was being pulled along on a travois. When it finally came to a halt, Native American women surrounded me singing and chanting, clipping hair from my hair, left armpit, and pubic area. They placed this hair in a pouch made of hide and inserted the pouch into my abdomen. One of the women then took my left toe between her thumb and forefinger and began swaying my foot left to right while chanting. I am not sure, but I think the body I occupied during this part of my vision was dead.

Since childhood I have always felt a deep pull to Native American traditions. Through this hospital and vision and experience, I have realized that there is no dichotomy between suffering and joy. Whenever I am graced with the sight of a soaring hawk, my mind becomes still, the hawk's spirit channels through my heart, and I am reminded of my connection to the Earth and all my relations. Because of this vision, I have followed my heart and its path, which has joyfully intersected with the paths of many with the same heart.

Since my vision, I have consumed many books about Native American traditions, history, art, etc. Through my independent research of these traditions, namely the mortuary customs of the Brule or Teton Sioux of the Lakota alliance, I have come to believe that the last part of my vision may be part of a past life experience. However, books and restrictive habits always led to a dead end; I felt there was more, but lacked the knowledge to clear the way.

When I decided to enroll at YSU, I entered with the hope of affirming this vision. I needed to know that my vision was not a mere hallucination. It was been through your classes that I have found the affirmation I was seeking and want to thank you once again for all that you have imparted.

This experience ruptures so many of our conventions that many readers may be tempted to throw up their hands. The idea of reincarnation is challenging enough, but how can someone actually experience being a hawk and seeing what a hawk sees? More radically, how can someone "become" the environment or become "one with all that was, is, or ever will be." It must have been the drugs, the skeptic in us says. She says she was always interested in Native

American lore. Perhaps she just hallucinated the entire episode under the residual influence of the anesthesia.

Some will find it easier to accept this conjecture, and that's all it is, than take her experience at face value. But her vision does not unfold like an hallucination—fluid, slippery, and fragmented. Rather, it unfolds clearly, smoothly, and elegantly. It lifts the human spirit and its effects are beneficial and long-lasting in her life. In the end, I think the clarity and majesty of her experience silence the grumbling of the critics. After a long period of suffering, a great gift was given her. The perennial cry of Oneness broke through, once again affirming the inherent wholeness of life—"I AM the universe. There is no beyond, only a forgetting of this truth."

It is not my project to argue these things here. Instead, I will simply remind the reader that many spiritual traditions have held that the experience of being one with all existence is the deepest, most satisfying experience a person can have in life. It is a rare and privileged experience, realized by few but highly valued in many cultures. If it is possible to become one with the whole of existence, then certainly merging with an individual part of existence such as a hawk would be possible. Unusual, of course, but possible. Shamanic cultures have been claiming this possibility for millennia, and contemporary explorers of nonordinary states of consciousness have reported similar experiences of fusion with other life forms.[2]

In the end, what recommends all these accounts, I think, is not their exotic features but their humble origins. These are not the experiences of elite mystics or reclusive hermits but of ordinary people, undergraduates at a modest state university. Because there is nothing unusual about my classroom, it's a safe assumption that these experiences are percolating inside all our classrooms in every state, every valley and plain. If other professors are not seeing them, they must be actively repressing them. When we give our students permission to speak their own truths, these are the kind of stories that surface.

CHAPTER 10

Conversion Experiences

Spiritual experiences come in many shapes and sizes, but there is one particular experience that is so widespread that it deserves separate attention—the conversion experience. By conversion experience, I don't mean conversion to a specific creed or faith but the experience of coming to a breaking point in one's life, and at that critical juncture being confronted with an intelligence that challenges and redirects your life. This intelligence sometimes "speaks" and people "hear" a voice. Where does this voice come from? What is its source? What theories should we invoke to explain its sudden appearance and dramatic impact on our lives?

Some would suggest that we accept the voice at face value as coming from an outside intelligence—God, an angel, or a spiritual guide. Others suggest that although the voice appears to come from without, it actually rises from a deeper within, that it comes from some hidden level of our own being, from the unconscious that surrounds our conscious awareness. This second line of thought is often hijacked by the reductive tendencies of the modern mind, leading to the dismissive conclusion that it is *"just* your mind talking to you" or *"just* a projection of your unconscious." But this conclusion pretends that we actually know the true dimensions of our consciousness, and that's not an accurate read of our intellectual landscape today. The truth is that as the twenty-first century opens, we do not have a consensus among professionals on either the scale or scope, the height, breadth, or depth of our own minds. We do not have a consensus on the boundaries of consciousness.

Many academics think of the mind as a finite entity, a private bubble of awareness surrounding our brain. Whatever wisdom the mind possesses, they say, it has compiled and synthesized this wisdom from our experience of parents, friends, relatives, books, movies, songs, and so on. It maps these experiences onto our brain and from this database it computes its best recommendations for our lives. Others, however, have suggested that our minds are not private, finite entities at all, but fields with open boundaries. For many in the consciousness community, the personal mind is a fractal phenomenon, discrete but sourced in deeper patterns of collective intelligence running throughout the fabric of the universe. From a transpersonal and integral perspective, the unconscious is a vast territory whose front door is the ego and whose back door is the mind of the Cosmos itself. If something like these far-reaching vistas is true, then the wisdom that rises from "our" unconscious could be rising not just from some hidden corner of our private mind but from some deeper psychological landscape, perhaps from the Ground of Being itself.

Perhaps we cannot at present say exactly where this voice comes from, but it is clear that in times of deep personal crisis, some people have found themselves being addressed by an intelligence, a consciousness, a knowing that is larger, more insightful, and wiser than their conscious personality. Contact with this intelligence some-times splits them open to their core and triggers a turning point in their lives. Those who have had this experience often report that what they encountered was "bigger" than they were, more potent, more full of knowledge. To name it they often use the categories available to them from their cultural backgrounds, but collectively these terms point to something that has the capacity and the right to speak defin-itively to them about their lives. More than what is said, it is often the experiential contact with this intelligence that means the most to them. It is not words that drive the conversion experience, but communion.

The following three stories that follow all come from men who did tours of duty in various branches of the military. The first two were ex-marines and the third, if my memory serves me correctly, had served in the navy. They never met because they were in different courses in different years, and none of them ever discussed in class what they wrote about in these essays.

The first student looked to be in his late twenties and still carried the physical conditioning of his military training. He was a good-looking fellow with an outgoing personality. He had been in sales at one time and you could see why. Words came easily to him. When he spoke in class, he spoke with enthusiasm. But more than words, he was a natural leader. Extravert by nature, he lived life by engaging it. It didn't surprise me to learn that he had risen to the top of whatever he had tried. But then in the middle of his success, he had gotten lost and had to find himself at a deeper level. Here's his account of the turning point of his life.

This chapter and this part of the course have helped me understand myself and the world much better than before. Many of my life experiences were explained to me. Approximately four years ago I had an extraordinary spiritual experience that I would like to share with you.

About two years after my near death episode and shortly after leaving the service, I was working as a car salesman in northern Virginia. I was making exceptionally good money too! I owned two new cars, my own townhouse, and all the money I could spend; and hundreds of folks around to manipulate. At that time I was seeing people as objects and not as subjects. I was one of the most miserable people in the world.

To complicate things, I was chemically dependent on alcohol and cocaine. I didn't know I was an addict at the time. I thought it was just something I did.

Finally the drugs got to me and I lost my job. I sold one of my cars, gave the other to my mom and dad and locked myself into my townhouse for three months to figure out the cause of my unhappiness. I walked everywhere I went and began to read for the first time in my life.

Somehow I became very interested in astrology. I began reading books about it. From my Christian background I was fighting the idea of astrology being evil. Then I began to question everything. Eventually I realized that what astrology did for me was to introduce me to the universe and to my "self."

Next I read a book entitled *How I Raised Myself from Failure to Success in Selling*. This book introduced me to the concept of cause and effect (karma) and my life began to change. I realized that I was not going to be able to understand the universe and its laws unless I read more and sought its knowledge.

I started to keep a journal. I carried it with me everywhere. Every time I noticed a significant event or thought, I wrote it down.

One special night, November 24, 1983, something happened. I was reading (just got a chill) in Revelations and I felt God was talking directly to me. It was overpowering. His, hers, or its presence was overpowering. I hid my cigarettes in the bottom of the wastebasket. I was *terrified*. I was afraid to read more but I had to! I had read the first few chapters of Revelations and I got to the part about being called, accepting this call, and there was something about "and they (the saints) were all looking down on me." I was very ashamed of my life and I could only put my head down to cry. Crying was something I never did. The verses went on to say something about taking in the words and they would make me sick. They did. The feelings went from emotional sadness to physical sickness. Terrible nausea.

What was significant about the event was that I was compelled to write down what I felt God was saying to me. I found out that I was living in a fog. A fog created by the dogmas of society, a fog spawned of ignorance. I learned that the fog was very thick and the road would be long and rocky if I wanted to get to the other side of the fog bank. I was given a choice at that time to either stay in the fog or to follow a path that would be revealed to me as I went along.

I realized that power, money and prestige were not working for me. I had experienced power as a sergeant in the Marine Corps, money from the car business and was looked up to by my peers. I became a sergeant at 19 years of age after being in the corps only two years. I was an instructor with awards for outstanding classes. I had won several sales awards, trips to Mexico, Atlantic City, and so on. I had money, women, cars, everything but peace.

I chose the path.

It was at this point that I started to notice synchronistic events and things began to stick out that I hadn't noticed before.

Whatever was on my mind, answers would appear out of nowhere. TV, radio, conversations suddenly became significant. Picking up a book I had never seen before, opening to some page in the middle and, bingo, another question answered and another arrow pointing to a turn.

I began seeing God in everything, people, plants, animals, trash cans, clouds, dirt, wind, rain, sunshine.

When I was low on money I would suddenly turn into a store, buy an instant lottery ticket and fifty dollars was there.

I began to change the way I treated all life. I respected everything. I forgave people and became someone with an understanding and direction in life.

Events are still happening the same way. For example, about six months ago, the idea of reincarnation began popping up. Then your classes [that addressed reincarnation]. Last semester I went to the free yoga classes at the Women's Center. Now I practice at home. I read books and listen to tapes on how to still the mind.

I've been to counselors, read many self-help books and listened to hundreds of tapes. People give me books or I find them on the ground.

Education seemed to be important at the beginning of the journey, but that changed to knowledge.

I have begun to have a relationship with the universe that is more profound than anything I've ever experienced before.

C. G. Jung observed that when his clients came to a point in their therapy at which they made deep life-pivots, they often found themselves encountering synchronicities in their daily lives. It was as if the circumstances of their lives suddenly "came alive" in order to confirm a breakthrough they had made or to point the way ahead. In a similar manner, this ex-marine, after emptying himself and committing himself to living more cooperatively with the universe, found himself being guided by circumstances that seemed to reflect a deeper intelligence and intentionality—keeping him moving along, learning, experimenting, practicing, growing. Was he delusional, simply paying better attention, or was life actually responding to the choices he was making as if to guide him? I guess what answer we choose depends on whether we think the processes of life are themselves alive at some deeper, implicate level. Is life intelligent or not? Integrated or not? Purposive or not?

The second essay comes from an African American student who came to our university from somewhere in the South. He was a little older than the other two men, in his late thirties I'd guess. He carried himself with a noticeable poise and discipline, always sitting erect in class, and he spoke to me as though I had earned his respect simply by getting advanced degrees. He understood rank and in his mind I seemed to be the equivalent of a captain. He didn't speak much in the course, but in his journal he wrote long, lyrical essays employing a beautiful free-flowing style that reflected the oral traditions of his southern roots. Having been born and raised in the South, I shared those roots, and I loved the way he wrote—free, honest, and immediate. In one essay, he decided to tell me about the experience that changed his life.

First I would like to tell you about myself. As you probably could remember from some of the other work I turned in, even as a child I have always had the feeling that something was always missing and as I stated before I grew up in the church. Some say you was made to go to church but I believe it was a way of life. Every Sunday the family would get ready to go to church and we come back home and have Sunday dinner so it was not like making somebody go to church, it was a family tradition that we went to church. Moreover, we had a large family. I had three sisters and three brothers. We were poor but happy and out of all my brothers and sisters, I was the only one that would not commit my self to joining the church and being baptized. I just wasn't ready I guess, it wasn't time for me and I wasn't ready for it. I thank God that my mother and father did not make me or persuade me to do this.

[He describes being drafted and serving in Vietnam, narrowly missing being killed.] I returned back from Vietnam without even one scratch and knowing that so many others came back crippled, one arm, one leg, no legs, mind disordered and some came back dead. Was it just luck that I came back without a scratch or scar, without any deformities at all and in my right mind?

Anyway, when I returned back from Vietnam, my life took a serious change. I found that I had become quite a drinker and my drinking grew larger and larger but I would not get drunk to a point that I did not know who I was or what I was doing and I could not walk straight. It look like I would get to a point of drunkenness and then get sober and then go right back into the stage of drunkenness again. Needless to say this had a tremendous effect on my marriage. We had quite a bit of marriage problems and I did not realize it at the time but when a person drinks he imagines a lot of things, he hallucinates, he believes in things that are not really there. I went a long ways after that never realizing what the real problem was, then finally I ended up getting a divorce.

I ended up in despair, ended up lost. Then nothing, no one cared, no one had any remorse for me, no love for me at all, not even my mother and father. It seemed like I couldn't even see the love they had for me at all. To be in a condition where you feel that no one cares, no one loves you is an awful state to be in.

Anyhow, at this point of depression in my life, I remember so clearly that I was in a club as usual and had been drinking quite a bit. At the clubs down where I was at in Texas, you brought your bottle into the club and all you had to do was buy your ice and pop, whatever you wanted to go with it and this got to be an everyday thing for me. So one night after I went to the club and I drunk and danced and laughed and talked and as I was getting ready to go home. I remember it was a Saturday night and the moon was shining bright. I said before I go home I was going to go across the border to a little town in old New Mexico and buy me two more bottles and I will go to the barracks and go to sleep and then the next day I would do the same thing all over again, but when I left from Texas and went to New Mexico which was only seven miles away, on my way back that's where the experience started.

As I started from the little town in New Mexico to El Paso making my way back to the west side of Texas, I stopped at a red light and something began to talk to me. The reason I say something is because no one else was in the car with me. But it so happened that at this red light there was a little white church on the right side. I happened to glance at it and what made it catch my eye was the moon was full and the church was painted white and it kind of had a glow to it and I said, Oh, what kind of building is this? Then I looked and there was a sign and it said Unity Missionary Baptist Church and at the church is where I stopped looking at the light and that's when the talking began and it said, Boy, when was the last time you been to church? And I said, It's been a long time and there's the same old thing in church, there's nothing happening there, people fantasizing and believing in this and believing in that. But then that's when it said, You know, all the problems you got, maybe that's why, and then, Maybe there is something more to that. Then it said—Go to church tomorrow! Simple as that, so I said, Okay, good idea.

Now I know that I must have been sitting there a long time, because the light had been red and when I looked up it was still red, it seemed like this person had been talking to me for a long time. Oh, it was like time didn't exist, not my thoughts and things around me. I had to look back and it felt like to me if I had been there fifteen or twenty minutes but obviously it couldn't have been that long, and of course I said this was real late at night so there was no traffic at all

I went to the barracks and went to bed. I took a shower and got dressed remembering that thought, out of all the drinking I had been doing, that thought stayed with me. When I first got up in the morning my first thought was I must go to church, so I got dressed and I made my way to church.

But I was scared to enter in. So I pulled up in a public parking lot and I said I will wait to see who goes in there. Will it be black or white, Mexican or what. Then I said, if it's a white church, I going ahead about my business because I know I had no business in a white church. And if it was a Mexican church or any other, the same thing goes. By the time all these thoughts ran in my mind, a little elderly woman came down the street and went into the church. She was a black lady but that still didn't satisfy me. I thought to myself that I would go and come back next week. So I started the car and went to pull off, but I had to hit the brakes because of some rocks and a ditch in the parking lot. And when I hit the brakes, the two bottles of whiskey that I had brought back from old Mexico rolled from underneath the seat of the car.

Then something told me even more to go ahead to the club and have a good time and go to church next Sunday. And as I drove out of the parking lot this voice that had spoken to me the night before came and said, You better go to church today. It was something about that voice, something so rightness about it. By this time I was out of the parking lot and on the way down the street so I had to turn around and come back to the parking lot. There I was parked in the parking lot scared to go into the church. Not just scared to go in but scared to get out of the car. At this point in time there was no voice to help me, should I go or should I stay. But when I thought of that voice, that rightness in the voice, I went in the church. Still scared but I had to go.

When I entered the church I sat on the last row. I was so scared that I couldn't make it any further if I wanted to. While the order of service was going on, the singing and the praying, I got a sensational good feeling, a feeling that I had known before, a feeling that I had missed and longed for, a feeling of peace, a peacefulness that consumed me. It just took over. And as the service went on the preacher came and started preaching, and his subject was divorce and what he was saying seemed like he was looking just at me. I know he was right, how I don't know, but I know he was. It hurt but he was right, the words that he read from the Bible drew me and pulled at me. I wanted to cry and laugh at the same time. The words cutting and hurting but yet that peaceful feeling that I was lost but have found my way, like I had been on a trip for a long time and now I was back home. I joined the church and began to read the Bible and my life has not been the same.

In a postscript to his story, he mentions one later occasion when the voice spoke to him again.

As I continued with going to church reading my Bible and prayer, I found that I seemed to be so close to God. And I didn't want anything to come between me and him. Not even my family who I love. I found myself drawing away from my family, they seemed to be so much in with the things I no longer wanted to be part of. Like rock and role, jazz, television. Something had took me away from that and it was beginning to cause more problems in my home. That is when that voice came to me again and told me he did not call me to leave my family. To this I thank God and began to take some time out with my family. Now my family has a love that we never had before. The same one that drew me also drew my family to a greater understanding.

What force interrupted this man's life? What set of circumstances conspired to bring him to his knees and reverse his deeply entrenched, self-destructive habits? Clearly, the man in my class was not the drunkard described here. Instead, he was a balanced, grounded, modest, and sincere man set on improving his life. The voice that turned his life around spoke to him in his own idiom, tuned to his circumstances and dialect, and it seemed to possess an authority and foresight that dwarfed his conscious personality.

Do we find it strange that this voice of authority would speak to this man in a black idiom? Does this confirm the skeptic's opinion that this man was simply speaking to himself? Perhaps. But did this familiar way of speaking dilute the impact that the voice had on his life or diminish the wisdom it conveyed or the fortuitous circumstances of timing and place? Besides, why not speak in a southern black idiom to a southern black man? How would we expect the "voice of God," the voice of a higher wisdom, to sound like to this man—like a scholarly English don? If there is a larger intelligence saturating life, an intelligence that sometimes rises to address us in times of crisis, would it not take the form appropriate to the person it is addressing, "speaking" Polish to the Poles, Ukrainian to the Ukraines, and French to the French? Could it be any other way?

The last essay comes from another African American man who also served in the military. He passed through two of my courses near the end of his college career en route to divinity school. He was a tall, well-dressed, and carefully groomed man in his late twenties. He wanted to be a pastor. I don't know whether he fulfilled that goal, but I hope he did because he had something to give.

People experience conversion in different settings. His conversion took place in the middle of a carefully planned and consciously chosen attempted suicide. For that reason, it skirts the edge of being a near-death episode. Though he alluded to this experience during the course, it was not until after the course had ended that he sent me the following account of the experience that had turned his life around.

In August of 1997 [6 years prior] I was very depressed. For almost 6 months prior to August I contemplated suicide on almost an everyday basis. At the beginning of the month I decided that I was going to go ahead with my decision. I felt that there was no reason for me to be here (on earth) any more. In my decision process I decided that I would give myself a month because there was only one thing that I wanted to do before I went and it would probably take about a month's time to do it. What I wanted to do is spend time with everyone that I truly loved before I died. I guess I figured if I was not ever going to have the opportunity to see them again, I wanted them to have peace of mind and know beyond a shadow of a doubt that I loved them.

During this time I kept a personal journal on the events of each day. I think one of the reasons I kept this journal was to see if things were getting better so that I could change my mind about my decision that only I was aware of. Yet, August proceeded to go on in the same manner, maybe even worse than the prior six months.

Finally, August 30, 1997 came and I was sure that I was going to go through with my decision. Most of the day I spent at home alone. In the evening I went out and visited some of my family members and close friends at the time. At around 2 A.M. I picked up my brother and we rode to the gas station. I filled up my gas tank and drove home. I told my brother to go in the house, that I would be in later, that I was going to listen to a couple of CD's of mine. He went in the house and I pulled into the garage.

After seven months or so of contemplation, the time had finally come. I thought that inevitably this would be my end, but it became the end that begins for me.

As I sat there I felt myself getting very tired. I knew that I was leaving this earth. I didn't feel any pain or anything. It just felt like I was going to sleep. Then I heard a voice that said, *"Worship Me."* I tried to ignore the voice although it was very apparent that the voice was there. The more I tried to ignore the voice the louder it got. Finally, I listened to the voice and began to worship God. I had never had an experience like this before and I can't say that I have heard a voice like that before, but I knew that it was God. The voice never identified itself as such. Yet, it was confirmed in every fiber of my being that the voice that was commanding me to worship Him was God.

As I began to worship God I saw a bright light. The light was not around me, the light was in me. Words can't describe this and years later I know that I am giving this story no more justice verbally than I would have been able to in 1997. All I know is that in the light I saw what I could best describe as a movie.

The movie was very fast, it didn't slow up at any part. If you could imagine watching a movie that you have never seen on your DVD while it was being fast-forwarded. Although it was very fast, I recognized every part. The reason I recognized every part was because it was my life. I saw every situation that ever had happened in my life up to that point in a matter of seconds. I can't say that I could feel how I felt or how other's felt in the movie like some of the NDEers have stated. Yet, I can say that I can remember clearer the parts of the movie that were bad parts of my life.

Then the movie went forward in time and I saw myself in places that I had never been before doing things that I would never have imagined myself doing. Then all of a sudden the voice said, *"The reason I let you go through all these things was so you could become the person I purposed you to be."* Instantly, I had peace about every situation that had ever happened to me that was less than desirable and even the situations that had led up to the decision I had contemplated for many months.

I never learned what string of circumstances had pushed this young man past his breaking point, but the person I met was centered, eager to learn, and going somewhere positive. I did not feel one ounce of proselytizer in him; instead, his experience of being touched by something "higher" just when he had completely given up on life seemed to have left him a humble man. Readers who are familiar with the literature on near-death episodes (NDEs) will recognize some common features in his account. Often NDEers encounter a bright light and experience a life review. Though it is rarer, some NDEers also experience a life preview as this young man did, a glimpse into what lies ahead for them if they choose to continue their present life. Another theme shared with NDEers is the experience of being completely reconciled with his past and the peace that flowed into him as a result of that reconciliation.

Each of these young men experienced an intervention in their lives that occurred in the middle of a personal crisis. And yet, if there is a wisdom that rises from our depths to guide us in moments of extreme crisis, isn't it likely that this same intelligence is also trying to get our attention in the ordinary workings of our day-to-day lives? Is it that the voice comes and goes or is it that we are only sometimes paying enough attention to hear it? If we were to give this inner wisdom more attention every day, we would likely get off track less often and require fewer dramatic interventions. We might even live in a state of perpetual joy, transparent to the great mystery that everywhere surrounds us, in continual communion with the Cosmos and always rooted in our true purpose for being here. The words of Rumi come to mind:

Human beings come into this world to do particular work.
That work is their purpose, and each is specific to the person.
If you forget everything else and not this, there's nothing to
    worry about.
If you remember everything else and forget your true work,
    then you will have done nothing in your life.

CHAPTER 11

Touched by Death

Through the years, I've received more stories from my students about death than any other single subject. Death touches all our lives. Many of my students have lost family members or friends; some have brushed up against death themselves. It's the universal encounter, the one truth that frames all other truths—everyone dies. And yet death is infrequently discussed in our college curriculum. A course here or there, but for the most part silence. You would think that, given how universal death is, we would pay it more attention, but not so. It is as though given the materialist worldview that dominates higher education today, we simply cannot bear to look at death for very long. For if it's true that when our bodies fail we vanish without a trace, then life is more pointless and unfair and cruel than we can stand to face for more than a few minutes at a time.

And yet, when we place several bodies of research side by side, a very different picture of death emerges. I am thinking here of research on people who nearly die (NDEs),[1] on those who approach their impending death consciously,[2] on reincarnation,[3] and on nonordinary states of awareness in which persons get glimpses of a world that appears to lie beyond space-time reality.[4] Taken as a whole, this body of evidence strongly suggests that we live in a universe in which death is *not* the final end, but a portal in a much larger trajectory of living.

You would think that a convergence of professional opinion bearing such good news would be welcomed by academics, but sadly most don't pay it any attention at all. It's considered "fringe stuff" not to be taken seriously. It simply does not get on their radar. I am continually amazed by the ease with which faculty who pride themselves on being critical thinkers brush aside research that provides strong evidence that death is not the end of one's conscious experience. Here one sees the pervasive and, in this case, corrupting influence of cultural paradigms that shape our perceptions of what is and is not possible, what counts as evidence and what doesn't. Our current materialist paradigm doesn't allow for survival of death except as a statement of faith. Our success in parsing and manipulating the physical universe has conned us into believing that matter is all that exists, the rest is illusion. But what rubbish this is. When science has proven nothing of the sort, why have so many intelligent people been hoodwinked into thinking it has?

It is not only our research but the voice of the people that keeps telling us that death is not the end but a transition in a much larger cycle of living. Because death is a universal constant in life, many students are carrying stories about death—unusual things that happened around someone's death, changes in a family member after a near-death experience, contact with relatives who have died, a loved one's spiritual opening as death approached. As you can imagine, these kinds of stories don't go over particularly well on campus where the general consensus is that no one can *really* know what happens after death. If students share these stories with their professors, they run the risk of being seen as uncritical, naïve, or gullible. And so, as with their spiritual experiences, students learn to chest their cards and keep quiet about these things.

Because I teach a course that takes a critical but open-minded approach to death and what lies beyond, I've collected quite a few such stories. I share a few of them here not to try to prove anything about the survival of death, for that would require a much more rigorous analysis best left to another time and place. I share them simply to honor the unofficial stories that continue to percolate in everyday life underneath the official academic story that our minds are generated by our brains and are destined to disappear as soon as our brains stop functioning.

The first story comes from a middle-aged man who was previously introduced in chapter 9. He was a gentle soul who had been anything but gentle when he was younger. Time and life had seasoned him, however, and when he showed up in my class, he had transformed himself into a much respected therapist in the community. The night he nearly drowned was the turning point in his life's journey. The following account was written ten years after the event.

It was the summer of 1980, a warm night and I can't sleep. I remember walking out onto the causeway which crosses the lake near my summer cottage. I lift my foot to cross the safety cable and catch the toe of my sandal on the cable. Over and over I go, thirty-five feet down the rock embankment. I can feel every rock as I tumble to the water, then nothing. All that I notice is the presence of something large and living surrounding me, and I am peaceful. I can see blurry pictures of me as a child in my room; it is storming and I am afraid of the lightning; then again the presence of this living thing all around me and I am not afraid.

There are more scenes but they aren't always clear, and I wonder where I am. I realize I am dead. I know that I am lying on the bottom of the Pymatuning Lake and the moon is shining through the surface of the water above me, and it is beautiful. There is the sound, this music like the wind blowing through the strings of an instrument, it is coming from inside my chest. I can feel the most wonderful vibrations penetrating my entire being. I am a part of everything that has ever been or will ever be, and I am no longer separate.

Now I am in another place, I cannot describe it, it is within me and outside me at the same time. I have come home, I have been here before. I am with someone, I know somehow that it is me I am with, I can't explain because it is not a "self" in the normal definition. I know all of this information, I think I have known it for a long time. This place is perfect, everything is beyond words. The sound, all sound, a harmony that is total, beautiful, and yet silent at the same time. There are no voices, but someone or something is giving me messages. I know I cannot stay here, all is necessary. How can I go back, I have all these answers, all this "stuff." I am not even concerned about it.

Someone is shaking me, I must be dreaming. Oh the pain! I remember I am dead. I will stay very still and I will go away again.

The next morning I was greeted upon my awakening by *pain*. I was able over the next few days, while beginning my recovery from 5 broken ribs and other less serious multiple trauma, to piece together the story of my rescue. Two fishermen had seen my fall and had come to my rescue. They told my friends at the cottage that it had taken them a long time to find my submerged body, and they were amazed that I was alive when they pulled me from the lake.

The experience of almost dying changed this man, as it has many others. It changed not only how he thought about life and what he valued, but something deeper inside him. It shifted the center he lived from. He goes on to describe those changes.

A little less than one year later I put down alcohol and drugs, they were not necessary any longer. So many of my life-long wounds had begun to heal. . . .

Today I have become content, most of the time, to allow the Universe to unfold in all its perfection. I am on a new journey, a new path. I know that we are all exactly where we are supposed to be at this moment. We have a simultaneous existence, physical and non-physical. For this place and time we need to experience a separation of the two realities. It does not matter which "side" we are currently on; we are always on the correct side. As for all the knowledge I became aware of when I was there, it is here, somewhere inside me, and I know it, but at the same time it is hidden. That is as it should be. Also, I am here; in the physical, because there are things I need to learn, and tasks I need to complete. I remain unfinished.

The next story comes from a woman in her senior year in college. In the midst of studying some of the literature on near-death episodes, she was moved to share the story of her father's death. While the previous story gives us some insight into the inner experience of (almost) dying, her story looks at death from the outside, at how it changed her father and the odd graces that surrounded his passing. She titled her story, "Things my father never told me . . . until."

In his last year of life, my father had cardiac arrest close to twelve times. One of the first times this happened, he told us about his ride to the hospital with the paramedics. He said he was lying on the stretcher and could see the men working on him, but he was watching from somewhere outside his body. He could hear the men calling him and asking him to work with him. A few months after this episode, my father was taken to the Cleveland Clinic and his first day there, he had a stroke. Again he described the same kind of phenomenon. I remember not really thinking anything of it until now, and pieces of a puzzle are falling into place.

After the first few cardiac failures, the change in my father was unreal. The major change was that my dad began to tell us how much we meant to him. Before, we knew our father loved us, but he never came right out and told us until then. He became more aware of small commonplace things, like the beauty of a sunset or a quiet (or not so quiet in my house) family meal. He started going to church, because he had found good friends there during his illness. I think he knew that the church people would be a comfort to us after his death. He laughed more, he cried more.

I don't really know what happened to my father when his heart stopped beating, but I do know that he was more comfortable with his death than we were.

The last week of my father's life was tremendously hard on all of us. Some strange things happened to me personally. I remember I had made lunch and my dad and I ate together. Suddenly my chest felt constricted. I thought it was from the heat, or allergies, so I told my dad I would be in the air conditioning lying down. I gave him a big hug and I said "I love you, Dad." He said with a smile, "I love you too, Katie." (Those were the last words I said to my dad.) I was upstairs with the chest constriction getting worse when my brother came up to tell me dad wasn't breathing. At that moment I knew this was it. Dad wouldn't be coming home again. I was 16, he was 50.

This is where the other strangeness kicks in. I always knew that I would be with my dad when he died and that he was going to die when he was fifty. It wasn't fear, it was the way things would happen. When I told people that, they thought I was more than a little crazy, but I believe it's possible now, because I realize how enmeshed we all are.

The morning my father died, his heart had stopped seven times. My family decided not to resuscitate him on the eighth time. My mother went in to see my dad at around seven o'clock. For the first time in three days, he opened his eyes, looked at her, squeezed her hand and died. He was reassuring her that death was not the end and he was finally free. Perhaps he'd already experienced what was ahead of him.

As a note to you: I hadn't remembered a lot of this until you started talking about NDE research. Then things about my dad started making sense and I was able to remember the sad things (for us the living) and the joy of my father's life. Thanks for making the puzzle come together!

Death is such a powerful event, is it surprising that it would be surrounded by intuitions, forewarnings, and synchronicities? A sense of when, the kindness of a last touch. Such things are actually quite common. People often second-guess these experiences after the event has passed because our culture tells them to, but our culture is nearly blind in these matters.

The stories my students tell about death echo many of the features reported in the research literature on NDEs—separation from the body, entering a tunnel, experiencing a life review, meeting deceased relatives, encountering a white light, even anger at the medical team who disrupted their bliss by reviving them. They often bracket their stories with disclaimers, like the young woman who said: "If anyone other than my mother would have told this story to me, I probably wouldn't have believed it, but she wasn't the type to exaggerate." When a family chooses to hold on to these stories, they become part of its family lore, a tradition of stories that will be passed along across generations. You can see this already happening in the next account, another story from a daughter about the death of her father.

The story begins in August 1983 with the death of my father. He had been ill for many months; however, in the last few weeks of his life he began to feel better and made some astonishing progress. During this time he had mentioned to my mother how in the critical stage of his illness in January 1983, while hospitalized, he had experienced a near-death episode. He recounted how he had experienced the sight of a brilliant light and how he felt a sense of peace and happiness. During this episode he knew no pain—which previously he had been experiencing in extreme proportions because of his illness. He further stated that he had seen many relatives who had preceded him in death. He especially mentioned seeing his sister, Virginia, who had just died in December, 1982. Virginia had told him that when it was his time to pass on, she would come for him. My mother never mentioned this account to anyone.

Later in August 1983, on the morning of my father's death, I had my own supernatural episode. While sleeping I felt an overwhelming sense of sorrow and began crying. I felt as if my shoulder were being shaken by my father and that he was speaking to me. (This entire perception confused me, because it was impossible for my father to approach me due to his bed-ridden condition.) I recall crying and saying out loud, "No . . . No, you can't die. No! . . . go away . . . Leave me alone! No . . . No!" All the while my father's voice kept repeating, "Good-bye . . . I love you . . . I'm going now . . ." At that, completely upset and startled, I remember sitting up in bed and feeling the strongest presence of Aunt Virginia there in my room. Just at that moment, my mother called for me to go immediately to my father's room. As I leaped from bed, I grabbed my stethoscope from the top the dresser and ran downstairs. While running down the stairway I recall thinking that I did not need my stethoscope or anything else because my father was already gone. There in his room, seeing my father's body, I realized that my perception was true.

It was not until two years later in 1985 that my mother disclosed all the information of my father's earlier near-death experience to me. Once I had this information, all the pieces of the puzzle finally fell into place.

Stories like this become teaching stories in a family that will be repeated when death draws near again. The same is true for the next story, one that a female student wrote about a vision her mother had of her deceased grandmother. The teller of the story is a traditionally aged college sophomore.

When I was in the seventh grade, my mother's mom died at the age of 83. My grandma had been sick and we anticipated her death. She had told my mother before she died that she felt she had lived a good long life. She also requested that no one mourn over her. If they cried that was okay, as long as they didn't carry on. Her outlook on death was something I'll never forget. She wasn't afraid but was ready to meet her maker with the confidence of having done his will while she lived.

About four months after she died, on the anniversary of her death, my mom remembers praying for her, as she does my other grandparents, and then going to sleep. During the night she felt someone kiss her on the cheek and assumed it was me. She opened her eyes and saw her mom standing there! My grandmother said, "Thank you for all those prayers." My mom was surprised because my grandma never spoke a word of English, just Polish. My mom said, "Ma, how beautiful you speak English." As she went to get out of bed to reach for grandma, my grandma smiled and was gone.

All aspects of death need to be honored, including the terrible sorrow that death brings. Even if death does not mean the true ending of someone's life, it does tear the fabric of relationships, separating us for a time from those we love. This sorrow cut particularly deep for the young man who wrote the following poem. Two years before, he had lost both of his parents to cancer within three months of each other.

> They've gone
> Each day you live in memories,
> You search,
> They've gone,
> Somehow, someway you must reach them.
> Old photos, memories, diaries, bills, anything to be close.
> Somehow to know them better.
> They're gone.
> Where? I don't know.
> What do I know?
> They're not with me.
> I can't talk to them. It hurts so bad.
> It's not an ache in the heart
> It's an emptiness in the mind.
> It's a hurt you don't get over.
> You just learn to live with it.
> Months, years from now.
> Something will happen
> You'll cry

Why? It still hurts.
It's confusing, frustrating, and maddening,
But above all it hurts,
Even though it hurts you search for
every bit of information about them.
What were they like.
They weren't perfect,
They made mistakes.
But you loved them
And you hurt.
Just to know more about them and their lives.
It hurts but still you feel better
somehow,
When you know more about them.
It hurts you.
But at least you learn
Why you loved them so much.
Maybe then the hurt will be worth it.
I don't know.
I still miss them
and it still hurts.

There is no blunting the edge of this young man's suffering. "It's a hurt you don't get over. You just learn to live with it." And yet, when death is placed in the larger context of a universe in which life changes but is never extinguished, surely it helps.

I wish I could describe better the flavor of the author of the next story. She was an older student who came into the course through the university's 60+ program that allows seniors to sit in on classes on a space-available basis. She was a no-nonsense woman with a wonderful sense of humor who would never mind my mentioning her age, which she never tried to hide, letting her hair grey naturally for all to see. With piercing eyes, and sharp features, she carried herself with a grace and elegance that seemed to come from an earlier time. Although under no obligation to write any of the papers for the course, she always did, with a prose that reflected a lifetime of prac- tice. And so it was in a course in transpersonal psychology that she came to write the story of the death of her son.

The first-born, how many wonders of the world can there be? He unleashed in me all at once a terror and a love unlike anything I had ever known. The terror subsided as I learned that he will keep breathing even when I look away. I had four children and they opened up dimensions of my soul that no other experience could. I became aware that through them I would learn the life lessons I was back in the "earth school" to learn. I should say the major "life lessons" of joy and tragedy, because one learns so much from every day and every encounter and every one.

David was my second child. There were differences that I attributed to my experience, but there was one all encompassing difference that I became aware of when he was still an infant. David was an old soul, or as I called it, a wise soul, one that had seen it all. Souls don't grow old, or do they?

When David received his first shot, he baffled the pediatrician with total indifference, not even a whimper. I was to witness this behavior through several tough athletic injuries, and once when both the surgeon and I asked if he did not feel the pain, he answered, "I feel it but it does not matter." What do you do with a kid like this? Most young people will gladly sit-in, march, or talk about compassion but no sacrifices please. This child rarely talked but he was well-known at the YMCA and the school for the handicapped. He worked at every menial job he could lay his hands on. He supported a child in the Philippines through the Children's Christian Fund, without our knowledge.

This child knew no strangers. His heart was as open as his hand. His humor and his athletic abilities as well as the girls kept him very normal and well removed from sainthood. Around his first birthday, I hugged him wildly and said that I wished every mother could have one just like him. I repeated that wish in a letter to him on his twentieth birthday, and it was as sincere as the first time. Four days later, we received a phone call from him. He had leukemia. Five months later, on March 3, 1978, David died.

With that phone call, the purification of my soul began. There are no words to describe my agony. I sat alone in a dark room one night and waited for the presence of God. I asked Him to cure David and the answer was, "No, I will not cure David, but I will heal David." I knew that a cure would only postpone what my soul had to experience, but the healing would erase the intense longing that I so often saw in David's eyes. It was five months of sheer hell for our family.

I would write pages of episodes in David's life that confirmed over and over my awareness that, as we sometimes kidded, he was from another planet. I am forever thankful for the bond and the deep communication that existed between us, rarely in an exchange of words. It was just there.

In David, shock at the diagnosis dissipated into a calm acceptance of the prognosis. Never "Why me?" but once "Why does one get leukemia?"

and no one could answer him. If I was drowning in a bottomless pit, my spirit also frequently soared in David's presence. He was in and out of the hospital and I never left it, unless he could. We were all on an accelerated life course, but he and I were more so. My sixth sense sharpened to sustain us both in bad moments. For example, he fell in the bathroom, looked at me tearfully and said, "I cannot walk anymore, Reinette." (He had a way of using my first name when he was deeply touched.) "You will walk again, David," I answered and in that moment I knew that we both knew that we would experience such a time. I knew from the beginning that I would be alone with him when he left. We sustained him but he nurtured our souls then and now. He drew friends to us in a strange town. When I thanked one couple afterwards, they answered, "We are the ones who are thankful that we met Dave."

The night David died, he refused all medication and further treatments. The physician assured him that he would die soon. For one brief moment he reached for me and uttered, "Mom, please help me! I don't want to die!" It was my final glimpse at us in the mother and child roles. I assured him, and we both believed, that his father was on his way to take us home. The medical staff gathered around his bed. A nurse sang a spiritual in a tremulous voice. Close to his ear, I reminisced about our happy times with a calm and peace inside me that belied the five months we had just completed. There was joy, even laughter from the staff when I reminded him of his birthday parties, when he was supposed to invite only his closest friends and we ended up with kids hanging from every branch in the backyard! Later one of the staff said that if there is such a thing as a beautiful death, she witnessed it that night. I have never witnessed a death before, but that night I was in the presence of the Holy.

When David drew his last breath, everyone left the room and we were, as at the beginning of his life, mother and child. I could only repeat his name over and over while giving into the tears that I could no longer control and then the most sublime experience followed. I saw David leave the body on the bed. He surrounded me and I was comforted in a way that defies description. Our roles were reversed. He was the father and I was the child. He was healed and my deepest pain was only beginning. He was now face to face and I was still looking through a glass darkly. In that moment he also reassured me that my pain was real but that it did not really matter. I sensed a detachment from me but not indifference and then he left the room. It was in the early hours of a new day and from that bed where I sat I was aware of him striding through the hospital in his blue jeans and ski-jacket and out the front door. He was walking again and we both knew it! We both smiled.

Out the door and gone, but not forever. Reinette was sure she would see David again. Souls like David's don't pop into existence from nowhere, she thought, or disappear simply because the body poops out. They are crafted in the womb of history, polished in the trials and joys of many lifetimes of learning. If some souls are old, then some relationships are also old, steeped in centuries of contact. She felt that her relationship with David was like that. Not begun in this lifetime nor ended here, only continued, deepened. Another chapter added to a much larger story.

The last story I'd like to share with you continues this theme. It is not about dying but the return from death—rebirth and the continuing cycle of life. It's about the deathless soul and the marks of age that parents sometimes see etched in their children, signs that they have been here before. Like strands of DNA, our minds store maximum information in minimum space. When we look into the eyes of our children, we can sometimes see time and experience folded up and compressed inside them, as this mother did when she gazed at her daughter.

This account comes from a tall, middle-aged, jovial woman. If you saw her at the supermarket, you would never suspect that she harbored such unorthodox ideas as reincarnation. She is one of the invisible 25 percent of Americans whom Gallup polls say believe in rebirth. Reincarnation had not been part of her family's beliefs, nor was it endorsed by her religion. It was something she came to on her own, and it was her experience with her daughter that pushed her in this direction.

From the day my daughter was born she was different. I could never put my finger on what I felt but as she grew from infancy through the stages of childhood, family and friends also saw and often commented on her being different. She seemed wise beyond her years.

One confirmation to me of her rebirth was one evening when her father told her to pick up her toys and she told him "No." The third time he told her, she questioned "Why?" By this time he was frustrated and told her in no uncertain terms because he said so and that she would do what he told her because he was her father. Her response was "Only in this lifetime." She was approximately 3 1/2 years old when that clue occurred.

I always felt my daughter knew something that others did not know and those feelings were confirmed many times in her childhood. [*Here she gives an example that is too complicated to reproduce concerning some unusual names her daughter had for her grandparents.*] The last time my daughter gave any clue to her rebirth was when she was approximately 11 years old. At that time I was going through divorce proceedings and I was reassuring her that even though her parents were separating, we loved her and if we had not been married she would never have been born. She emphatically told me that we had nothing to do with her being born. She told me it was time for her to be born and if she had not been born to us, someone else would have been lucky enough to be her parents.

My daughter is now 17 and still wise beyond her years. The majority of the time she is just a normal teenager, but when I least expect it, her old soul shines through.

The cycle of life in which death is eventually followed by rebirth does not mean there is no heaven, but it dramatically expands our vision of the scale and scope of the enterprise we are part of. Just as our estimate of the age and size of the universe expanded exponentially in the twentieth century, our estimate of the age and depth of the soul seems destined to expand exponentially in the twenty-first. Why would we think that an Intelligence that is willing to invest four billion years developing a planet would spend only a hundred years perfecting a soul? In the vision of death that is emerging from research on the one hand and everyday experience on the other, death is a doorway back to the Mother Universe, a passage to rest, rejuvenation, and reunion, a cause of celebration and joy. It is also a portal in the larger cycle of the soul's journey.[5]

CHAPTER 12

Personal Discoveries

The last set of stories I'd like to share with you are four jewels that students have shared with me about personal discoveries they have made in their lives. While not as dramatic as some of the stories that involve death, out-of-body experiences, or sudden conversions, each of these stories reflects a hard-won insight, something that the student had wrestled with in life. Not exactly statements of faith, these are more statements of discovery, something they've learned from life and now hold as important truths. Commentary is redundant. All that is required is setting.

There is enormous pressure on students today to think of college as primarily career training. The more technologically advanced the workplace has become, the more colleges must prove their worth by producing employable students, so much so that the classical view of college as a time of intellectual exploration has been surrendered by many students. This trend is particularly strong in communities that have been hurt by our changing economy, as where I teach. The list of courses required for majors in technical fields get longer while distribution requirements that have traditionally ensured intellectual breadth shrink, often under the guise of "strengthening the core curriculum." Times are hard, good jobs are getting more difficult to find, and the students know it.

And yet college still remains a treasure trove of new opportunities for the adventuresome student who is willing to buck this trend. Even in our challenging economic environment, some students still take the risk of putting their education first. Some have seen the price that their friends have paid for success in careers that were chosen primarily because they paid well. Or perhaps they've experienced the early symptoms of this disease in their own lives. This was the case for the student who gave me this first story, a woman who came back to college in her late twenties. Responding to a lecture outlining the different spiritual paths in Hinduism, she described her own search for a spiritually fulfilling career. She titled her essay "Following My Bliss."

I can relate this philosophy to the decisions I have made in my own life.

For the past nine years I have been working in a factory, earning good money and benefits. I gradually became dissatisfied with my life, with my basic goals being making money. Eventually I started college, majoring in computer technology for the purpose of getting a better job. After a while I became dissatisfied with my studies, and my goal of getting out of the factory was just not enough. I didn't really like computers and had to push myself to continue. I finally decided I had made a wrong choice and quit school.

After much contemplation I started back to school, this time doing something because it is what I truly love—majoring in Art. I have no idea yet what, if anything, I will do with a Bachelor of Fine Arts degree. My goal now is to learn all I can and develop a talent I am still discovering.

I have never been so sure of any decision I have ever made in my life as I am of this one. I have gone beyond searching for job satisfaction and monetary rewards to bringing out something that is coming from deep within me. A new kind of faith is evolving within me that I don't yet understand. I am looking deeper and deeper within myself and discovering a me that I never knew existed, finding qualities I never knew I had. I have suddenly turned my attention inward and am looking at myself with a whole new perspective.

This Hindu philosophy is helping me to understand better what I am experiencing and encourages me to continue these explorations into myself.

As I was working on this book, I wondered whether the gamble this woman had taken had paid off for her in the long run. Did she still feel as enthusiastic about her decision as she had when she was an undergraduate? I usually remove the names of the students from their essays, but hers I happened to still have, so, with the help of the university alumni office, I tracked her down. I sent her a copy of her original essay, and asked how her gamble had turned out and whether she ever regretted her decision. She answered with a long letter that answered my question and added new layers to her story. Teaching is an act of faith. One seldom sees where the ideas we share with our students go or what they do with them. It was gratifying to learn that our time together had served her well.

Reading the essay brought back the memories and feelings of that transitional period of my life. My father died in May of 1985, and I took my first class with you the following spring. The timing for me could not have been better, with my emotions still so close to the surface because of the grief I was still experiencing at losing my Dad. You introduced me to a philosophy that was very new to me. Before taking your class I knew very little of any other religion other than Christianity, and most of what I did know was highly distorted. Even the information you presented on Christianity clarified so many things for me—so much more than 12 years of Catholic school ever did! What I learned in your classes has stayed with me all these years and has evolved into a very private and unique spirituality.

I never regretted my decision to choose fine arts as my major. Although it never materialized into a career for me, it served as an important stepping stone for many of the choices I have made since. I came to Alaska on vacation in 1989 and fell madly in love with this place. I knew then that I had found a place where I belonged. Shortly after I graduated from YSU in 1992, I moved here. I am still in awe of the beauty around me, even after 13 years.

She has stayed gainfully employed all this time and her college exposure to different faiths has helped deepen her relationship with her partner, an Alaskan Tlingit native who follows the religion of his father, a Russian Orthodox priest. "We have both learned so much about our religious and cultural differences in the last 12 years," she added. "Our relationship could not have survived without recognizing and respecting those differences."

The second jewel comes from a young man in his early twenties who took a course on Eastern religions with me many years ago. During the course he wrote an essay in which he described the spiritual journey he had been on for almost ten years, an odyssey that had led him to explore meditation deeply. Without the help of a spiritual teacher, he had pushed ahead on his own. His story is a reminder of the treasures that lie inside each of us if we will simply take time to look within.

His spiritual awakening began when he was thirteen years old. He had a spontaneous out-of-body (OBE) experience as he was going to sleep one night. His detailed description of the sensation of separating from his body, floating toward the ceiling, seeing himself lying on the bed below, and the sudden jolt of reentry into his body left little doubt—he had had a genuine OBE. This jarring experience led him to begin asking questions of his friends, teachers, and relatives. Some told him it was just a dream, but his brother believed him and sent him to the library where he discovered accounts of people who had had similar experiences. One book led to another and he became a seeker, devouring many books on spirituality, Eastern religions, and meditation. He began to practice meditation diligently, using books as his guide. In time his practice matured, and he began to understand that meditation was not just a psychological technique but a lifestyle that required discipline and devotion. As his practice continued to deepen, his mind relaxed and he began to enter increasingly subtle states of awareness.

He concluded his essay by trying to put into words the most personally meaningful insights that had surfaced in his meditation practice. His commentary may sound somewhat enigmatic to nonmeditators, for he is trying to describe states of consciousness in which the usual distinction between self and other is dissolving into an encompassing non-dual expansiveness. He gives voice to the splendor of a Oneness that contains everything that exists, including all the levels and dimensions there are to existence. This is his statement of discovery, a statement so original that it surely reflects his own experience. He called it "Going beyond 'It'."

I learned that to transcend this world one must be able to leave it as it is. That is, one must be willing to accept all as "It" is in order to go beyond "It."

But what do you find when you go beyond "It"?
Well, if "It" is all there is, then even to go beyond "It"
is only to find more of "It."
So "It" is something that can never be comprehended.
"It" is fluid.
"It" fills any and every shape.
"It" is the formless form we all realize exists
yet feel so overwhelmed by "Its" nature that we feel
insignificant in "Its" shadow.
But we need only realize that we are part of "It."

Then we know that "It" is ourselves.
WE CHOOSE LIFE!
All that you want to be, you will be, in the end.

Everything you want to know you will know because you
  choose to know.

Your perception of life is directly related to your degree of
  experience of life.
The more experience, the broader your perception.
Your openness to the situation determines how much you
  learn from the situation.
The more you learn, the more you understand.
The more you understand, the more at ease you are.
The more at ease you are, *THE EASIER IT IS FOR YOU TO
  ACCEPT "IT" ALL.*
Then "It" reveals more of Itself to you.

The third jewel comes from a student in his early thirties who took
a course on Eastern religions with me many years ago. It was summer
and campus was in bloom when he wrote an essay in which he
summarized his personal beliefs. Many students have done something
like this, but this student's statement struck me as a particularly clear
and poignant description of a critical challenge that the entire human
family is facing in this century.

For tens of thousands of years, our greatest cultural heroes have
been those who have been willing to fight and die (and kill) for their
country. The legacy of military valor runs deep in our collective
psyche and is continually reinforced by our movies, books, and
national holidays. And yet military technology has now taken
humanity into new territory, producing weapons so destructive that
we will lose everything worth fighting for if we dare use them. This
new fact of life, which we are all trying to absorb, is driving us to find
a new definition of heroic valor and a deeper understanding of the
values that guide our lives. This was certainly true for this student.
Having incorporated reincarnation into his thinking before he came
into the course, he saw this historical drama being acted out in the
very center of his soul. He titled his essay "The Eternal Warrior."

A belief system is something that is hard for me to put into words. I know
what I have come to believe through years of reading and evaluating other
people's work, but I have never collected these thoughts into one organized belief system. I know that I believe in a higher being that "is" the
universe and everything in it. I have gotten beyond the belief that everything happens by chance. Given the complexity of the universe that we

live in, I do not think that God would go at it halfheartedly. I am also beyond the concept that we are the only life in this or any other universe. I am not that conceited.

As for where I fit in this world, this is something that I have taken a great deal of time contemplating. I believe that I am an incarnation of an eternal warrior who is now faced with the task of having to live in a society where war is no longer an option. I have dreams from time to time of battles in other times, in other bodies that make me feel as if my soul is very old. Because of these beliefs I have found that I do not have a fear of death but a fear of failure. I have come very close to death while in military service, and dying did not scare me, but knowing that I would have to repeat this life if I did not complete my mission was frightening.

I have finally come to understand that I am not here for some war that has not yet been waged, but to learn to live without war. To really live a life with no battles, no killing, no hatred. To learn to love. It is in this that I think my final lives will be spent, trying to understand the people that for so many centuries I have tried to destroy.

Our last jewel comes from a fifty-five-year old woman who clearly had a gift for writing. I don't know what she may have learned from me, but I learned much from her. She had a highly developed personal philosophy before we met. Like the previous student, she too believed in reincarnation and unfolded this belief in an essay that took the form of an extended meditation on a maple tree. Married, mother of several children, seasoned with life's disappointments and joys, she saw her life reflected in a maple tree down to the tiniest details. Her essay is a distillation of her life experience, the nectar of her realization, her statement of discovery. She titled her essay "The Maple Tree."

As I write this, it is early June and this beautifully shaped, sixty-foot silver maple tree opposite my study window is luxuriant with new leaves. Forty feet across, the tree is a solid, intricately designed, elegantly decorated work of nature.

I wonder to myself how many leaves it bears. It is so lush that even an estimate would be only a broad guess. Let us start with the trunk which has three major divisions beginning five feet above the ground. Suppose that each of those divisions has ten large branches, each of those has fifteen medium branches, each of those has ten smaller branches, each of those has six tiny branches, each of those has ten twigs, and each twig sprouts four leaves. That would total one million eighty thousand leaves. Are we getting close? Should it be a tenth or ten times that number? If the tree has a million leaves which average five inches from top to bottom not counting the stem and if I line them up in a straight row, they will reach almost eighty miles! What an amazing abundance God is able to pack into a single tree!

I see the tree as a model of my life down to the smallest detail. The leaves represent the individual bits of knowledge I have gained from my moment by moment experiences, the twigs the events of my hourly existence, the tiny branches my days, the larger branches my weeks, months and years, the big divisions in the tree my lifetimes, and the trunk my eternal spiritual existence. I am currently fifty-five years old. That is 660 months, 2860 weeks, over 20,000 days. Suppose each day involved twenty separate experiences and each experience produced three of the most elementary bits of permanent knowledge. That means that in my half-century-plus I have accumulated well over a million particles of knowing, a mass which forms the substance of my present life. I cannot consciously remember one in ten thousand, but they are all within me, helping or hindering my progress each day.

The tree I am looking at today is not the same tree I saw last season. The old tree is hidden within the current one. Now it has new leaves, a slightly more extensive root system, an imperceptibly larger girth. If I were to look at a cross-section of the tree, I would find a profile of its past lives, between each of which it seemed to die. Yet each season it has been reborn, bearing within itself the accumulated memories of all its past season-lives.

The same is true for me. Hidden within the textures of my spiritual being are the impressions of all my past lives. I am the combined wisdom and experience of all those former journeys through time, even though they lie so deep within they are lost to my conscious awareness.

As the sap rises recurrently in the tree to bring it to new life, so the spirit rising within me brings me back to life again and again. I am reborn so that I can experience a new season: another lifetime of gathering specks of wisdom one at a time, of growing new leaves of awareness which reach out to the light and bring me nourishment of truth.

The only true gift I have for the world is this intricate web of unique experiences which forms my individuality. It is for the assembling of this unique creation that God has sent me into the world. He is waiting to see what I will produce; the wonder is that even he considers it of importance. You and I are generating the substance of human awareness—feeling, suffering, victory, failure, pain, loss, hope, love. God waits patiently to receive this material, because from it he plans to weave his consummate creation—the *Kingdom of Heaven*.

NOTES

Introduction

1. Tarnas, 1991:280; for a cogent telling of the story of the emergence of the modern self, see Tarnas, 1991:223–413. In her book *For Love of Matter*, Freya Mathews presents a philosophical defense of panpsychism (the view that all material reality is invested with some form of subjectivity) that includes an excellent critique of Descartes' severing of mind from matter and his locating mind in isolated, separate human beings. Here she writes: "The proposition that I exist, where "I" is understood to refer to a finite individual being whose essence is to think, does not in fact follow straightforwardly, as Descartes supposed, from a state of direct awareness of certain thoughts.... [His argument] assumes that, in reflexive states of awareness, what is registered is the content of a discrete individual mind. It does not allow for the possibility that, in such states, *what is registered might be merely a point of local reflexivity in a wider field of awareness.* Our immediate experience cannot reveal to us who the real subject of our subjectivity is, whether it is a global or a finite individual subject. Hence the individual mind, and self, that Descartes purports to infer from his cogito argument is in fact presupposed: he has simply assumed the discreteness of his subject that then enables him to sever mind from the rest of reality" (2003:37; my emphasis).
2. "End of the Line," Mike Tobin, *The Cleveland Scene*, April 8, 1999, http://www.clevescene.com/issues/1999-04-08/feature.html; "Crimetown USA—The city that fell in love with the mob (Youngstown, Ohio)," David Grann, *The New Republic*, July 10, 2000, http://www.highbeam.com/library/doc3.asp?DOCID=1G1:63330703.

Chapter 1. Resonance in the Classroom

1. On synchronicity, see Jung, 1973; Combs and Holland, 1990; Peat, 1987; and Progoff, 1987.
2. Bache, 2000.
3. For more on the perennial tradition, see Schuon, 1974, 1986; Smith, 1992. For an important recasting of this tradition, see Ferrer, 2001.
4. In Indian philosophy, there are said to be seven distinct spiritual centers called *chakras* ("wheels") that anchor seven levels of awareness ranging from the grounded fight-or-flight response to the highest state of God-realization or non-dual awareness. Kundalini is the name given to the energy that moves upward from the lowest chakra to the highest chakra, opening the chakras as it rises and triggering various shifts in awareness. The chakras that are most relevant to the discussion here are the heart chakra, said to be the seat of compassion, the throat chakra, the seat of creativity,

the brow chakra, the seat of insight (especially insight that reaches beyond the physical senses), and the crown chakra, the seat of non-dual awareness. (See Swami Ajaya, 1983; Mookerjee, 1983.)

5. One does not have to have permanently crossed this boundary for these synchronicities to occur. Using Ken Wilber's vocabulary, one does not have to stabilize "states" of transpersonal consciousness into "stages" of transpersonal development for these patterns of resonance to manifest. My experience is that even temporary immersion into various transpersonal states, if sufficiently deep, will elicit these responses (Wilber, 1997).

6. Two points here. First, "nearness" may be physical proximity or it may be "karmic proximity," meaning people with whom we have a particularly strong internal connection. Often it is both simultaneously. Those who are near us physically are often those with whom we have strong karmic connection. These kind of karmic ties show up frequently in our careers. For a teacher, therefore, the classroom is often a hotbed of karmic connections. Second, if a person's spiritual breakthroughs influence those around them, the same would also seem to apply to our spiritual failures. When any one of us fails to step up to some personal challenge, those with whom we have connection are all dragged down to some degree. The resulting tension between all the pulling "up" and "down" establishes the common denominator of the collective human psyche, C. G. Jung's collective unconscious.

7. Satprem, 1993:291. In discussing Aurobindo's attempt to transform the single body of humanity, Satprem writes: "But then, if the body is *one* with all other bodies, it means that all the other bodies are right there inside it, along with all the falsehoods of the world! There is no longer only one person's battle; it becomes the whole world's battle.... There is only one body" (1993:286–287).

8. von Durckheim, 1971:206–207; cited in Samaya, 1986:80–81.

9. While all forms of spiritual practice can be said to serve the general goal of spiritual awakening, when you get down to specifics, they approach this goal differently and often conceptualize the goal itself differently. It's important, therefore, not to oversimplify or overgeneralize here. See Jorge Ferrer's important observations on the participatory nature of spiritual practice in his book *Revisioning Transpersonal Theory*, 2001.

Chapter 2: Group Fields, Group Minds

1. Levi, R., 2004. See her Web site: www.theresonanceproject.org.
2. Novak, 1976; quoted in Rupert Sheldrake, 2003:40. See also Murphy, M., and White, R., 1978.
3. *What Is Enlightenment?*, May–July, 2004:15. See his book *Sacred Hoops*.
4. Quoted in Rupert Sheldrake, 2003:40.
5. Rowe, W. D. 1998:569–583; quoted in Radin, 2006:103.
6. Emerson, 1969, in R. Cook (Ed.), *Ralph Waldo Emerson: Selected Prose and Poetry*. San Francisco: Rinehart; quoted in R. Kenny, 2004.
7. In his novel *The Killer Angels*, Michael Shaara tells a story that gives the flavor of such an exchange. The setting is the eve of the battle of Gettysburg, the decisive battle that marked the beginning of the end of the Civil War. The speaker is Colonel Lawrence Chamberlain, previously a professor of rhetoric at Bowdoin College, here speaking to seasoned veterans from his home state of Maine. It is a tense situation. The veterans believe, with some justice, that they have fulfilled their original military obligation and want to go home, and Chamberlain is trying to persuade them to stay for one more

critical battle—Gettysburg. Chamberlain is new to his command and he must influence deep to reach these men.

> He bent down, scratched the black dirt into his fingers. He was beginning to warm to it; the words were beginning to flow. No one in front of him was moving.... Once he started talking he broke right through the embarrassment and there was suddenly no longer a barrier there. The words came out of him in a clear river, and he felt himself silent and suspended in the grove listening to himself speak, carried outside himself and looking back down on the silent faces and himself speaking, and he felt the power in him, the power of his cause. For an instant he could see black castles in the air; he could create centuries of screaming, eons of torture. Then he was back in sunlit Pennsylvania. The bugles were blowing and he was done. He had nothing else to say. No one moved. He felt the embarrassment return. He was suddenly enormously tired. (2003:30)

Chamberlain's deep convictions had been transmitted to his men. They chose to stay.

8. 1988: chapter 10.
9. For an especially insightful analysis of Sheldrake's theory of morphic fields and its far-reaching implications for science, see Frank Poletti, "Why do so many scientists reject Rupert Sheldrake's morphic fields?" (unpublished manuscript). Poletti points out that the concept of fields has historically been applied to widely varying phenomena such as light and gravity, and now with Sheldrake to memory, giving the term a semantic and scientific ambiguity that requires further clarification. Poletti can be contacted through the Esalen Center for Theory and Research Web site at www.esalenctr.org.
10. McDougall, 1938; cited in Sheldrake, 1981: 186–191; also 1988:175.
11. Crew, 1936; cited in Sheldrake, 1981: 186–191;also 1988:175.
12. Agar, 1954; cited in Sheldrake, 1981:186–191;1988:175.
13. For a careful survey of these developments, see Tarnas, *The Passion of the Western Mind*.
14. This quote came from the Internet. Unfortunately, I have lost the original source and have been unable to relocate it. Colin Hall died in 2005.
15. Palmer, 1998:3, 31, 11, 120.
16. 1990:154, 165.
17. Palmer, 1998:01.

Chapter 3: The Science of Fields

In order to make it easier for readers to consult the references cited in this more technical chapter, I have included the full citation for journal articles.

1. See *The Hidden Heart of the Cosmos* (1992), *The Universe Story* coauthored with Thomas Berry (1994), and *The Powers of the Universe* (DVD).
2. *Sunday Mirror*, February 8, 2000, p. 26; cited in Playfair, 2003:116.
3. *Counterblast: Where Scientists Fear to Tread*, BBC 2, April 23, 1998; cited in Playfair, 2003:116.
4. Quoted in Strogatz, 2003:151–152.
5. Dennett, 1991:33.
6. See www.consciousness.arizona.edu/Tucson2006.htm and www.mindandlife.org/mission.org_section.html.
7. Hall, 1977:72–77. Cited in Bloom, 2000:76.
8. William S. Condon. Communication: Rhythm and Structure. In *Rhythm in*

Psychological Linguistic and Musical Processes, ed. James R. Evans and Manfred Clynes, Springfield, IL: C. C. Thomas, 1986:55–77. Cited in Howard Bloom, 2000:76. For brain wave patterns spiking in unison, personal communication between Condon and Howard Bloom.

9. Bloom, 2000:75.
10. First quote, Bloom, 2000:76; my emphasis. Second quote, Bloom, 2000:219. To be fair, Bloom does not include psi in his overview. He tends to eschew all discussion of psi and to address material processes exclusively. Given the historical split between mind and matter going back to Descartes, he follows modern convention, jettisoning mind and studying the exquisite subtlety and complexity of matter, thinking that physical processes alone will account for the emergence of the global brain he is arguing for.
I would argue that it's not this simple, that where we find matter organizing itself into a global brain, we will also find a parallel process of conscious-ness organizing itself into a global mind. Ken Wilber has argued persuasively that complexity in one of these domains will mirror complexity in the other. Similarly, I would agree with Christian De Quincy in *Radical Nature* that this ontological split between mind and matter is a mistaken concept in the first place. Eventually we need to move to a more refined metaphysics that De Quincy, following Whitehead, calls panpsychism.
11. Goleman, 2006:4.
12. The frequency of psi is especially strong for identical twins. Identical twins represent a particularly fascinating opportunity to study what some have called bioentanglement. Consider, for example, the true case of two iden-tical twin boys who were raised separately and yet who were both independently named Jim. Furthermore, each Jim married a woman named Betty, divorced her, and then married a woman named Linda. Both became firefighters and both built a circular white bench around a tree in their back-yard. Even the strongest proponent of genetic determinism has a hard time explaining such an unusual string of coincidences. See Guy Lyon Playfair, 2003: cited in Radin, 2006:17.
13. http://www.collectivewisdominitiative.org/papers/kenny_science.htm
14. Bem, D. J., and Honorton, C. (1994). Does psi exist? Replicable evidence for an anomalous process of information transfer. *Psychological Bulletin,* 115, 4–18, cited in Radin, 2006:117.
15. Dunne, B. J., and Jahn, R. G. (2003). Information and uncertainty in remote perception research. *Journal of Scientific Exploration,* 17 (2), 207–241; cited in Radin, 2006:98.
16. Sherwood, S. J., and Roe, C. A. (2003). A review of dream ESP studies conducted since the Maimonides dream ESP studies. In J. Alcock, J. Burns, and A. Freeman (Eds.). *Psi Wars: Getting to Grips with the Paranormal.* Thorverton, UK: Imprint Academic; cited in Radin, 2006:109.
17. Schmidt, S., Schneider, R., Utts, J., and Walach, H. (2004). Distant inten-tionality and the feeling of being stared at: Two meta-analyses. *British Journal of Psychology,* 95, 235–247; cited in Radin, 2006:134.
18. Standish, L. J., Kozak, L., Johnson, L. C., and Richards, T. (2004). Elec-troencephaolographic evidence of correlated event-related signals between the brains of spatially and sensory isolated human subjects. *Journal of Alternative and Complementary Medicine,* 10, 307–314; cited in Radin, 2006:137.
19. Kenny, 2004; fn. 176.
20. Schlitz, M., Radin, D., Malle, Bertram, Schmidt, S., Utts, J., and Yount, G.

(May–June 2003). Distant healing intention: Definitions and evolving guidelines for laboratory studies. *Alternative Therapies and Health Medicine*, 9 (3 Supp), A31–43; cited in Kenny, 2004.

21. Sheldrake, 2003:83.

22. Boone, 1970:74–75. Quoted in Sheldrake, 2003:152–153. Sheldrake follows this quote with four pages of testimonials from professional hunters and wildlife photographers on the sensitivity of animals to the thoughts of those who stalk them.

23. Sheldrake, 1999:57–63 and Appendix B. This pattern was replicated in a subsequent experiment with Jaytee carried out by Dr. Richard Wiseman, but by creating an arbitrary criterion for judging Jaytee's behavior, Wiseman concluded that Jaytee had failed the test. He decided that Jaytee's "signal" for Pam's return would be the first time he visited the window for more than 2 minutes for no obvious external reason. Once this "signal" was given, no other data was taken into account. Wiseman does not contest that in his experiment Jaytee was at the window only 4 percent of the time for the main part of Pam's absence, 48 percent of the time in the 10 minutes prior to her return, and 78 percent of the time while she was actually returning. Is it significant that Dr. Wiseman is a consulting editor of the *Skeptical Inquirer*, the organ of the Committee for the Scientific Investigation of Claims of the Paranormal, an organization committed to debunking claims of psi? For the details, see Wiseman, Smith, and Milton (1998) and Sheldrake (1999a).

24. Potts, W. K. (1984). The chorus-line hypothesis of coordination in avian flocks. *Nature*, 24, 344–345. Sheldrake, 2003:114–116.

25. Sheldrake, 2003:117–118.

26. Marais, E. *The Soul of the White Ant*. Harmondsworth, England: Penguin, cited in Kenny, 2004.

27. Wilson, E. O., 1971; cited in Sheldrake, 1995:231.

28. Sheldrake, 1995:83–84.

29. Sheldrake, 1995:80–81.

30. If human psi is anchored in animal psi, we might ask how far down the evolutionary ladder psi actually goes. How complex must an organism be to show signs of psi? I would not want to hazard a guess, but consider the work of Eshel Ben-Jacob at the University of Tel Aviv on bacteria.

Ben-Jacob has demonstrated that some genetic mutations in bacteria appear not to be random, as classical Darwinian theory would predict, but instead are "custom-tailored" to overcome stressors in their environment. That is, bacteria intelligently reshape their genome in response to environmental pressures. This by itself is a remarkable finding with revolutionary implications, and it has been borne out in the laboratory. In one experiment, for example, researchers took a community of intestine-dwelling bacteria *E. coli*, separated it from its normal food source, and offered it a food that is inedible to bacteria—salicin, a pain reliever made from the bark of willow trees. An individual bacterium can extract nourishment from salicin only if it undergoes a step-by-step sequence of two genetic breakthroughs. The odds against pulling this off through random mutation are more than ten billion trillion to one, yet *E. coli* consistently manages to pull it off. The question is, how does it accomplish this Herculean task?

Ben-Jacob hypothesizes that the answer lies in networking. A "creative network" of bacteria, he says, invents a new set of instructions to beat the challenge. Different colony members take on different parts of the task.

Some study the outside environment while others puzzle over the genome "like race-car designers tinkering with an engine." The bacterial "supermind" even draws in lessons from other colonies. Such is the power of what he calls the bacterial "creative web."

I suspect that Ben-Jacob assumes that this network operates through purely physical mechanisms and he may be right. Nevertheless, his language is remarkably similar to Sheldrake's description of morphic fields—"supermind," "creative web," "creative network." Will bacteria turn out to "know" things in ways that mirror how birds "know" how to fly in close formation? Some experiments on distant healing intention already suggest that bacteria are at the very least able to receive (perceive?) the mental influence projected to them by healers. We will have to wait to see what future research turns up. See Eshel Ben-Jacob (1998). Bacterial wisdom, Gödel's theorem and creative genomic webs. *Physica A*, 248, 57–76, discussed in Bloom, 2000: 44–46.

31. Hagelin, J. S., et al. (1999). Effects of group practice of the Transcendental Meditation Program on preventing violent crime in Washington, D.C.: Results of the National Demonstration Project to Reduce Crime and Improve Governmental Effectiveness in Washington, D.C., June–July, 1993. *Social Indicators Research*, 47, 153–201.

32. Dillbeck, M. C. et al. (1981). The Transcendental Meditation Program and crime rate change in a sample of 48 cities. *Journal of Crime and Justice* 4, 25–45. The statistics given are for a reduced sample of twenty cities and twenty control cities necessitated by a change in how the police reported crime statistics to comply with the FBI standard for reporting the Uniform Crime Report index.

33. Orme-Johnson, D. W., et al. (1988). International peace project in the Middle East: The effects of the Maharishi technology of the unified field *Journal of Conflict Resolution*, 32,776–812. See also Dillbeck, M. C., et al. (1988). Test of a field model of consciousness and social change: The transcendental meditation and TM-Sidhi program and decreased urban crime. *Journal of Mind & Behavior* 9, 4, 457–86; Dillbeck, M. C. (1990). Test of a field theory of consciousness and social change: Time series analysis of participation in the TM-Sidhi program and reduction of violent death in the U.S. *Social Indicators Research*, 22, 399–418; and Gelderloos, P. et al. (1988). Creating world peace through the collective practice of the Maharishi Technology of the Unified Field: Improved U.S. Soviet relations. *Social Science Perspectives Journal*, 2 (4), 80–94. The TM organization has summarized their research efforts online at www.mum.edu/tm_research/tm_biblio/socio_c.html

34. Radin, 2006: chapter 11. On PEAR's research, see their Web site: www.princeton.edu/~pear/.

35. The following references are provided by Radin, 2006: Nelson, R. D., Bradish, G. J., Dobyns, Y. H., Dunne, B. J., and Jahn, R. G. (1996). FieldREG anomalies in group situations. *Journal of Scientific Exploration*, 10, 111–142; Nelson, R. D., Jahn, R. G., Dunne, B. J., Dobyns, Y. H., and Bradish, G. J. (1998). FieldREG II: Consciousness field effects: Replications and explorations. *Journal of Scientific Exploration*, 12, 425–454; Radin, D. I. (1997). *The Conscious Universe*. San Francisco: HarperEdge; Blasband, R. A. (2000). The ordering of random events by emotional expression. *Journal of Scientific Exploration*, 14, 195–216; Radin, D. I., Rebman, J. M., and Cross, M. P. (1996). Anomalous organization of random events by

group consciousness: Two exploratory experiments. *Journal of Scientific Exploration*, 10, 143–168; Yoichi, H., Kokubo, H., and Yamamoto, M. (2002). Anomaly of random number generator outputs: Cumulative deviation at a meeting and New Year's holiday. *Journal of International Society of Life Information Science*, 20 (1), 195–201; Yoichi, H., Kokubo, H., and Yamamoto, M. (2004). Anomaly of random number generator outputs (II): Cumulative deviation at New Year's holiday. *Journal of International Society of Life Information Science*, 22 (1), 142–146; Bierman, D. J. (1996). Exploring correlations between local emotional and global emotional events and the behavior of a random number generator. *Journal of Scientific Exploration*, 10, 363–373; Kokubo, H., Yoichi, H., and Yamamoto, M. (2002). Data analyses of a field number generator. *The Japanese Journal of Parapsychology*, 7, 11–16 (in Japanese); Hirukawa, T., and Ishikawa, M. (2004). Anomalous fluctuation of RNG data in Nebuta: Summer festival in Northeast Japan. *Proceedings of Presented Papers*, Parapsychological Association, 2004; Hagel, J., and Tschapke, M. (2004). The local event detector (LED): An experimental setup for an exploratory study of correlations between collective emotional events and Random number sequences, *Proceedings of Presented Papers*, Parapsychological Association, 2004.

36. Radin, D. I., Taft, R., and Yount, G. (2004). Possible effects of healing intention on cell cultures and truly random events. *Journal of Alternative and Complementary Medicine*, 10, 103–112. Also Radin: 2006; chapter 11.

37. Radin, 2006:193–195. Though the study of Princess Diana's funeral preceded the official establishment of the Global Consciousness Project, it was the precipitating cause for creating the GCP and the research protocol was the same as for subsequent studies. For convenience of summary, therefore, I have treated it as part of that project.

38. Nelson, R. D., Radin, D. I., Shoup, R., and Bancel, P. (2002). Correlation of continuous random data with major world events. *Foundations of Physics Letters*, 15 (6), 537–550.

39. Radin, 2006:198.

40. Nelson, R. D. (2002). *Terrorist disaster: September 11, 2001*. Available: Global Consciousness Project, http://noosphere.princeton.edu. Bringing together the research on the Maharishi effect and the Global Consciousness Project, shortly after the 9/11 tragedy TM practitioners gathered in Iowa for five days "to meditate together to create an influence of stability and peace." On September 26, 2001, when the highest number of meditators had gathered (1,800 individuals), Nelson found that the GCP network showed a departure from expectation that was "steady and unusually strong, leading to a final result that has a chance likelihood of about one in 1000." This was a post facto observation, however, not an a priori prediction, and therefore did not follow a formal scientific protocol. It does lend some small support, however, to Maharishi's claim that meditators' collective experience of a unified field of consciousness creates greater coherence in the collective psyche of humanity. See Nelson, R.D. (2002). *MUM peace meditation*. Available: Global Consciousness Project, http://noosphere.princeton.edu/mumspeak.html, cited in Kenny, 2004.

41. Radin, 1977:160–161.

42. Theories of Psi, ANPA (*Alternative Natural Philosophical Association*) *West Journal*, 1977, 7 (1).

43. Aczel, 2001:70; quoted in Radin, 2006:226.

44. Brooks, M. (March 27, 2004). The weirdest link. *New Scientist*; quoted in

Radin, 2006:14.

45. Nadeau, R., & Kafatos, M., 2001: 81; quoted in Radin, 2006:261–262, Radin's italics.

46. See Radin, 2006: chapters 12–13.

47. Radin, 2006:263–264. Radin points out that in order to explain various forms of psi, it is not necessary to assume that the mind is fundamentally different from the brain (dualism) but only that the mind/brain behaves as a quantum object.

Chapter 4: Working with Fields

1. I am not conversant with Rudolph Steiner's writings on education, but I have been told by people who are that some of the recommendations I am making here were foreshadowed in his thought and are incorporated into the training of Waldorf teachers. I must leave it to others to draw out these parallels and chart the history of these concepts.

2. The distinction between "physical" and "nonphysical" dimensions is a crude one that begs for more discussion than I can give here. I'm not a dualist who thinks that there are two types of "stuff" in the Cosmos, physical stuff and nonphysical stuff. That course twists us into mental pretzels trying to explain how two different types of reality can influence each other. By nonphysical dimensions, I mean simply dimensions of the Cosmos that are beyond the four-dimensional universe we inhabit, invisible to ordinary sense perception. My basic cosmological convictions go in the direction of monism and panpsychism (de Quincy, 2002; Mathews, 2003), but I don't have a particular theory about the nuts and bolts of how a multi-dimensional universe unfolds. For that discussion, one might consider the insights of Ervin Laszlo (2003, 2004, 2006).

3. It's important to distinguish the *concept of evolution* from particular *theories of evolution*. The concept of evolution is the concept of progressive complexification, the view that the universe is growing itself into increasingly complex forms over vast stretches of time. This concept is quite distinct from specific theories that have been proposed to explain *how* this progressive complexification is taking place. Classically, the theory has been that life evolves through chance variation screened by natural selection. However, it is becoming clear to many scientists that these two principles alone cannot explain the complexities of life that actually emerged in the relatively short timeframe of 13.7 billions years that the universe has existed. See, for example, Stuart Kaufman, *At Home in the Universe*. When I speak of evolution, therefore, I am referring to the concept of progressive complexification and am not endorsing any particular theory of how progressive complexification takes place, which I consider an open question. See Laszlo, 2004, 2006.

4. For Christianity to incorporate rebirth into its theological vision, it will be necessary only to expand the size of stage of salvation history and the age of the players. On the compatibility of reincarnation and Christianity, see MacGregor, 1978, and Bache, 1990.

5. See Ian Stevenson, *Twenty Cases Suggestive of Reincarnation* (1974), *Cases of the Reincarnation Type, Vol. I–IV* (1975–1983), and *Reincarnation and Biology, Vol. I–II* (1997). Stevenson has had his critics, of course, most notably Paul Edwards (1986–1987, 1996). Edwards, however, has failed to make his case against Stevenson, as Robert Almeder has convincingly demonstrated in his book *Death and Personal Survival* (1992). Almeder shows that Edwards does not refute Stevenson's evidence so much as refuse

to consider it seriously, and he does so because he is absolutely convinced that the materialist paradigm is true. Therefore he "knows" in advance that consciousness cannot exist independently of one's brain, even for a short period of time. Almeder's critique applies equally well to Edward's later criticism of Stevenson (1996).

6. See Fiore, *You Have Been Here Before* (1979) ; Lucas, *Regression Therapy* (1993); Netherton, Shiffrin, and Viertel, *Past Lives Therapy* (1978); Newton, *Journey of Souls* (1994) and *Destiny of Souls* (2000); Whitton and Fisher, *Life Between Life* (1986); and Woolger, *Other Lives, Other Selves* (1988).

7. See Grof, *LSD Psychotherapy* (1980), *The Adventure of Self-Discovery* (1988), *The Cosmic Game* (1998), and especially *The Ultimate Journey* (2006b).

8. For a convenient overview, see Cranston, *Reincarnation: An East–West Anthology* (1970); and Cranston and Williams, *Reincarnation: A New Horizon in Science, Religion, and Society* (1984). We may not be accustomed to thinking of reincarnation as a component of Western religions, but it is—in their mystical branches at least. Mainstream Judaism, for example, does not endorse reincarnation, but the contemplative branch of Judaism, Hasidism, does. Similarly, while mainstream Islam does not embrace the concept of rebirth, Sufism, the contemplative branch of Islam, does.

For Christianity the picture is more complicated. Reincarnation is affirmed in the early Christian Gnostic gospels and has repeatedly surfaced among Christian believers throughout history, but it has also been aggressively repressed by the ecclesiastical authorities, as in the Albigensian crusade of the thirteenth century. Reincarnation was officially rejected by the Second Council of Constantinople in the sixth century, but Scottish theologian Geddes MacGregor believes it did so not because the concept was incompatible with the gospel message but because rebirth was seen as undermining the centralized authority of the young church by giving individuals too much responsibility for their own salvation (1978).

9. For more on *Chöd*, see *Machig Labdrön and the Foundations of Chöd* by Jérôme Edou (1996) and Tsultrim Allione's biography of Machig Labdrön in her book *Women of Wisdom* (2000).

Chapter 5. Café Conversations

1. Brown, 2005:271.
2. A very useful online resource for introducing students to Café principles is www.theworldcafe.com.
3. Brown, 2005:113, 117.
4. Sheldrake, 1988:113–114.

Chapter 6. Waking Up in the Classroom

1. Kaufman, 1995: 25.
2. In a thought-provoking paper, Terrence Deacon, an anthropologist at the University of California, Berkeley, distinguishes different orders of emergence. He identifies self-organization as example of what he calls "second-order emergence" and evolution as an example of "third-order emergence." He concludes his essay with this passage:

> Human consciousness is not merely an emergent phenomenon; it *epitomizes the logic of emergence in its very form*: the locus of an immense

confluence, condensation, amplification, and dissemination of topological constraint and bias that continually deviates from and undermines old patterns of causality and amplifies new ones: causality transcending itself. (Deacon, 2003; my emphasis.)

3. "Why Reading Matters," *Parade*, September 2, 1990. For more on synchronicity see Jung, 1973; Combs and Holland, 1990; Grof, 2006b and Peat, 1987.
4. Palmer, 1998:10, his emphasis.
5. Palmer, 1998:32.
6. Capra, 1975:92.
7. All three quotes are cited in Laszlo, 2004:104.
8. Swimme and Berry, 1994; Swimme, 1996.
9. Laszlo, 2004:112.
10. Elgin, 2000:58; see also Elgin's forthcoming *The First Miracle*.
11. James, "The final impressions of a psychical researcher." *The American Magazine*, October 1909. Reprinted in Murphy and Ballou, 1961. Cited in Radin, 2006:234.
12. For the full text of the Avatamsaka Sutra, see Cook, 1977.

Chapter 9. Spiritual Experiences

1. Development of the College Students' Beliefs and Values Survey, and Spirituality and the Professorate: A National Study of Faculty Beliefs, Attitudes and Behaviors at www.spirituality.ucla.edu.
2. See, for example, Grof, 1988:54–62.

Chapter 11. Touched by Death

1. Ring, 1980, 1984, 1998; Sabom, 1982.
2. Singh, 1998; Osis and Haraldson, 1978.
3. Stevenson 1974, 1975–1983, 1997; Woolger, 1988.
4. Grof, 1980, 1988, 1998, and especially 2006b; Newton, 1994, 2000; Whitton and Fisher, 1986.
5. I particularly recommend the following books on death and dying: *Lessons from the Light* by Kenneth Ring; *The Grace in Dying* by Kathleen Singh; *The Ultimate Journey* by Stanislav Grof; and *Journey of Souls* by Michael Newton. On reincarnation, one might see *Many Lives, Many Selves* by Roger Woolger and my book *Lifecycles*.

BIBLIOGRAPHY

Agar, W. , et al., 1954. Fourth (final) report on a test of MCDougall's
  Lamarckian experiment on the training of rats. *Journal of Experimental
  Biology* 31:307–321.
Ajaya, S. 1983. *Psychotherapy East and West*. Honesdale, PA: Himalayan
  Institute.
Allione, T. 2000. *Women of Wisdom*. Ithaca, NY: Snow Lion.
Almeder, R. 1992. *Death and Personal Survival*. Lanham: Littlefield Adams.
Bache, C. 1990. *Lifecycles*. New York: Paragon House.
———. 2000. *Dark Night, Early Dawn*. Albany: State University of New
  York Press.
Bloom, H. 2000. *Global Brain*. New York: Wiley.
Boone, J. A. 1970. *The Language of Silence*. New York: Harper and Row.
Brown, J. 2005. *The World Café*. San Francisco: Berrett-Koehler.
Capra, F. 1975. *The Tao of Physics*. New York: Random House.
Combs, Allan, and Holland, Mark. 1990. *Synchronicity*. New York:
  Paragon House.
Cook, F. 1977. *Hua-Yen Buddhism: The Jewel Net of Indra*. University
  Park: Pennsylvania State University Press.
Cranston, S. 1970. *Reincarnation: An East–West Anthology*. Wheaton, IL:
  Theosophical Publication House.
Cranston, S., and Williams, C. 1984. *Reincarnation: A New Horizon in
  Science, Religion, and Society*. New York: Julian.
Crew, F. A. E. 1936. A repetition of McDougall's Lamarckian experiment.
  Journal of Genetics 33:61–101.
Deacon, T. 2003. The Hierarchic Logic of Emergence: Untangling The Inter-
  dependence of Evolution and Self-Organization, in Weber, B., and
  Depew, D. (Eds.), *Evolution and Learning*. Cambridge: MIT Press.
Dennett, D. 1991. *Consciousness Explained*. Boston: Little, Brown.
de Quincy, C. 2002. *Radical Nature*. Montpelier, VT: Invisible Cities Press.
DeSalvo, L. 1999. *Writing as a Way of Healing*. Boston: Beacon Press.
Edwards, P. 1986–87. The Case Against Reincarnation: Parts I–IV. *Free
  Inquiry* Vol. 6, No. 4:24–24; Vol. 7, No. 1:38–48; No. 2:38–49; No.
  3:46–53.
———. 1996. *Reincarnation*. New York: Prometheus.

Edou, J. 1996. *Machig Labdrön and the Foundations of Chöd*. Ithaca, NY: Snow Lion.

Elgin. D. 2000. *Promise Ahead*. New York: William Morrow.

Ferrer, J. 2001. *Revisioning Transpersonal Theory*. Albany: State University of New York Press.

Fiore, E. 1979. *You Have Been Here Before*. New York: Ballantine.

Goleman, D. 2006. *Social Intelligence*. New York: Bantam Dell.

Grof, S. 1980. *LSD Psychotherapy*. Pomona, CA: Hunter House.

——. 1988. *The Adventure of Self-Discovery*. Albany: State University of New York Press.

——. *The Cosmic Game*. Albany: State University of New York Press.

——. 2006a. *When the Impossible Happens*. Boulder: Sounds True.

——. 2006b. *The Ultimate Journey*. Ben Lomond, CA: Multidisciplinary Association for Psychedelic Studies.

Hall, E. 1977. *Beyond Culture*. New York: Anchor Books.

Huxley, A. 1944. *The Perennial Philosophy*. New York: Harper and Row.

Jackson, P., and Delehanty, H. 1995. *Sacred Hoops*. New York: Hyperion.

Jung, C. G. 1954. The Collected Works of C. G. Jung: The Symbolic Life. Reid, H., Fordham, M., and Adler, G. (Eds.). Princeton: Princeton University Press.

——. 1973. *Synchronicity*. Princeton: Bolligen.

Kaufman, S. 1995. *At Home in the Universe*. New York: Oxford University Press.

Kenny, R. 2004. "What Can Science Tell Us about Collective Consciousness?" http://www.collectivewisdominitiative.org/papers/kenny_science.htm.

Laszlo, E. 1993. *The Creative Cosmos*. Edinburgh: Florish Books.

——. 1999a. *The Interconnected Universe*. Singapore: World Scientific Publishing.

——. 1999b. *The Whispering Pond*. Boston: Element Books.

——. 2003. *The Connectivity Hypothesis*. Albany: State University of New York Press.

——. 2004. *Science and the Akashic Field*. Rochester, VT: Inner Traditions.

——. 2006. *Science and the Reenchantment of the Cosmos*. Rochester, VT: Inner Traditions.

Levi, R. 2004. Group Magic: An inquiry into experiences of collective resonance. Doctoral dissertation from Saybrook Graduate School and Research Center, San Francisco, CA.

Lucas, W. 1993. *Regression Therapy, Vol. I & II*. Crest Park, CA: Deep Forest Press.

MacGregor, G. 1978. *Reincarnation and Christianity*. Wheaton, IL: Quest Books.

Marais, E. 1973. *The Soul of the White Ant*. Harmondsworth, England: Penguin.

Mathews, F. 2003. *For Love of Matter*. Albany: State University of New York Press.

McDougall, W. 1938. Fourth report on a Lamarckian experiment. *British Journal of Psychology* 28:321–345.

Mindell, Arnold. 2000. *Quantum Mind*. Portland: Lao Tse Press.

Monroe, R 1970. *Journeys Out of the Body*. Garden City: Anchor Press.

———. 1985. *Far Journeys*. New York: Doubleday.

———. 1994. *Ultimate Journey*. New York: Doubleday.

Mookerjee, Ajit. 1983. *Kundalini*. New York: Destiny Books.

Murphy, G., and Ballou, R. (Eds.). 1961. *William James on Psychical Research*. London: Chatto and Windus.

Murphy, M., and White, R. 1978. *The Psychic Side of Sports*. Reading: Addison-Wesley.

Nadeau, R., & Kafatos, M. 2001. *The Non-Local Universe*. Oxford: Oxford University Press.

Netherton, M., N. Shiffrin, and J. Viertel. 1978. *Past Lives Therapy*. New York: William Morrow.

Newton, M. 1994. *Journey of Souls*. St. Paul: Llewellyn.

———. 2000. *Destiny of Souls*. St. Paul: Llewellyn.

Novak, Michael. 1976. *The Joy of Sports*. New York: Basic Books.

Osis, K., and Haraldsson, E. 1977. *At the Hour of Death*. New York: Avon.

Ouspensky, P. D. 1950. *In Search of the Miraculous*. London: Routledge & Kegan Paul.

Palmer, P. 1998. *The Courage to Teach*. San Francisco: Jossey-Bass.

Peat, F. David. 1987. *Synchronicity*. New York: Bantam.

Playfair, G. L. 2003. *Twin Telepathy*. London: Vega.

Poletti, F. "Why do so many scientists reject Rupert Sheldrake's morphic fields?" (unpublished manuscript).

Progoff, I. 1987. *Jung, Synchronicity, and Human Destiny*. New York: Three Rivers Press.

Radin, D. 2006. *Entangled Minds*. New York: Pocket Books.

Ray, Paul, and Anderson, Sherri. 2000. *The Cultural Creatives*. New York: Three Rivers Press.

Ring, K. 1980. *Life at Death*. New York: Coward, McCann and Geoghegan.

———. 1984. *Heading Toward Omega*. New York: Morrow.

———. 1998. *Lessons from the Light*. Portsmouth, NH: Moment Point Press

Rowe, W. D. 1998. Physical Measurements of Episodes of Focused Group Energy. *Journal of Scientific Explorations,* 12, 569–583.

Sabom, M. 1982. *Recollections of Death*. New York: Harper and Row

Samaya, Mike. 1986. *Samadhi*. Albany: State University of New York Press.

Satprem. 1993. *Sri Aurobindo or The Adventure of Consciousness*. Pondicherry: Sri Aurobindo Ashram.

Schuon, F. 1974. *The Transcendent Unity of Religion*. New York: Harper and Row.

———. 1986. *Survey of Metaphysics and Esoterism*. Bloomington: World Wisdom Books.

Schwarz, B. 1971. *Parent-Child Telepathy*. New York: Garrett Publications.

Senge, P., Scharmer, C., Jaworski, J., and Flowers, B. 2004. *Presence*. Cambridge, MA: Society for Organizational Learning.

Shaara, Michael. 2003. *The Killer Angels*. New York: Random House.

Sheldrake, R. 1981. *A New Science of Life*. Los Angeles: J. P. Tarcher.

———. 1988. *The Presence of the Past*. New York: Vintage.

———. 1991a. *The Rebirth of Nature*. New York: Bantam.

———. 1991b. Commentary on a paper by Wiseman, Smith and Milton on the "psychic pet" phenomenon. *Journal of the Society for Psychical Research* 63, 304–309.

———. 1995. *Seven Experiments That Could Change the World*. New York: Riverhead Books.

———. 1999. *Dogs That Know When Their Owners Are Coming Home*. New York: Crown.

———. 2003. *The Sense of Being Stared At*. New York: Crown.

Singh, K. 1998. *The Grace in Dying*. New York: HarperCollins.

Smith, H. 1992. *Forgotten Truth*. New York: HarperCollins.

Stevenson, I. 1974. *Twenty Cases Suggestive of Reincarnation*. 2nd rev. ed. Charlottesville: University Press of Virginia.

———. 1975–1983. *Cases of the Reincarnation Type, Vol. I–IV*. Charlottesville: University Press of Virginia.

———. 1997. *Reincarnation and Biology, Vol. I–II*. Charlottesville: University Press of Virginia.

Surowieck, J. 2004. *The Wisdom of Crowds*. New York: Anchor Books.

Swimme, B. 1996. *The Hidden Heart of the Cosmos*. Maryknoll, NY: Orbis Books.

———. 2007. *The Powers of the Universe*. DVD.

Swimme, B., and Berry, T. 1994. *The Universe Story*. New York: HarperCollins.

Tarnas, R. 1991. *The Passion of the Western Mind*. New York: Crown.

von Durckheim, K. 1971. *Hara*. London: George Allen and Unwin.

Whitton, J., and Fisher, J. 1986. *Life Between Life*. Garden City, NY: Doubleday.

Wilber, K. 1997. *The Eye of Spirit*. Boston: Shambhala Press.

Wiseman, R., M. Smith, and J. Milton. 1998. Can Animals Detect When Their Owners Are Returning Home? An Experimental Test of the 'Psychic Pet' Phenomenon. *British Journal of Psychology* 89, 453–462.

Woolger, R. 1988. *Other Lives, Other Selves*. New York: Bantam.

Zukov, G. *The Dancing Wu-Li Masters*. New York: William Morrow.

INDEX